FROM FAMILY TREE TO FAMILY HISTORY

Edited by Ruth Finnegan
and Michael Drake

 CAMBRIDGE
UNIVERSITY PRESS _in association with_ The Open University

Published by the Press Syndicate of the University of Cambridge in association with The Open University
The Pitt Building, Trumpington Street, Cambridge CB2 1RP
40 West 20th Street, New York, NY 10011-4211, USA
10 Stamford Road, Oakleigh, Melbourne 3166, Australia

First published 1994. Reprinted 1995

Edited, designed and typeset by The Open University

Printed in Great Britain by Butler and Tanner Ltd, Frome

A catalogue record for this book is available from the British Library

Library of Congress Cataloging-in-Publication data
Studying family and community history: 19th and 20th centuries/
series editor, Ruth Finnegan.
       p.   cm.
   Includes index.
   Contents: v. 1. From family tree to family history/edited by
Ruth Finnegan and Michael Drake
      ISBN 0-521-46001-8 (hardback). ISBN 0-521-46577-X (paperback)
      1. Family – Great Britain – History. 2. Family demography – Great Britain.
3. Great Britain – Genealogy. I. Finnegan, Ruth.
II. Drake, Michael.
HQ613.S78 1993
306.85'0941 – dc20   93-32697
                       CIP

ISBN 0 521 46001 8   hardback

ISBN 0 521 46577 X   paperback

CONTENTS

PART III: AN ILLUSTRATION

CHAPTER 5: HOW FAMILIES LIVED THEN: KATHARINE BUILDINGS, EAST SMITHFIELD, 1885–1890   129
Rosemary O'Day

PART IV: REFLECTING ON THE ISSUES

CHAPTER 6: CONCLUSION   167
Ruth Finnegan and Michael Drake

LIST OF FIGURES AND TABLES

CONTRIBUTORS

Michael Drake, Emeritus Professor and first Dean of Faculty of Social Sciences, The Open University; Visiting Professor of History, University of Tromsø

Ruth Finnegan, Professor in Comparative Social Institutions, Faculty of Social Sciences, The Open University

Rosemary O'Day, Senior Lecturer in History, Faculty of Arts, The Open University

viii

PREFACE

Many thousands of people are currently exploring their family trees or investigating the history of their localities. It is an absorbing hobby – and more than just a hobby. It combines the excitement of the chase and the exercise of demanding investigative skills. It also leads to personal rewards, among them perhaps an enhanced awareness of identity, achieved through the process of searching out your roots within the unending cycle of the past, and something to hold on to in the confusions of the present.

At the same time scholars within a series of social science and historical disciplines are increasingly realizing the value of small-scale case studies, extending and questioning accepted theories through a greater understanding of local and personal diversities. Sociologists now look to individual life histories as well as generalized social structure; geographers emphasize the local as well as the global; demographers explore regional divergences, not just national aggregates; historians extend their research from the doings of the famous to how 'ordinary people' pursued their lives at a local level.

This volume and the series of which it is a part have as their central purpose the encouragement of active personal research in family and community history – but research that is also linked to more general findings and insights. The series thus seeks to combine the strengths of two traditions: that of the independent personal researcher into family tree or local history, and that of established academic disciplines in history and the social sciences.

Now is a particularly appropriate moment to bring these two sides together. The networks of family and local historians up and down the country have in the past had scant recognition from within mainstream university circles, which (in contrast to the active involvement of further education and extra-mural departments) have sometimes given the impression of despising the offerings of 'amateur researchers'. Explicitly academic publications, for their part, have been little read by independent investigators – understandably, perhaps, for, with a few honourable exceptions, such publications have been predominantly directed to specialist colleagues. But there are signs that this situation may be changing. Not only is there an increasing awareness of the research value of micro studies, but higher education as a whole is opening up more flexible ways of learning and is recognizing achievements undertaken outside traditional 'university walls'. Our hope is to further this trend of mutual understanding, to the benefit of each.

There are thus two main aims in these volumes, overlapping and complementary. The first is to present an interdisciplinary overview of recent scholarly work in family and community history, drawing on the approaches and findings of such subjects as anthropology, social and economic history, sociology, demography, and historical geography. This should be illuminating not only for those seeking an up-to-date review of such work, but also for anyone interested in the functioning of families and communities today – the essential historical background to present-day concerns. The second, equally important aim is to help readers develop their own research interests. The framework here is rather different from traditional genealogy or local history courses (where excellent DIY guides already exist) since our emphasis is on completing a project and relating it to other research findings and theories, rather than on an unending personal quest for yet more and more details. It differs too from most conventional academic publications, in that the focus is on *doing* research, rather than absorbing or reporting the research of others. These volumes are therefore full of practical advice on sources and methods, as well as illustrations of the kinds of projects that can be followed up by the individual researcher.

Given the infinite scope of the subject and the need to provide practical advice, we have put some limits on the coverage. The timescale is the nineteenth and twentieth centuries, a period for which the sources are plentiful and – for the recent period at least – oral investigation feasible. (The critical assessment and exploitation of primary sources within this timescale will, of course, develop skills which can be extended to earlier periods.) There is no attempt to give a detailed narrative of nineteenth- and twentieth-century history. Rather we present a blend of specific case studies, findings and theoretical ideas, selected with a view to giving both some taste of recent work, and a context and stimulus for further investigation.

In terms of area, the focus is on the United Kingdom and Ireland, or, to put it differently, on the countries of the British Isles (these and similar terms have both changing historical applications and inescapable political connotations, so since we wish to write without prejudice we have deliberately alternated between them). This focus is applied flexibly, and there is some reference to emigration abroad; but we have not tried to describe sources and experiences overseas. Thus while much of the general theoretical background and even specific ideas for research may relate to many areas of the world, the detailed practical information about sources or record repositories concentrates on those available to students working in England, Ireland (north and south), Scotland and Wales.

The emphasis is also on encouraging small-scale projects. This does not mean that larger patterns are neglected: indeed, like other more generalized findings and theories, they form the background against which smaller studies can be set and compared. But small, manageable projects of the kinds focused on in this volume have two essential merits. First, they link with the emerging appreciation of the value of research into diversities as well as into generalizations: many gaps in our knowledge about particular localities or particular family experiences remain to be filled. Second, they represent a form of research that can be pursued seriously within the resources of independent and part-time researchers.

This opening volume focuses on the family and its history, relating ideas for research in this field to recent academic writings on the history of the family. It can be read on its own, but it is also linked to the other volumes in the series which complement and amplify the topics considered here. The companion volumes (listed on p.ii) turn the spotlight on migration and community (Volume 2); family- or community-based activities that can be studied at a local level such as work, social mobility, local politics, religion, or leisure (Volume 3); and, in Volume 4, on some of the many sources and methods that can be used to conduct and communicate research in family and community history.

This book forms one part of the Open University course DA301 *Studying family and community history: 19th and 20th centuries* (the other components are listed on p.ii). DA301 is an honours-level undergraduate course for part-time adult learners studying at a distance, and it is designed to develop the skills, methods and understanding to complete a guided project in family or community history within the time constraints of a one-year course – comparable, therefore, to the dissertation sometimes carried out in the final year of a conventional honours degree. It also looks forward to ways in which such a project could be extended and communicated at a later stage. However, these volumes are also designed to be used, either singly or as a series, by anyone interested in family or community history. The introduction to recent research, together with the practical exercises, advice on the critical exploitation of primary sources, and suggestions for research projects, should be of wide interest and application. Collectively the results of such research should not only develop individuals' investigations but also enhance our more general understanding of family and community history. Much remains to be discovered by the army of amateur and professional researchers throughout the British Isles.

Since a series of this kind obviously depends on the efforts of many people, there are many thanks to express. As in other Open University courses, the material was developed collaboratively. So while authors are responsible for what they have written, they have also been both influenced and supported by other members of the course team: not just its academic contributors, but also those from the editorial, design, and production areas of the university. There was also the highly skilled group who prepared the manuscript for electronic publishing, among them Molly Freeman, Maggie Tebbs, Pauline Turner, Betty Atkinson, Maureen Adams, and above all Dianne Cook, our calm and efficient course secretary throughout most of the production period. For advice and help on various points in this volume we would especially like to thank Stella Colwell, Jacqueline Eustace, Monica Shelley and Wendy Webster. For the series generally we are greatly indebted to four external critical readers who provided wonderfully detailed comments on successive drafts of the whole text: Brenda Collins, particularly for her informed advice on Ireland; Janet Few, both in her own right and as Education Officer of the Federation of Family History Societies; Dennis Mills, with his unparalleled command not only of the subject matter but of the needs of distance students; and Colin Rogers of the Metropolitan University, Manchester, for sharing the fruits of his long experience in teaching and furthering the study of family history. Finally, particular thanks go to our external assessor, Professor Paul Hair, for his constant challenges, queries and suggestions. Our advisors should not be held responsible for the shortcomings that remain, but without their help these volumes would certainly have been both less accurate and less intelligible.

Our list of thanks is a long one and even so does not cover everyone. In our case its scope arises from the particular Open University form of production. But this extensive cooperation also, we think, represents the fruitful blend of individual interest and collaborative effort that is typical in the field of studying family and community history: a form of collaboration in which we hope we can now engage with you, our readers.

USING THIS BOOK

Activities

This volume is designed not just as a text to be read through but also as an active workbook. It is therefore punctuated by a series of activities, signalled by different formats. These include:

(a) *Short questions*: these provide the opportunity to stop and consider for a moment before reading on. They are separated from the surrounding text merely by being printed in a different colour.

(b) *Exercises*: these are activities to be carried out as part of working through the text, requiring anything from ten minutes to an hour to complete. Follow-up discussion comes either immediately after in the main text or (when so indicated in the exercise) in the separate comments and answers at the end of the book.

(c) *Questions for research*: these are suggestions for longer-term research projects to follow up selectively according to personal interest or opportunity *after* working through the relevant chapter(s). Note that although there are frequent references to 'your family', in practice any family (or set of families) in which you are interested will do equally well. In fact taking a family on which there are *locally* available records may be more practicable, as a first stage at least, than chasing the details of your own.

Schemas

These are lists of questions, factors or key theories which can help in formulating research, providing a kind of model or template against which research findings can be compared.

References

While this book is free-standing, there are cross-references to other volumes in the series which appear, for example, in the form 'see Volume 4, Chapter 6'. This is to aid readers using all the books.

The lists of books or articles at the end of each chapter follow the scholarly convention of giving details of all works cited; they are not intended as obligatory further reading. The asterisked items in these lists are useful starting points for those wishing to go further into the subject.

RUTH FINNEGAN

INTRODUCTION

by Michael Drake (section 1) and Ruth Finnegan (section 2)

1 FROM FAMILY TREE TO FAMILY HISTORY

To create a family tree is one way of doing family history. But there is another approach: linking work on a single family into findings about families in general. The purpose of this volume is to explain this other way of doing family history, and suggest how to go about it. Not that the two ways are totally different; for instance, the same documents are used, and both originate in the comparatively recent realization that history is not just about the great and the good, kings and queens, nation states, empires, parliaments, politics, etc. We all have our histories. What our forebears did for a living, who they married, where they lived, what they thought – all this is of interest to those of us who carry their genes as well as to a wider audience that regards the family household as the arena for a wide range of activities that now occupy centre stage.

In this volume, then, we start by taking a look at a number of individual cases and some of the widely accessible sources they draw on: a family tree, part of a nineteenth-century census enumerator's book, a photograph from a family album, a letter. From these we try to tease out some general issues. We then reverse the procedure by examining some general findings, for example about marriage, to see what developments have taken place over the past two hundred years. These findings can subsequently be examined in the light of your own individual family histories, so giving them an added dimension.

But to go further, to increase what we know about the family in the past (and, by extension, our understanding of the family today) *you* need to carry out research. For that you need a strategy, and here we give you a choice of two. Both have their strengths and weaknesses. Our 'hypothesis testing strategy' is more suited to the examination of a new body of evidence in the light of existing knowledge. As its name suggests, we derive a hypothesis (or likely explanation) from this knowledge (it could be a formal theory or a generalization of one sort or another) and see if it is borne out or refuted when we test it against *our* evidence. Our answer could be a clear yes or no, but is more likely to be qualified in some way. The strengths of this strategy lie in the limited (and therefore more controllable) nature of the enquiry; the probability of being able to focus on a single source; the good chance of coming up with a definite answer and, not least, the near certainty of adding something, however small, to our existing knowledge. The weaknesses of the strategy are the mirror image of these strengths: the narrowness of the enquiry, the very predictability of the exercise, and the likelihood that the outcome may not go beyond the dotting of an 'i' or the crossing of a 't'.

Our 'questioning sources strategy' is much more open-ended, suited to a piece of research that goes from the particular to the general, or vice-versa. Its strengths lie in this open-endedness; in the excitement of moving from source to source (in some cases, not all); of reformulating questions in the light of one's findings; of producing an entirely novel outcome. Again, the weaknesses are inherent in the strengths. The open-endedness can lead to an ever greater accumulation of notes in search of a structure; a difficulty in knowing when to stop the search for new material; an intoxication with the plethora of questions there for the asking; and the very real chance of ultimate disappointment when the 'history' fails to materialize on the page.

I have spent a little time on the strategy aspect because it is such a central element of the book. Indeed, much of what you will find elsewhere in it is designed to show how the two strategies work in practice, the sort of materials they are suited to, and the type of questions they help you answer.

1

These questions are essentially of two kinds. On the one hand, we consider such central issues as birth, marriage and death: how many children did people have; how many were conceived before marriage; who married whom; why were certain times of the year more popular for weddings amongst Catholics than amongst Protestants in Ireland, or for the inhabitants of northern Scotland than for those of south-west Scotland; what happened to infant mortality over the years; what can we say about those major killers – cholera, TB, typhoid? Then there is the size and composition of the families and households our forebears lived in: how many people lived together, who were they, what differences can we discern between different classes, parts of the country, periods? On the other hand, we seek to tackle questions about people's perceptions and experiences and about the active strategies and relationships developed within families: how family members got on with each other, for example, or what they did for each other. This leads to a further set of questions. How did families manage to make a livelihood in the past? Do we support our relatives more or less than we did a hundred or two hundred years ago? And what meaning can we find in the memories, myths and legends we pass on from one generation to another?

The climax of the book is a study of working-class family life in a block of London flats in the period 1885–1890. Here is brought together much that, for study purposes, we have treated separately in earlier chapters. Thus we come across a variety of sources: a ledger describing the inhabitants (a gem!), photographs, maps, plans, correspondence, a diary. We examine the size and composition of the families, the occupations of husbands and wives, their illnesses and disabilities, their sources of income. We also see what the middle-class rent collectors and (some would say) 'do-gooders' felt about the tenants of Katharine Buildings and what the tenants felt about them. Again and again we find instances of the gulf between the classes. Though the overarching strategy is that of 'questioning sources' – to use our terminology – we can discern elements of 'hypothesis testing' too. As for the presentation itself, we find tabular, literary and visual matter.

We hope that by the end of this book you may not only have come to see your own family tree in a different light, but will want to extend your research in at least some of the ways we have suggested and that you will have both the confidence and the tools with which to do it.

2 HOW WILL YOU BE STUDYING FAMILY AND COMMUNITY HISTORY?

by Ruth Finnegan

Setting individual cases into a wider perspective is, therefore, the overall approach of this volume, and it is the route you will follow in your own research. But before getting into that, let's pause a moment, for it is only fair to apply the same procedure to the approach of this and the following volumes, putting *them* in perspective too. At some point you are bound to wonder how typical our particular approach really is. How does it fit with other approaches to family and community history, and to intellectual developments in history and social sciences more widely? (If you are not concerned now, by all means just skim this section lightly or leave it till later – but sooner or later someone else will ask you about it, even if you don't yourself!)

2.1 FEATURES OF THE APPROACH IN THESE VOLUMES

Two points stand out immediately. One is the interdisciplinary nature of our approach. We have drawn on such disciplines as social and economic history, sociology, demography, anthropology and historical geography. But rather than presenting them separately or sequentially, we are seeking to combine their insights. For the study of family and community history we believe this provides an illuminating background to both academic understanding and practical research.

The second point is the particular interdisciplinary blend that we have chosen. It is drawn primarily from history on the one hand, and a series of social science disciplines on the other, subjects which have sometimes been taken as belonging to different and perhaps mutually exclusive intellectual traditions.

This contrast is worth considering (even if it has perhaps never been quite as radical as some twentieth-century protagonists have made out). Historians have tended to look at single, unique cases as against social scientists' concern to establish general theories that apply to all or most of these cases. Social scientists have argued that these generalizations (about the process of industrialization, for instance, or the effects of the class struggle) are what make sense of the single examples, while historians have retorted that 'reducing' individual cases in this way means distorting their unique and historically specific qualities. Similar arguments have featured in the claimed contrast between historians' interest in 'facts' – investigating what actually happened on the ground, the historical specificities – as against social scientists' focus on the concepts and theories which give meaning to what would otherwise merely be unintelligible data (see, for example, Jones, 1976). Furthermore, historical research has, unsurprisingly, emphasized changes over time, at least partly through narrative accounts about individuals' choices and actions (especially those of the powerful!). Where social scientists have been strong, by contrast, is in analysing the workings of a social system, group or community at a particular point in time, with less concern for historical change. This has enabled them to reveal the constraints on individuals' actions resulting from their membership of a wider system and how it functions.

One way of summing up such contrasts is given in Schema A.

Schema A: Some contrasting interests and methodologies – or are they?

Individual	Collective
Single unique cases (*ideographic*)	General theories (*nomothetic*)
'Facts'	'Theories'
Individual actions	External social constraints/structure
Change (*diachronic*)	Continuance (*synchronic*)

Note: the italicized technical terms can safely be ignored unless they are ones you already find familiar and helpful.

Looking at Schema A, into which column would you place history and social science respectively?

The answer may seem obvious. History is in the left-hand column, social science the right.

But wait. Not only have some researchers never observed the distinction, but the divisions themselves are now under challenge. Increasingly there is a cross-over. Nowadays some historians too invoke general concepts (such as 'class', 'family', 'community') and draw out the external constraints as well as individual choices. And social scientists concern themselves with individual cases and engage in research that builds on the detailed investigation of personal life histories, small localities, and individual case studies (see, for example, the discussions in Burke, 1991; Elliott, 1990; Hareven, 1991; Smith, 1982). Gone too is the unquestioning assumption that social scientists can safely neglect specific historical changes, while many historians on their side have been going beyond their traditional focus on the actions of the powerful to consider everyday popular culture and the broader patterns within social and economic history.

The changes of emphasis are perhaps not so extreme that we need to *reverse* the attributions in Schema A, though one teasing suggestion is that some historians and social scientists now seem to be rushing past one another 'like two trains on parallel tracks' (Burke, 1992, p.20). But it is true that the increasing convergence of historians and social scientists is opening up opportunities to build jointly on insights which in the past have too often been kept separate.

If this convergence is one feature of the approach of this series, another reflects further recent developments in historical and social scientific thinking. Of particular importance for the study of family and community is a growing awareness that such overarching concepts as 'the Industrial Revolution', 'urbanization' or 'modernization' do not represent simple uniform entities, but are multifaceted processes, worked out and shaped in specific localities by particular groups adopting varied local and personal strategies (for some relevant discussions see Davis, 1991; Hareven, 1991; Hudson, 1989; O'Brian and Quinault, 1993; Phythian-Adams, 1991). Understanding industrialization, for example, needs to include *both* looking at what was happening within a single small village *and* relating this to the regional or national contexts in which it functioned (this is well illustrated in Mills, 1993).

These developments form part of a more general intellectual move within a number of disciplines. In a recent editorial in the leading British journal *Sociology*, Liz Stanley and David Morgan express the kind of comment being heard from many sides, when they speak of the current 're-thinking and re-seeing in intellectual life in general' (Stanley and Morgan, 1993, p.1). They characterize this as, among other things, 'the rejection of the older dichotomy between "structure" [or external social constraints] and "action"', and comment on new ways of looking at individuals which involve 'Steering a course between the over-determinism of some varieties of socialization theory, and the opposite extreme of seeing selves as entirely unique individuals … Questioning and rejecting conventional sharp distinctions between … individual and collective' (Stanley and Morgan, 1993, p.2).

Put more concretely, social scientists *and* historians are increasingly interested in individual lives, in specific family or neighbourhood experiences, or in particular localities, but do not see such interests as stopping them from relating these to wider patterns and theories (see, for example, Hareven, 1991; Elliott, 1990; Hastrup, 1992; Rapport, 1992; Schürer, 1991). In other words they – like you – are trying to pay some attention to *both* sides in Schema A.

Our interdisciplinary approach builds on these recent intellectual developments and provides a framework so that your research can contribute to them. Admittedly, the tensions between differing emphases still continue. And like other scholars, both the writers in this volume and you in your own work will at times be sucked too far into individual cases or pulled too much towards general theories. In fact these tensions are enlightening and useful ones that are worth attention from any serious researcher into family and community history.

Thus it has proved helpful to approach our subject from two angles. On the one hand we need to balance the larger (and once unquestioned) conclusions about, say, '*the* impacts of industrialization' or the 'one-way progress' view of history, by micro studies of specific groups and historical contexts which can amplify or challenge such theories. On the other hand we lose out if we rest content with merely describing individual cases in their own terms, without any relation to the comparative findings. Our assumption is therefore both that the general can be illuminated by research into specific detailed cases, *and* that these gain further meaning when seen in the perspective of their social context and historical background – something which, in turn, our understanding of the more general theories can help us appreciate.

Small-scale case studies therefore play a central part. These can be drawn from your own experience and researches in genealogy or local history, or from those presented by the authors here: such studies are not only interesting in their own right, personal, unique, enlarging our awareness of the importance of detailed experience and of complexity; they also form a kind of exemplar and testing ground for the wider insights and questions they raise and with which they are interconnected.

We have spoken about two related characteristics of our overall approach: its interdisciplinary nature, and the way it bridges older divides both within and between history and the social sciences. These two characteristics really boil down to one – an approach consonant with the emerging interdisciplinary movement which is increasingly combining interests in both the individual case *and* the comparative patterns. Your interests and work in linking the two are thus at the forefront of contemporary intellectual endeavour, and can make an important contribution to it.

This last point leads on to the third feature of our approach, namely its emphasis on active research. The aim is not just to read the history others have written, but to write it yourself; not to philosophize *about* history, but to *do* it. We recognize that this leaves many issues on one side – for example the debates about post-modernism, ideology, the relativity of 'truth', or post-structuralist views of reality which loom large in some academic writing and teaching (and which you may indeed have encountered elsewhere). As you will see, we have mostly kept away from such topics. It is not that they are unimportant, but rather than encouraging you to spend your time listening to scholars' abstract arguments about the elusiveness of 'facts' or how far any source can really be 'primary', our priority is to enable you to develop the necessary critical skills to be able to *do* research, and so to work out these issues for yourself as you encounter them in practice.

The series does, therefore, take a distinctive approach in trying to bridge older divides, to stress the value of specific case studies, and to encourage individual research set in the framework of our existing knowledge. On such points you will find a broad consensus among our authors. It would be wrong, however, to imply total uniformity. Some authors prefer to test hypotheses or use quantitative methods; others prefer more open-ended questioning, perhaps drawing on a variety of sources; some look primarily to documentary sources, others to oral evidence; some are concerned with questions of power or economic constraints, others with human meanings, memories or culture. The approaches that you prefer and choose to follow up will give yet another twist to the final outcome.

2.2 WHAT DO WE MEAN BY 'FAMILY HISTORY' AND 'COMMUNITY HISTORY'?

Finally, let us turn to this crucial question: it is an important one, if only because these terms have more than one meaning.

The quick answer is that by 'family history' we mean something wider than 'genealogy'; and by 'community history' we mean something that goes beyond 'local history'. A more considered response to the question might be: wait and see how *you* define them after working through the volumes in this series and (equally important) conducting your own research – the proof of the pudding being in the eating.

A medium-term answer would be to relate the questions to the approach we have just been describing. In both family and community history we are dealing with interaction between the general *and* the specific. 'Family history' as we understand it is *not* just about single families but about the wider experience of family life through time, an approach sometimes described as 'the history of the family'. However, it draws on micro studies and appreciates the value of individual cases and diversities, and is thus more down to earth than the vaster speculations sometimes put forward about the evolution of 'The Family' through many millennia. It deals with historical processes and the theories developed to illuminate them within particular periods and areas. Above all it constantly moves backwards and forwards between individual families and more, or less, general patterns and theories (this is illustrated further in Chapter 1; see especially Figure 1.7).

The same applies to 'community history'. This is elaborated in Volumes 2 and 3 in the series, but, briefly, it is something more than just the tracing of unrelated events in a particular locality over the centuries (though, as with genealogy, this could form a useful starting point). It is partly a matter of putting investigations of a particular place within a wider framework, of relating them comparatively to more general findings and theories about how 'communities' are constituted and function. It also means ultimately aiming to set them in the context of the interacting political, economic, religious and cultural processes within (and beyond) a given community, both at a particular point and over time. Dennis Mills sums up the distinction between local history – concerned with the history of 'any aspect of human endeavour at the local level' – and community history:

> Community history ... has begun to focus more sharply on a particular group of concepts ... relating to the problems of *defining* communities; ... of *relationships* between individuals and households *within* communities; and ... of *relations between* communities. ... The pursuit of these complex webs of activity forms one of the hallmarks of community, as opposed to simply local history.

(Mills, 1993, pp.281–2)

This first volume focuses on one particular aspect of family and community history – the structure, functioning and relationships of family life over the last two centuries – and does so within the framework just described. It illustrates how individual studies of a particular family can be related to more general themes and contexts, leading on to the broader study of the history of the family; and it closes by highlighting links with contemporary debates about the nature and history of 'the family', inviting you to relate your own research to such issues.

The emphasis is on starting from where you are (from previous research or some current interest) and on conducting a small study at a family or community level. This is not simply because small studies are more manageable, but because we believe that such studies, once put in wider perspective, have a vital role to play in developing our historical understanding.

REFERENCES AND FURTHER READING

Note: suggestions for further reading are indicated by an asterisk.

Burke, P. (ed.) (1991) *New perspectives on historical writing*, Cambridge, Polity Press.

Burke, P. (1992) *History and social theory*, Cambridge, Polity Press.[*]

Davis, G. (1991) *The Irish in Britain 1815–1914*, Dublin, Gill and Macmillan.

Drake, M. (ed.) (1994) *Time, family and community: perspectives on family and community history*, Oxford, Blackwell in association with The Open University (Course Reader).

Elliott, B. (1990) 'Biography, family history and the analysis of social change', in Kendrick, S. *et al.* (eds) *Interpreting the past, understanding the present*, Basingstoke and London, Macmillan for British Sociological Association. Reprinted in Drake (1994).[*]

Hareven, T. (1991) 'The history of the family and the complexity of social change', *American Historical Review* 96, 1, pp.95–124. Reprinted in an abridged form as 'Recent research on the history of the family' in Drake (1994).

Hastrup, K. (ed.) (1992) *Other histories*, London, Routledge.

Hudson, P. (ed.) (1989) *Regions and industries: a perspective on the Industrial Revolution in Britain*, Cambridge, Cambridge University Press.

Jones, G.S. (1976) 'From historical sociology to theoretical history', *British Journal of Sociology*, 27, pp.295–305.

Mills, D. (1993) 'Community and nation in the past: perception and reality', in Drake (1994).[*]

O'Brian, P. and Quinault, R. (eds) (1993) *The Industrial Revolution and British society*, Cambridge, Cambridge University Press.

Phythian-Adams, C.V. (1991) 'Local history and national history: the question for the peoples of England', *Rural History*, 2, 1, pp.1–23.

Rapport, N. (1992) 'From affect to analysis: the biography of an interaction in an English village', in Okely, J. and Callaway, H. (eds) (1992) *Anthropology and autobiography*, London, Routledge.

Schürer, K. (1991) 'The future for local history: boom or recession?', *The Local Historian*, 1991, pp.99–108.

Smith, D. (1982) 'Social history and sociology – more than just good friends', *Sociological Review*, 30, pp.286–308.

Stanley, L. and Morgan, D. (eds) (1993) *Auto/biography in sociology*, special issue, *Sociology*, 27, 1.

PART I

PERSPECTIVES ON YOUR OWN STUDY

❖ ❖ ❖

Chapter 1

STARTING FROM WHERE YOU ARE

by Ruth Finnegan

Just about everyone knows something about their family background: about their parents, most likely, and where they come from; or about their brothers and sisters, or, perhaps in due course, their spouse and children. My family, at its most basic, is shown in Figure 1.1.

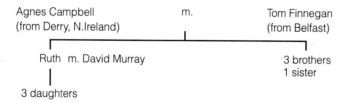

Figure 1.1   Ruth Finnegan's family

The links in Figure 1.1, as also in more elaborate family trees, are principally biological and marital: parents–children; husband–wife. Some families, of course, are based on adoption or fosterage, or result from non-marital unions. These links too provide a framework for family formation and investigation. This knowledge of our family background, however incomplete, gives us a place to stand – some consciousness, whether painful or happy, of who we are through the past and the present.

It can also give us a place to 'dig'. Indeed the commonest advice in genealogy and local history is precisely this: begin from your own family, your own workplace, your own locality, before extending back in time or out in space. That same strategy will start off our studies of family and community history.

So where are you now? Let us begin by looking at the possible points at which you may now be standing.

You may already have some background in social sciences or social history, and want to apply this to the study of family or community history without as yet having gone very far into the history of your own family or locality. Alternatively, you may have amplified the sketchy knowledge most people already have about their family background by some investigation of your own family tree or locality, but have less experience of relating this to the history of the family more generally. Each of these starting points is valuable. But, equally, neither is sufficient in itself. Our plan here, therefore, is to take each in turn and bring them together progressively throughout this chapter. As befits the title of this volume, the focus is more on family than on community, but the general lessons can equally be applied to local history (this is followed up in Volumes 2 and 3).

1 FROM THE PARTICULAR TO THE GENERAL

So where might you be if you have already worked on researching your own family history? You may already have arrived at some such overall picture as that in Figure 1.2 (though your own example may so far be less – or maybe more – full than this one). Note that the family tree shown in Figure 1.2 should be regarded as a working document only – it does not adhere to all the conventions of family tree construction as followed by genealogists.

Look more closely at Figure 1.2. How can it lead to more general questions?

Well, in one way it is just another unique family tree: fascinating for Arnison descendants perhaps, but maybe of little wider interest? But it *does* also include information we could build on. Notice, for example, the different occupations between and within the generations: we could investigate how far these mirrored similar diversities among other families. Are the changes between generations linked to the diversification in occupations and the move out of farming that came with the industrial revolution? Did the experience of this family fit in with – and form the basis for – what we know about urbanization and industrialization during the nineteenth and twentieth centuries? And can we draw on more general findings to say more about the kinds of domestic groups they were likely to live in, how they kept up family links with relations outside their immediate households, or how they organized their family affairs?

Raising such questions inevitably draws us into wider issues. Some lead us into recent research on migration (examined in Volume 2), occupations or social mobility (treated in Volume 3, which incidentally tells more about the fortunes of the Arnisons). Others link into questions treated later in this volume: for example demography and family structure (Chapter 3), findings about domestic economies and family resources (Chapter 4), or debates about the history of the family (see section 2 below and Chapter 6, section 2). Our knowledge of one particular family – the Arnisons or any other – can both contribute to, and be illuminated by, the more general patterns.

Alternatively you may have explored the composition of your family and how it lived in earlier times by discovering its household make-up in a nineteenth-century census entry. One example is reproduced as Figure 1.3.

This is a valuable document containing a great deal of information. Indeed, as you may know already, the census enumerators' books (commonly abridged to CEBs) are key sources for studying the family in Britain for the period 1841–1891 (in Ireland 1901, 1911). They have formed both the basis of and the testing ground for many theories about, for example, the relation between family or locality, or the size and structure of households (further comments on CEBs can be found in Chapters 2 and 3 and in Volume 4).

Look carefully at the entry shown in Figure 1.3, especially the first Goodaire family. What further questions does it raise?

One immediate question that springs to mind is whether most nineteenth-century households in the British Isles were made up in the same way as the one presented here. What about the other entries on this page, or elsewhere? Did all families have servants? How did household size and structure vary according to date, region or wealth? How did it change with different stages in the family's development: for example, did sons stay or move out on marriage? Was it usual for the wife not (apparently) to be in employment? Did relations often live near each other? We will be returning to the Goodaires in Chapter 3, where you can find a transcript of part of this facsimile (see p.87) and answers to some of the questions. But the more general point is that this and any similar entries inevitably lead us on to larger questions about demography, household structure, the domestic cycle and family economy, all explored in later chapters in this volume.

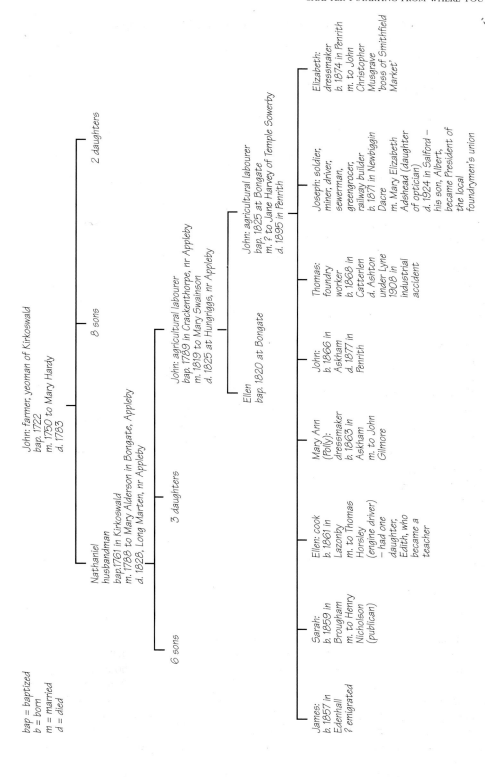

Figure 1.2 Part of the Arnison family tree: the Manchester Arnisons (Source: Monica Shelley)

11

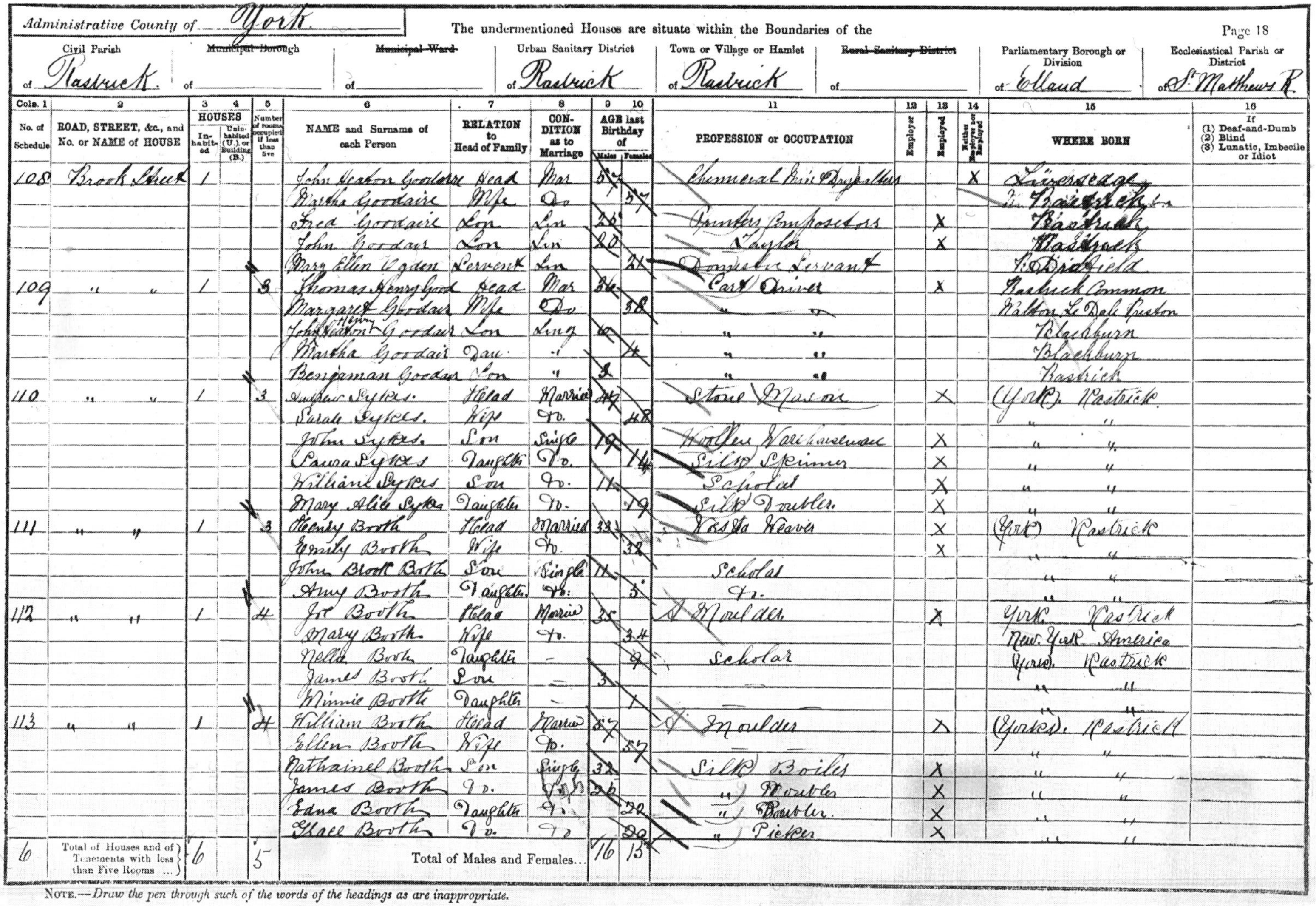

Administrative County of York

The undermentioned Houses are situate within the Boundaries of the

Page 18

Civil Parish	~~Municipal Borough~~	~~Municipal Ward~~	Urban Sanitary District	Town or Village or Hamlet	~~Rural Sanitary District~~	Parliamentary Borough or Division	Ecclesiastical Parish or District
of Rastrick	of	of	of Rastrick	of Rastrick	of	of Elland	of St. Matthews R.

Cols. 1 No. of Schedule	2 ROAD, STREET, &c., and No. or NAME of HOUSE	3 HOUSES Inhabited	4 HOUSES Uninhabited (U.) or Building (B.)	5 Number of rooms occupied if less than five	6 NAME and Surname of each Person	7 RELATION to Head of Family	8 CONDITION as to Marriage	9 AGE last Birthday of Males	10 AGE last Birthday of Females	11 PROFESSION or OCCUPATION	12 Employer	13 Employed	14 Neither Employer nor Employed	15 WHERE BORN	16 If (1) Deaf-and-Dumb (2) Blind (3) Lunatic, Imbecile or Idiot
108	Brook Street	1			John Heaton Goodair	Head	Mar	57		Chemical Mix & Drysalter			X	Liversedge	
					Martha Goodaire	Wife	Do		57					[illegible]	
					Fred Goodaire	Son	Sin	25		Printers Compositors		X		Rastrick	
					John Goodair	Son	Sin	20		Taylor		X		Rastrick	
					Mary Ellen Ogden	Servent	Sin		21	Domestic Servant				S. Driffield	
109	" "	1		3	Thomas Henry Good[air]	Head	Mar	36		Cart Driver		X		Rastrick Common	
					Margaret Goodair	Wife	Do		38	"				Walton Le Dale Preston	
					John Henry Goodair	Son	Sing	10		"				Blackburn	
					Martha Goodair	Dau	"		4	"				Blackburn	
					Benjaman Goodair	Son	"	2		"				Rastrick	
110	" "	1		3	Arthur Sykes	Head	Married	47		Stone Mason		X		(York) Rastrick	
					Sarah Sykes	Wife	Do		48					" "	
					John Sykes	Son	Single	19		Woollen Warehouseman		X		" "	
					Laura Sykes	Daughter	Do		14	Silk Spinner		X		" "	
					William Sykes	Son	Do	11		Scholar		X		" "	
					Mary Alice Sykes	Daughter	Do		19	Silk Doubler		X		" "	
111	" "	1		3	Henry Booth	Head	Married	33		Worsted Weaver		X		(York) Rastrick	
					Emily Booth	Wife	Do		32			X		" "	
					John Brook Booth	Son	Single	11		Scholar				" "	
					Amy Booth	Daughter	Do		5	Do				" "	
112	" "	1		4	Joe Booth	Head	Married	35		Moulder		X		York Rastrick	
					Mary Booth	Wife	Do		34					New York America	
					Nellie Booth	Daughter	–		9	Scholar				York Rastrick	
					James Booth	Son	–	3						" "	
					Minnie Booth	Daughter	–		1					" "	
113	" "	1		4	William Booth	Head	Married	57		Moulder		X		(Yorks) Rastrick	
					Ellen Booth	Wife	Do		57					" "	
					Nathainel Booth	Son	Single	32		Silk Boiler		X		" "	
					James Booth	Do	[illegible]	26		" Doubler		X		" "	
					Edna Booth	Daughter	Do		22	" Doubler		X		" "	
					Grace Booth	Do	Do		20	" Picker		X		" "	
6	Total of Houses and of Tenements with less than Five Rooms	6		5	Total of Males and Females...			16	13						

NOTE.—*Draw the pen through such of the words of the headings as are inappropriate.*

Figure 1.3 Facsimile of entry from census enumerator's book for Rastrick, Yorkshire, 1891 (Source: Public Record Office)

Figure 1.4   Image of a family: photograph of the family of John Maxwell Finnegan of Belfast, with his second wife, Susanna (c. 1903)

Photographs are another common source. Figure 1.4 is an example from my own family. At first sight such photographs merely give information about some members of a particular family at one point in time. But even this can lead on to further questions. In fact, as I know from other sources, the elder two children were those of John Finnegan's first (deceased) wife. We tend to picture 'the family' as ideally from two common parents – but perhaps 'composite' families like this are and were not so uncommon? Look further: does this – and similar photographs – also indicate something about people's *ideal* image of the family or of the differing kinds of people within it? Were the photographs taken in a form and context to convey this? How do such images vary across, say, date, place or class, and link to presuppositions about internal family roles or relationships? Or again, are photographs associated with particular family rituals (such as weddings) when relations gather even if they are not otherwise close? (For further discussion of photographs see Volume 4.)

It may be that you know little about your earlier ancestors but are well informed about recent members of your family, especially those living near you or currently significant in your life. Your researches may thus extend laterally rather than vertically into the past, resulting in something like Figure 1.5.

Notice the horizontal rather than vertical family links. Perhaps this represents not just lack of knowledge by the researcher but also some more positive points about the way people sometimes live. Is this a case of recognizing kinship links according to situation and practicality rather than following purely genealogical links into the past? If so, 'relations' rather than 'ancestors' might be important. Maybe too this can be related to theories about extended kinship ties and their relevance, or to arguments about whether families 'support' each other more or less than in the past, and who does the 'supporting' and in what ways (a much discussed topic, see Chapter 4).

Horizontal kinship links like these may also be typical when people have migrated. With relations moving around and sometimes separated by great distances, contact and mutual

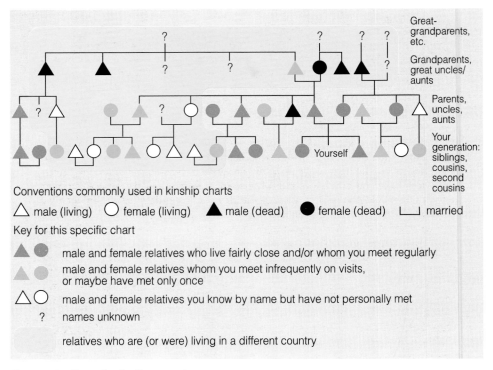

Figure 1.5 Chart of a family network

support may well be mostly between those living nearby, regardless of closeness in 'blood' terms, while other family links might just be exploited situationally as and when needed – for example, a visit to an otherwise unfamiliar relative overseas. If this is a common pattern, is it to be found here? Is it just confined to recent migrants? Studying present and earlier generations of this and comparable families could throw light on these questions.

Alternatively you may have heard about the earlier experiences of your family – or at least the family myths about them – from, say, a grandparent's spoken or written recollections. Or you may have autobiographies or recorded reminiscences from other members of your family from which you can build up some picture of their earlier life and times. Such sources can be of many different kinds, but the examples below illustrate some common forms.

The first source is part of an autobiographical extract published for the first time in John Burnett's collection *Useful toil* (1974). It is the story of a young girl who was born in Newcastle-upon-Tyne in 1906, the daughter of a blacksmith striker.

Lavinia Swainbank, house-maid

The year 1922 was not an easy time to be starting out on one's career. For those were the days of depression on the Tyne, when the shipyards were idle and pits closed down and every day the queue of sad-eyed men signing on for dole grew longer and hope of finding work grew more remote.

Passing the eleven-plus exam was just a matter of pride of achievement. One realized there was no money to spend on books or uniform. One could enter and pass the exams that meant a chance in one of the more exalted jobs, but here again one met with frustration time and time again, when it was pointed out (usually when one had succeeded in passing) that one needed to have graduated from a secondary school at least. The English teacher, too, who tried so hard, without success, to open the way to a career in journalism for a promising pupil must have realized from the start that he was fighting a losing battle, for where could the parents of the pupil find the necessary £50 premium?

Money alone was the key to success.

Thus at sixteen, I entered into a career of drudgery where long hours, low wages and very often inadequate food were accepted standards of a life that was thrust on one out of sheer necessity. The next six years of my life were to be spent in graduating from 'tweeny' in a Lakeland hotel, to second house-maid in gentlemen's service (strange term for a household comprising of mother and two spinster daughters). Ultimately I reached my peak as third house-maid in one of the stately homes of England. I took great pride in my work, and however menial domestic work was considered to be even at that time, I vowed to do it well and to the best of my ability. ...

My second venture was a definite improvement, as under-house-maid of two in a private house. The family consisted of mother and two spinster daughters. I was to receive 30s. per month and my keep. I had a room to myself here. The type of room I discovered through trial that one always expected in 'gentlemen's service' has an iron bedstead with lumpy mattress, specially manufactured for the use of maids, I suspect, a painted chest of drawers, with spotty mirror, lino-covered floor and a strip of matting at the bedside. Oh yes! The alarm clock. Here I was to familiarize myself with The Timetable. I had never before seen one of these and on first sight I could not see how one could possibly perform these duties in one day. This proved a splendid basic training, turning an ordinary human being into something resembling a well-oiled-machine whose rhythm and motion ran smoothly like a clock. To this day I have not lost the clockwork precision instilled into me by a succession of head house-maids and timetables forty-eight years ago. There were no vacuums, so carpets were brushed with a small hard brush with either tea-leaves or salt to settle the dust. In a kneeling position of course. There were awful open grates, with steel fire-irons thicker than my skinny arms, to be emery-papered each morning, the glass screen over the open grate to be washed with wash-leather, and finally the basin of whitening powder, with cloth for washing hearths. All this paraphernalia to be carried round from room to room. The rooms were always fitted out with syphons of soda water, which proved a boon to one overworked house-maid. Easier to squirt the hearth than make those endless trips back and forth for water to moisten the whitening.

(quoted from Burnett, 1974, pp.221–2)

This is only a snippet from one person's account of just a few details in her life. It has its limitations as a source, for her memories are no doubt coloured by hindsight, perhaps written with an eye to the reactions of her likely readers. (Autobiographies are useful sources, but need to be used with care; see Volume 4.) Even the whole autobiography cannot tell us *everything* about the social constraints on Lavinia Swainbank's life, let alone whether it was typical of such experiences.

On the other hand, this *is* a personal account of real experiences, even if written after the event. It is often precisely this subjective personal dimension that is missing in many accounts of the past, particularly for 'ordinary' men and women. It gives us a special insight, different from generalized accounts of occupations or of migration. It also cries out for more investigation into the *context* of this one life: what were the common processes of migrating within this country, for example, or the nature of domestic service? (These questions are followed up in Volumes 2 and 3 respectively.)

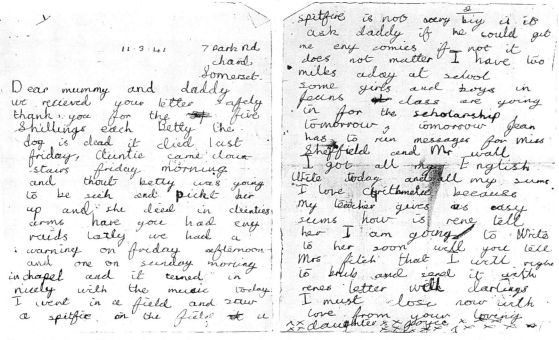

Figure 1.6 'Joyce Wright writes home': an evacuee's letter from the Second World War (Source: Wicks, 1988)

It is possible that you have personal letters from members of your family. As these are naturally most frequent between people separated from friends or family, they are a good source for that experience. Figure 1.6 gives one example.

What wider issues might this child's letter lead to? Perhaps it will bring back personal memories. It certainly reminds us that though we may prefer to picture 'the family' as living together – 'the family' and 'the household' as coterminous – the actual situation is often more complex. Over a million people were evacuated in the first week of the Second World War, and though many who moved in the first panic later went home, many children went through that same experience of living away from their parents – as have so many children at other times, through being away at school, being brought up by relatives while their parents were abroad, or in the absence of their 'own' parents through death or divorce. So how are children brought up? How typical or how factually based is our idealized notion of 'the family' as a constant co-resident unit? Was it different in the past? These are questions we will return to.

Here is another letter, this time from an earlier period and a greater distance. It is one of many sent by the Kerr brothers to their extended family in Antrim. Unlike Lavinia Swainbank's reminiscences, they were written at the time, unaffected by hindsight.

> 62 Jane Street
> New York
> U.S.A.
> June 12th 1847
> Dear Uncle,
> I wrote a letter to you last week which was to go by Packet on Monday last, wishing you to send out David [his younger brother], if he will come, as soon as possible; but as letters by this sailing Packet are sometimes lost and often detained, I sit down to write to you again on the same subject …

I can get David a place I have no doubt, to learn a trade I believe in this city ... I stated that I thought a Ship Carpenter a good trade, but I have been looking at them and I must say it is a very laborious business, and requires one to be out of doors generally summer and winter. So that it would require a strong frame and a person inured to the climate to stand this. The wages of Journeymen Ship Carpenters have been higher this year than usual; two dollars per day, that of pattern makers or Machinist 1 dollar 50 cents or 75 cents and then the latter work in a shop all the time or at least but seldom out of it. If David comes he can choose when here.

I wrote a letter to William [another brother, a policeman] along with the one to you. I did not just bid him to come and I held out no particular inducement, but I know he can do as well here as I am doing or as I have done and I would not exchange my chances here for the situation of a policeman in Ireland. If I were in William's place I would embark for America ...

If neither David nor William come I intend to go to sea, on a Whaling expedition, more for my health than anything else; although I could make 3 or 4 hundred dollars by the enterprise ...

I informed you in my letter last winter what kind of clothes David ought to bring ... Don't take his passage in Belfast but go to Liverpool, and avoid if possible an emigrant passenger vessel, for every one of those coming here has 40 or 50 bad in the ship fever, a bad kind of typhus. There are now 1300 sick in this fever at the quarantine ground near this city. So you see what a risk it is to come in one of these. There are vast numbers of emigrants coming here now; more than was ever known before.

It would be as well for David to bring with him what money he has, for he might need it more now than at any time hereafter. When he will have learnt his trade, there will be no fear of him; he can get work then almost anywhere in the United States. He may bring plenty of shirts and socks, both linen and check shirts and woollen and cotton socks ... If he will bring me a dozen of woollen and a dozen of cotton socks pick large ones, and half a dozen of linen shirts pretty fine, and keep an account of the price, I will pay him ... .

Besides I send in this my measure for a coat which you can get made in Magee's in Belfast or from any other good tailor there. You will get it cheaper at a merchant tailor. He is a merchant tailor and just by giving him the measure and choosing the cloth in his own shop, he will furnish the coat at whatever price you want ... I want the coat an invisible green or invisible blue rather dark. Price £2 or £2.5s. I would not care much if it should go £2.10s. but £2 will do. Let him make it as coats are generally worn in Belfast, pretty full in the skirts. If you are in a hurry he will make it in a day: such a coat would cost here 15 or 20 dollars, so I will save something.

I think this is all. William knows what to bring. When you have engaged the passage, write me and let me know the name of the vessel and when she will sail and I will look out for her. David must drink gruel when he is sick, and when better eat light food and sparingly for a while. Take a little salts every day from the first. Bring Molasses and use them. Give the old cook a shilling now and again. Bring oat bread and a little biscuit. Plenty of eggs, they will keep. Lend the sailors a hand now and again pulling a rope but don't venture aloft except on a calm day. Have your name on your trunks, and watch and always keep them locked. Keep yourself clean and stay on deck a good deal in the air.

Direct all your letters 62 Jane Street, New York. I must close. Give my respects to all, tell David to play the man and go ahead.

John Kerr

Tell David to keep his watch if he has one, and his knife, etc. in his trunk and take care that he does not lose his keys, for he will readily lose all overboard that he may have in his trouser pocket, put these in his trunk. I saw Wm. Kyle before I left Pittsburg. He was well, as were all. He cannot send his father any money at present.

(Source: Foy, 1989, letter 9, pp.55–7)

Once again this is a very individual letter, but it relates to recurrent themes in family history. Here too we find separated family members, but their separation is tempered by links through letters and continuing mutual concern: 'the family' as in one sense extending well beyond a single co-resident unit (a pattern we will meet again). David and William did in fact follow their elder brother – part of that great movement from Europe to America in the nineteenth century – and so too did two other brothers later, keeping up contact with members of the family on both sides of the Atlantic. We know from other sources that John, the eldest, was the first to emigrate at the age of 17, a move partly explained by his background – orphaned at the age of 15 and, together with his brother, living with his dead mother's brother, 'Uncle' James Graham, on his family's farm. Can we see a typical agricultural pattern here (further discussed in Chapter 4, section 1), with some members of a farming family leaving to seek a livelihood elsewhere since one farm could not absorb their labour or support them all? Though the Grahams and Kerrs appear to have been reasonably well off and protected from the worst shortages of the famine years, John Kerr himself had no land to inherit. His departure to seek his fortune across the Atlantic while keeping up his family links with home – for a time – was one characteristic feature, it appears, of family experience and composition in much of nineteenth-century Ireland. Further general issues arise about how typical it was for single men to emigrate, how far they kept up relationships with their families at home, and to what extent and when they became assimilated into the foreign society.

Not everyone will have access to the kind of letters quoted here (although published letters, as in Erickson's (1972) analytic collection, can provide rich sources). But similar themes will be surfacing in many contexts: above all the interaction between individual lives and the wider historical movements by which they were both affected and themselves helped to form. (There is further discussion of migration in Volume 2, and of private letters in Volume 4; see also Chapter 2, section 3 below).

Oral recordings of personal memories of the past are becoming increasingly common. Here is one example, recorded by an oral history group of seven women of African and Caribbean descent in a community education project in Southwark.

Wendy's memories of her grandmother

Who is really interested in me or my family and friends? Who cares that I met with my great uncle Stanley for the first time in Trinidad, August '88, who at 93 told me his grandmother was taken from Africa at the age of 15 and died in Grenada at the grand old age of 110! Who cares? Who wants to know that my grandfather was a genius inventing all sorts of domestic gadgets for people in a small village called River Road in Grenada? Who is interested that my great aunt was the first black woman to own and drive a Ford motor car in Aruba, West Indies and perhaps the first black woman in the world? Who wants to know? The point is that all of these facts and events happened and there were reasons which made them happen. ...

I never had the opportunity of meeting my other grandparents. My grandfather by my mother died when I was two and my father's grandparents died a few years ago in Grenada.

But, the one grandmother who has stood by me since birth is the gracious woman Molly Esther Baptiste. Well – she wasn't always gracious in my eyes. As a child my respect for her was like fear itself, not because she was an ogre, quite the contrary. She couldn't tolerate rudeness, unpunctuality and a lazy house cleaner. At one stage I was all three. So I was told off quite a bit – but it's the way she would tell you off – she'd never shout or hit – I can't remember being hit. She'd somehow get me to reflect on my actions to the extent where I could plainly see I was wrong. I used to hate that so much – she was right, I was wrong, and I couldn't run away from it. The fear I had therefore was not for my Granny but for being wrong and having to admit it.

I remember the days we used to play my mum up. Like not fulfilling house chores, being rude and killing a gallon of orange quash in three days – no wonder I had a chronic skin problem. When my mum lost her voice through shouting she'd call granny to finish it off: 'Anyway, uh ringing all you grandmoder – she go give you.' … We'd hear the fingers in the dial, then a pause, then 'Oh Gard mummy it's dem children – what I go do – dem children go kill me!' What an exaggeration we thought. Then my mum would call us, 'Wendy and Debbie – come you grandmoder want to talk to you.' I often felt as if I was being called up for sentencing.

The benefit of being 27 and not 14 is that I don't have to put up with that anymore. Unchanged, however, is my undying love for my granny and hers for me. Today we are great friends, I must see her weekly or I feel ill. I've grown up on her stories, they make me laugh, cry and think my gran is such a joker. She should have been a stand-up comic. Serious, my belly hurts every time I'm with her. What I look forward to most of all is her food – food so tasty I can't describe it so I won't bother. Have you ever had food so good you wanna cry? I can't talk when I'm eating her food – just savour. She gives you enough too and if you don't eat all of it you're in trouble. 'Com' – eat gierl – eat – there's more – eat me food you know – hum …'

Afterwards we talk and talk – I love to hear about her life back home and her stories of her childhood and the hows and whys of her moving to England. And how she worked hard to send for all her children. It's only then I realise how proud I am of this woman and how proud she is of herself, her achievements and her family. As she often says, 'Uh work hard and uh'm pleased for my children, grandchildren and great grans, I pray for them everyday. Anytime papa God ready he can take me – I am pleased – I'm satisfied – I'm at peace, my conscience is clean.'

Most of all I'm amazed that so many of us come from this one woman as she so readily boasts 'My dear, uh have nine children – three boys and six girls. Twenty-one grandchildren and nine great grandchildren.' We're still counting.

(Alo-wa, 1990, pp.4–5, 10–11)

This extract, of course, gives voice to just one person's memories. They are no doubt coloured by the grandmother's present situation and Wendy's own relationship to her as well as by the context in which the memories were recorded. The memories she reports of the earlier generations are dramatic, but the likelihood of being able to trace much of that earlier detail now is – it must be accepted – quite remote (speculative conclusions over far-back generations such as those in Alex Haley's moving book *Roots* (1976) are now regarded somewhat sceptically by modern scholars, even those sympathetic to Haley's personal quest). But personal memories can give rich clues to questions about the more recent past. Here we have the other side of the coin to John Kerr's emigrating experience – but perhaps with some similarities too? So how does this case fit with other patterns of migratory movement? Or with the importance of *women* in West Indian family patterns? Is this an individual illustration of the well-known phenomenon of 'chain migration', with one member of the family following another? If so, how did it work and were other families similar or dissimilar? On a different tack, how does Wendy's account fit with recent analyses of oral history as a method, or the role of family stories in a family's sense of identity? These are questions to which we shall return.

Finally you might have found something like the plan shown in Figure 5.3 on pp.134–5. In itself the plan is simple, but it leads into a host of questions about certain working-class families living in the Katharine Buildings of East London in the 1880s, and about some influences on how they lived. (You can find out some of the answers in Chapter 5.)

On the other hand you may already have gone beyond individual examples and engaged in the systematic collection and recording of memories not only from your own relations but also from others in the locality or elsewhere. Or you may have moved beyond just your own family to explore, for example, the wider patterns of household size, or of occupational and spatial distribution within a particular locality.

Whatever your background, does your knowledge or research so far overlap with any of the examples given here?

If you have touched on any sources or examples similar to those above, even if only spasmodically and unsystematically, you have something to build on. What is more, you have the incentive and insight given by starting from a personal interest which stirs you. Such examples are essential in putting flesh on what otherwise can seem merely abstract theorizing about 'the history of the family'. But it is also easy to fall into over-preoccupation with one individual case (a temptation that we all succumb to when exploring our own families!). Setting the single case in context means having to lift one's eyes to the wider horizons. We have to see how far it is or is not typical of wider patterns, how it can be more fully understood by setting it in context or applying new insights, and how it can in its turn contribute to our more general knowledge. So we begin from what we know (often more than we think) and what we have done already. But so as not just to stop there, a necessary next stage is to put it in wider perspective.

_____ *EXERCISE 1.1* _____

Spend a few moments glancing back through this section and making brief notes on:

1   the strengths and limitations of each of the examples above for the wider study of family history;

2   those examples you found (a) most interesting, (b) dullest.

Then go on to compare your reactions to the discussion that follows.

_____

Clearly all have their own strengths. Some of the sources are official documents, such as the CEBs. Others, like Wendy's, are oral reminiscences, privately written accounts or family letters. Searching out and using such sources for first-hand research challenges one's personal resource-fulness, motivation and sustained interest to a level often not required of conventional university students even at an advanced level. Reaching conclusions from them, furthermore, demands time spent discovering, analysing and putting together evidence from a variety of sources. The individual cases drawn from such research represent something of great value, not only for the researcher personally, but also for our enhanced understanding of the lives of ordinary people in the past – an insight which historians and social scientists are now increasingly beginning to appreciate.

But the examples have their limitations too. None of the sources or findings is comprehensive. The names or dates are obviously sometimes incomplete, and many potentially interesting details are lacking. Even more relevant for the purposes of this chapter are the following two points.

First, each example is (understandably) based on only a selection of sources, and highlights those facts which can easily be found in them – to the neglect of other aspects. Official documents such as the CEBs (as in Figure 1.3) or the records of the General Register Office (a major source for diagrams like Figure 1.2) provide valuable information about birth, marriage, death or residence, but are silent about personal experience: what people did and felt. The more personal accounts like Wendy's, John Kerr's or Joyce Wright's convey the experiential dimensions – often very vividly – but with few links into a more systematic framework. We might be able to go further if we could complement such findings through other sources, and scrutinize the sources critically in terms not only of what is there, but also of what is left out.

Second, each example really refers to just one unique case – one family, one household, one individual's experience. Each has its own richness and can grip us when it touches our own experience, but may seem to carry little interest when it belongs to others.

But relating each example to *other* cases is precisely the way both to make them more interesting to others and to see them in a wider perspective. So we come back to the kinds of questions raised earlier. Are these examples typical – and if not, how and why not? How can they be illuminated by, and themselves contribute to, wider historical debates or findings about recurrent patterns? Are they part of a more general history of the family? Such moves take us on from family history in the sense of genealogy – the personal exploration of a family tree – to the broader sense of family history which relates individual findings to more general patterns and to the current scholarly literature on the family, or, more broadly still, to the complex history of the family itself.

EXERCISE 1.2

Review the discussion above by spending a few moments jotting down any personal reactions on how you might apply it in the case of your own research (whether this consists of a family tree, a computer analysis of census data, or merely the first stirrings of interest in your own or another's family). Have you noticed any wider issues your own research could lead to?

You will come back to this question throughout this volume. Without doubt your answers will grow.

---

2   FROM THE GENERAL TO THE PARTICULAR – AND BACK

You might also start from the other end: beginning from general questions and findings, and only then going on to see how these relate to individual cases. This too is a strong background for research. Thus you may already have an established interest in, say, the role of the family in modern society or the history of the family generally. Or your focus may be broader still. Readers with an academic background in sociology or history, for example, may be familiar with debates about industrialization, urbanization, or the significance of 'family', 'community' or 'class' in modern as against 'traditional' society. These themes do indeed surface in this and subsequent volumes, and some prior acquaintance with such debates, and the kind of terminologies in which their exponents express themselves, is certainly an advantage.

On the other hand, researchers with this kind of background may have little experience of dealing directly with primary sources. Furthermore, traditional academic courses sometimes lay more stress on theories and generalizations than on the individual cases which ultimately form their basis. So here too – but starting the other way round – new insights can be gained by relating these general questions to investigations of the particular.

The strategy of looking at the general first and then trying to relate it to individual cases can take various forms. One is to start with some open-ended general question (say, 'how has marriage changed over the last century?'). The next step would be to refine that question as you discover more about detailed sources and complexities, eventually tying it down to a more limited investigation to suit the researcher's time and source constraints. Another standard strategy is to take an already limited statement – for example the interesting statement that in 1851 fewer than one in two people were living in the same place they had been born (Anderson, 1983, p.8). You could then test this out for people in a specific locality. Afterwards you could go back to the general accounts, perhaps finding they had been confirmed, perhaps that they need refining, rejecting or restating in new ways (further comments on these strategies are given in Chapter 2). Either way the central procedure is to relate the general to the individual, and vice versa.

Here is another example of this procedure, this time starting from some general statements made about the family and its history, and examining these by reference to specific examples. Moving like this between the general and the particular sharpens your understanding not just of wider scholarship but also of individual cases. (Even if you are already familiar with the evidence for or against these statements, give them another look for the purpose of this exercise.)

Look at the following assertions about the family and its history. They are ones you have probably come across either in the academic literature or (just as likely) in public speeches and everyday assumptions.

1   Families are so different that it is impossible to generalize about them.

2   Wherever it is found 'the family' differs little in essentials.

3   Life expectancy was lower in the past, with consequences for the structure of the family.

4   In both the nineteenth and twentieth centuries people chose to live near their relations.

5   'The family' in the past, unlike today, was a stable and harmonious unit.

Do you think these statements are true? (Try them on your friends too.)

How did you react? Perhaps you were clear on some, not sure on others, if only because some are too vague to 'prove' once and for all. Yet they are all commonly made assertions about the history of the family. So, are they true or not? As a start, can we get any help by looking at the evidence from the examples discussed earlier?

EXERCISE 1.3

First look again at each of the five statements above, noting down briefly what light (if any) seems to be thrown on them by

(a)   all or any of the examples referred to in section 1;

(b)   your own research or knowledge if relevant.

The individual cases certainly give some humanity to the large-scale statements and in one way form their basis: without them there *could* be no general statements. On the other hand, it is difficult to use them as final evidence for or against any of the statements as a whole. When I tried to reach conclusions, I did have some 'trues' and 'falses' from just these examples – but also a lot of 'can't tells' or instances of 'yes *and* no'. But let us see if any points can be drawn out.

How about the assertion that 'Families are so different that it is impossible to generalize about them'? Many of the examples give such a vivid personal impression that one entirely justifiable reaction is that no generalization could ever faithfully capture that individual richness. On the other hand, there are also some regularities to be found, even from what is stated in the personal accounts themselves. So one reason for wondering how far the examples here really provide evidence for or against the statements may be that we are not sure how much weight to attach to just one instance. How far can we take it as typical, not perhaps of *all* comparable cases, but at least of a significant number?

The marked *differences* in the examples also raise doubts about the theory that the family differs little in essentials or indeed that there is one set direction in which 'the family' is developing, though it also depends on what you consider as 'essentials'. As for the earlier 'stable-harmonious families', perhaps the examples cannot inform us about the far distant past, but for the last two centuries they certainly suggest exceptions to a constant state of 'stability'. Families were broken up by death, or re-formed to become composite groupings. Note too the many movements, far *and* near, with or without other family members. Even though people might have preferred to stay near their original homes and families if conditions had been different, these bonds were necessarily disrupted when Lavinia Swainbank, John Kerr, Molly Esther Baptiste, Joyce Wright and so many others left their homes. There is not much evidence about life expectancy, and having nearby relations has to be 'yes *and* no'. But the biggest problem again is the difficulty of coming to any conclusion about these general statements from these *single* cases.

One obvious way to make further progress is to examine more cases. (Other ways would be to look more closely into the details of the individual cases, or to refine the statements themselves more clearly, but let us leave those aside for now.) What about other comparable cases?

Here we can fortunately turn to an intensive study of a large number of cases by Michael Anderson. The article overleaf, written by Anderson and published in *The Guardian* in 1982, summarizes his conclusions briefly.

_____ *EXERCISE 1.4* _____

Read the article and answer the following questions:

(a) What does Anderson's account suggest about the truth or falsity of our five statements?

(b) How reliable do you think this account is?

For comments see p.179.

Anderson's article is not the end of the matter, of course. Each statement could be investigated further, and his conclusions interpreted or tested out for other contexts (in Ireland, for example). Indeed, several are followed up in later chapters. You might also have wondered how far you can trust a brief article appearing in a newspaper (fitting only too well, perhaps, the social liberal tone of *The Guardian?*): this is a very proper critical question, of the kind worth applying to any source you use.

On the other hand Anderson's account does take us further than scattered individual cases. Anderson is well known for his research into family structures in nineteenth-century Lancashire (Anderson, 1971) and for his analysis of a 2 per cent national sample of the 1851 census of Great Britain (further expanded in Anderson, 1983). Despite some limitations, then, the conclusions sketched here *are* based on a very large number of cases in Great Britain, and are worth highlighting.

Many scholars now take the same line as Anderson in being sceptical about such popular stereotypes as the idea that families were harmonious and stable in the past – the 'Golden Age myth' – or that families are always and everywhere the same. The idea of one set direction of 'family development' through the centuries is also suspect nowadays. Attractive this idea may be, and it is apparently buttressed by older theories about 'evolution' or 'modernization'; but there is now much evidence against any simple ladder of development such as that from 'traditional' extended families to 'modern' nuclear ones. There have indeed been changes – not least in life

Property, know-how, fertility. What's love got to do with it?

THE MOST striking omission in the debate over the crisis in marriage and family life today is the almost total lack of any historical perspective. Too often we see things as new which are not new, while failing to appreciate how profoundly the changes in society and economy of the last 50 years have undermined some of the basic props of our traditional family morality.

Let us consider first what is not new; already in pre-industrial Britain we find references to battered wives and children and to adultery by those who thought that they could get away with it undetected. Premarital chastity is certainly not part of our cultural tradition; pre-marital sex was normal in some parts of eighteenth century Britain, and the chances of a child being born illegitimate were almost as high in mid-Victorian Britain as they are today.

Frequent marital dissolution is not new either, though in the past death was more likely to be responsible than personal preferences – not that they did not sometimes play a part as well. Indeed, in most areas of Europe before the present century marriages were almost as likely to be broken in their early years as they are in the present divorce boom, and the proportion of children affected before the normal age of independence may very well have been larger.

As far back as we can go, we also find something else familiar; couples, on marriage or very soon after, typically set up households of their own, the household consisting normally of husband, wife, children and, in some cases, one or more servants. Behind this outward similarity, however, were concealed fundamental differences in the social and economic contexts of marriage and in what sociologists would call its functions.

The first priority of all but the most affluent had to be to organise their household economy so as to avoid starvation now and, if possible, in old age. Survival would require the interdependent work efforts of all family members – husband, wife and, as soon as they could do anything useful, children. Historians are still arguing about whether, or when, most couples "fell in love", in the sense that we understand it, but what is clear is that there were several considerations in choosing a spouse and in the timing of marriage.

One was the property – dowry, land, tools, a few pieces of linen or household equipment – which the partners had gradually managed to assemble. A second was the agricultural, industrial and domestic skills they had gradually learned. A third was the likely fertility of the wife (she should be fertile – but not too fertile). The results were that marriage had to be delayed so that the property and skills could be assembled – the average age was around 28 for men and 26 for women in the sixteenth to eighteenth centuries; though many had to wait much longer.

Older wives were often popular: they had more skills and property, and were likely to produce fewer children. If a spouse died, remarriage could be very rapid (a few weeks in some areas) – the household economy could not long survive without two adults at its head. In spite of continual opposition from the Church, premarital sex continued – there were important advantages in knowing that your intended spouse could have children.

Once married, social controls could be severe. Small communities, thin house walls and the frequent presence of non-relatives (servants, workmen or lodgers) in the house made keeping any secrets difficult. Until the eighteenth century, Church courts had sweeping powers of investigation and sanction – in England they included for a time the power to break into any house in which adultery was suspected. The local community, by public ridicule and abuse could readily sanction the wife beater or those whose morals were considered too loose.

Over the past 250 years, at an accelerating pace, these social and economic props to marriage and family living have gradually weakened, while the demands we have made on marriage have steadily increased. In the peasant household the marital couple organised the household's production, using its own labour and coordinating the contributions of all family members.

But under our kind of capitalist system of production, work is rewarded on an individual basis. One or more household members daily leave the home and are paid by outsiders in a way which seldom takes account

United in death: Thomas de Beauchamp, Earl of Warwick, and his wife - a marriage of love, or practical convenience?

of his or her family situation. The wage has become the personal property of the individual, dependent on his or her own activities and paid in private, leaving to negotiation between family members the question of how it is to be divided and used.

Today where both spouses enter the labour force and each receives a private reward for labour, their work is not naturally seen as a co-operative productive activity or even, often, as one involving a complementary division of labour. When career paths conflict, as they often do, work can become a source of mutual antagonism, rather than mutual interdependence rooted in the need to survive.

In addition, the aspirations of those entering a modern marriage are much more susceptible to change over time than those of preindustrial European couples. Basic survival, together or often even alone, is not usually their first concern. Love (or whether or not it is fun to go on holiday together or out for a drink together) is largely a matter of personal taste.

Outsiders could play a mediating and advisory role if a dispute occurred about farming skills or domestic capabilities necessary for survival. But outside mediation, even by trained counsellors, can only play a

lesser role if the conflict involves what one or both see as personal incompatibility, failing to "turn each other on", or the fact that being together isn't fun any more.

Outsiders can play a much less authoritative role over the timing of marriage and the choice of spouse if the main problem likely to arise is one of whether or not the couple will be happy together. Modern contraception, by separating the pleasures of sexual activity from the risks of conception has seriously undermined what was once an almost certain link between extramarital sex and its consequences and has thus taken away a principal prop of the Christian morality of premarital – and indeed marital – chastity.

From an historical perspective, therefore, the family today lacks many of the social supports which it had even in the not too distant past. But other changes are important too. Younger ages of marriage and an increase in life expectancy among adults have combined roughly to double the average duration of marriages unbroken by social dissolution. "Till death do us part" now means not far short of 50 years.

The fall in family size and the fact that most couples have their children soon after mar-

riage means that, for the first time, most of the life span of marriage does not involve the care of small children. What was once the prime familial role of women has shrunk in its significance. At the same time increased leisure has increased further the potential time available for unhappiness, in the one relationship in life which has increasingly become seen to have "being happy" as one of its central functions.

Far more so than in the past, we live in a society which emphasises the rights and freedoms of the individual and which sees personal relations as influenced by personal advantages. Increasingly it seems that these ideas have been carried over to family life with family relationships being seen as slightly special ordinary social relationships, to be evaluated in terms of their contribution to individual welfare and interests and to be made and broken on the same basis as other friendships.

Externally and superficially, then, the family and marriage today may look quite similar to the patterns of 300 years ago. A closer look suggests that their nature has changed in many subtle but important ways which are a direct reflection of the changed position of family and marriage in the wider society. We have inherited a set of expectations about marriage which have become increasingly unsupported by the social and economic context in which family life is lived.

The lesson of history seems to be that we could go back to a strict conformity with the morality of the past – a conformity which has never in fact existed totally – only by reverting also to the economic and social relations of the past. That is clearly impossible. We thus have to develop new institutions and new expectations to cope with new situations.

Source: *The Guardian*, 10 February 1982

expectancy – and variants at different times and places. But the processes are both more complex and more specific than were encompassed by older ideas about one irreversible line of evolution.

Besides querying common stereotypes, Anderson adds further positive conclusions. He points out that changing demographic patterns over the past two centuries in the ages of marriage and death or the number and spacing of children, have had direct effects on the operation of the family. Changes in social, economic and value systems also have implications for the family, related in Anderson's view to a more individual-based form of family life today.

An additional result, therefore, of Anderson's findings is a series of questions about how far his conclusions are generally applicable: what light can they throw on *individual* cases (yours for instance) – and vice versa? Such questions form the basis of further investigations in the following chapters.

3   'SPLITTING' AND 'LUMPING': FAMILY TREE, FAMILY HISTORY AND THE HISTORY OF THE FAMILY

Our key procedure here, then, is to move back- and forwards between particular cases and broader generalizations, or – to adapt Hexter's distinction (1979, pp.242 ff) to our own purposes – between 'splitting' or 'lumping': 'splitting' being a focus on *differences* and uniqueness; 'lumping' a concern about *likeness* and what is in common.

As we saw earlier, an exclusive emphasis on either can be misleading. The splitters can lose the wood for the trees, while the lumpers can merge multi-faceted variety into coarse-grained over-generalization. In practice, good research usually includes both lumping *and* splitting: both general theories *and* specific examples. Precisely where a study comes on this 'splitting–lumping continuum' (see Figure 1.7) varies according to the research topic and, perhaps, personal taste. But in a serious study of family and community history as envisaged in these volumes, the aim is to avoid falling too far to the misleading extremes in either direction, and instead reaching some useful combination of the two.

Splitting may seem relatively easy. It is where many of us start – with our own place or family, or with an in-depth study of a particular group or historical period. We need to be reminded to continue that but to 'lump' a bit too: i.e. to compare our case with others, relate it to the wider theories.

Lumping is sometimes harder, but it can also at times be the most tempting, particularly for those with little experience of individual cases. So it may be useful to reflect a little further on some differing forms of 'lumping' or ways of generalizing.

First, look at what the lumping covers: the *scope* of the generalization. It is actually impossible to engage in any kind of research without some encounter with regularities. This comes through even in the personal examples: Lavinia Swainbank was only one of many who left home for domestic service; John Kerr went abroad along predictable pathways, and with others; the Goodaires, the Finnegans and even the evacuees lived in the kind of household and family relationships we still recognize. Even in specific cases we automatically assume that there are some recurrent patterns and categories.

So even at the individual level, there are in-built regularities. Indeed, a common experience among researchers is that we gain a deeper understanding of individual actions or situations if we put them in the context of more general patterns: for example, of the expectations that people themselves held about what families or households should be like, the constraints within which they lived, or the opportunities they exploited – even the ways some broke through accustomed conventions to do something different.

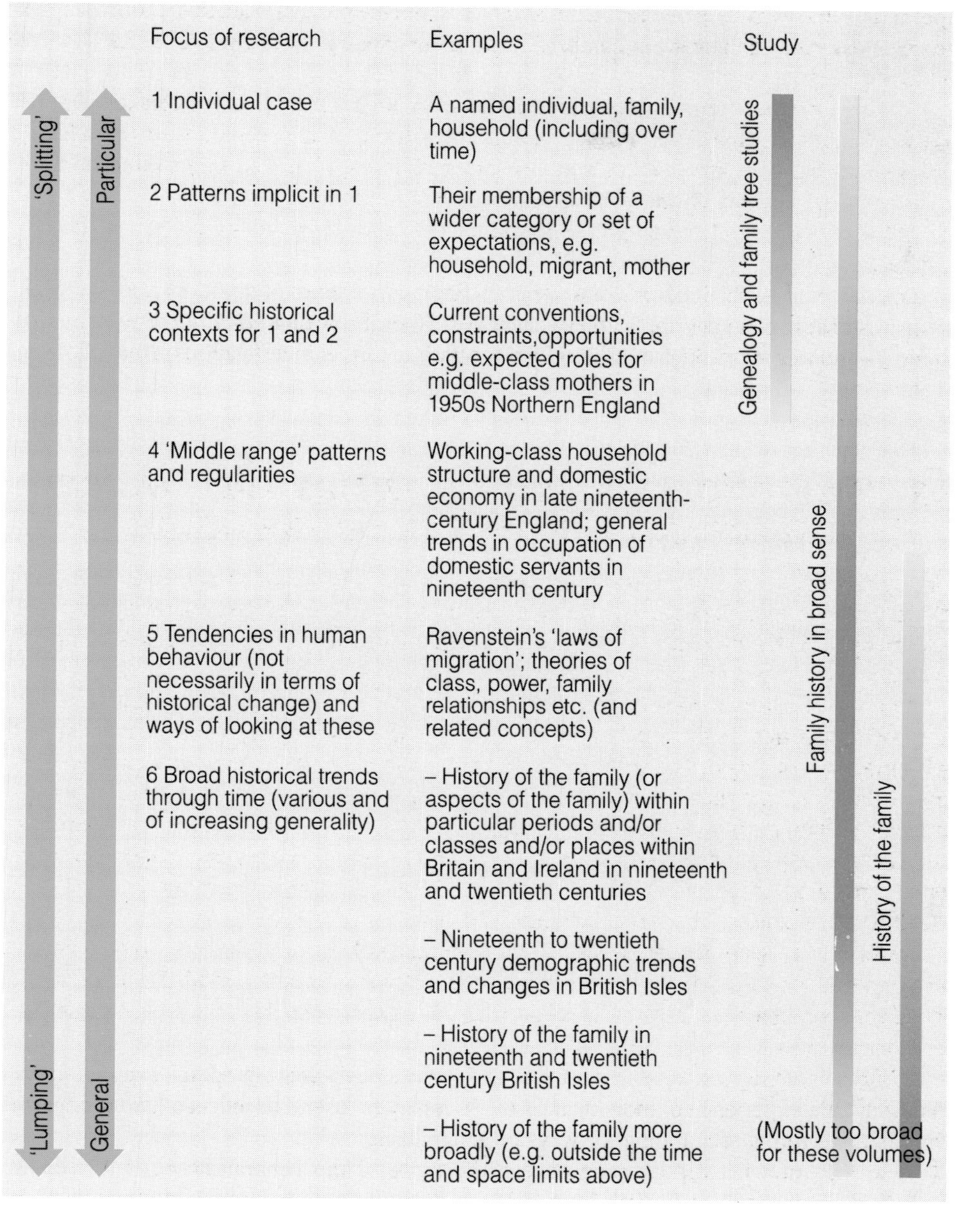

'Splitting' / Particular ↑ ... 'Lumping' / General ↓

Focus of research	Examples	Study
1 Individual case	A named individual, family, household (including over time)	Genealogy and family tree studies
2 Patterns implicit in 1	Their membership of a wider category or set of expectations, e.g. household, migrant, mother	
3 Specific historical contexts for 1 and 2	Current conventions, constraints, opportunities e.g. expected roles for middle-class mothers in 1950s Northern England	
4 'Middle range' patterns and regularities	Working-class household structure and domestic economy in late nineteenth-century England; general trends in occupation of domestic servants in nineteenth century	Family history in broad sense
5 Tendencies in human behaviour (not necessarily in terms of historical change) and ways of looking at these	Ravenstein's 'laws of migration'; theories of class, power, family relationships etc. (and related concepts)	
6 Broad historical trends through time (various and of increasing generality)	– History of the family (or aspects of the family) within particular periods and/or classes and/or places within Britain and Ireland in nineteenth and twentieth centuries	History of the family
	– Nineteenth to twentieth century demographic trends and changes in British Isles	
	– History of the family in nineteenth and twentieth century British Isles	
	– History of the family more broadly (e.g. outside the time and space limits above)	(Mostly too broad for these volumes)

Figure 1.7 'Splitting' and 'lumping': family tree, family history and the history of the family

We can sometimes go further, and discover the patterns followed by a large number of cases within a particular category (a specific occupation, say) in a specific area or period. One example would be the more general trends in domestic service in Britain which give a context to Lavinia Swainbank's experience. It had changed from a situation in the mid-nineteenth century where a high proportion of women had at some stage worked as domestic servants, to one where – as for Lavinia Swainbank – this occupation had declined in status and was mainly taken up by girls from the depressed areas, where opportunities for female employment were few (Burnett, 1974, p.135). Another example could be a general account of family structure in working-class families in the north of England in the late nineteenth century – a wider focus than just single families or a single area but certainly narrower than, say, 'the nineteenth-century family in Britain'.

Other lumping might take a broader scope still: for example statements about how 'the family' supposedly developed over the centuries, whether in the British Isles or in human history as a whole. One example would be the assertions – doubted by scholars nowadays, but still popularly believed – that industrialization resulted in a drastic change in the nature of the family, or that there has been a general evolution over the ages from larger extended families to the smaller nuclear families of today.

Another way of generalizing is to focus less on historical trends through time than on *tendencies in human behaviour*: patterns which arguably recur irrespective of specific times, or even, perhaps, of specific places. Sometimes this kind of lumping means looking to categories which could perhaps be applied across time and space: concepts like 'class', 'community', 'industrialization', or indeed 'family'; sometimes it means looking to theories (alternatively called 'laws', 'models' or occasionally 'hypotheses') which provide a more, or less, generalized account or explanation linking together separate instances. As you will see in later chapters, such concepts and theories can provide illuminating frameworks for gathering together disparate (but perhaps only *superficially* disparate?) examples, and are often a powerful incentive for further research and testing. At the same time they are, and must always be, open to the splitter's challenge of whether they are in fact meaningful terms when assessed against the historical record for a particular place or period.

There are, then, several forms of lumping – constructing general theories to account for and illuminate the evidence of specific cases – and also both lesser and greater degrees of 'splitting'. One way of representing these is along a scale, as in Figure 1.7, running from the extremes of individual 'splitting' at one end to that of the most generalized 'lumping' at the other. As you can see, 'family history' as understood in these volumes falls somewhere towards the centre: it is more general than genealogy or the study of name-based family trees; it is concerned among other things with the history of the family as experienced in various places and periods within the nineteenth- and twentieth-century British Isles; but it is less universalizing than the history of 'the family' over many centuries.

Figure 1.7 doesn't tell quite the whole story, however, for it is equally important not to stay just at one point along the continuum. Any good investigation needs both splitting *and* lumping, back- and forwards along the continuum. For one thing this makes it more interesting. For another, serious research within family and community history should mean constantly testing out our generalizations through more particularized evidence, and setting individual examples within some wider 'lumping' perspective, before finally bringing both elements together into a final conclusion.

Some strategies for achieving this combination of particular and general are illustrated in Chapter 2. For the moment I want to end by emphasizing again the many uncertainties and gaps in our knowledge of family and community history, both general and specific. Correspondingly, there are many opportunities for you to develop your own interests to add to our ever-increasing knowledge, to explore in one way or another the complex and rich interaction of the particular with the general.

REFERENCES AND FURTHER READING

Note: suggestions for further reading are indicated by an asterisk.

Alo-wa: Black Women's Oral History Group (1990) *Our story*, London, Willowbrook Urban Studies Centre and Southwark Women's Centre.

Anderson, M. (1971) *Family structure in nineteenth century Lancashire*, Cambridge, Cambridge University Press.

Anderson, M. (1982) 'Property, know-how, fertility: what's love got to do with it?', *The Guardian*, 10 February 1982.

Anderson, M. (1983) 'What is new about the modern family?', Occasional Paper 31, *The family*, London, OPCS, pp.2–16. Reprinted in Drake (1994).[*]

Burke, P. (1992) *History and social theory*, Cambridge, Polity Press.

Burnett, J. (ed.) (1974) *Useful toil*, London, Allen Lane.

Drake, M. (ed.) (1994) *Time, family and community: perspectives on family and community history*, Oxford, Blackwell in association with The Open University (Course Reader).

Erickson, C. (1972) *Invisible immigrants: the adaptation of English and Scottish immigrants in nineteenth-century America*, London, Weidenfeld & Nicolson.

Foy, R. H. (1989) *Dear uncle: immigrant letters to Antrim from the USA 1843–52*, Antrim, Antrim and District Historical Society.

Haley, A.C. (1976) *Roots*, New York, Doubleday.

Hexter, J.H. (1979) *On historians*, Cambridge, Mass., Harvard University Press.

Wicks, B. (1988) *No time to wave goodbye*, London, Bloomsbury.

CHAPTER 2

GOING FURTHER: TACTICS AND STRATEGIES

Sections 1 and 2 by Ruth Finnegan and Michael Drake;
sections 3 and 4 by Michael Drake

In this chapter we suggest how you can develop your own research. First there are some exercises to give you practice in using two commonly available sources: the census enumerators' books and oral recordings. Depending on how familiar you already are with these sources, you may or may not find the exercises taxing in themselves, but the point to look for is how they provide bridges between your own family or community and what we know of families and communities generally. This leads into section 2 of the chapter, where we present two alternative strategies for conducting your research. In section 3 we show how you can conduct a piece of research when you start with a source (in this case a third type of source, private letters). The chapter also draws together a number of threads in the study of families and their history.

1 LINKING INTO MORE GENERAL PATTERNS: PRACTICAL EXERCISES

Two pieces of research are taken to illustrate this linking process: one by Michael Anderson and the other by Lynn Jamieson.

You will already know of some of Anderson's work, if only from the article reprinted in section 2 of Chapter 1. The points made there are expanded in a later article, 'What is new about the modern family?' (Anderson, 1983), in which Anderson discusses recent findings about the history of the family in the nineteenth and twentieth centuries. Much 'popular thinking', he asserts 'contrasted the "modern family" with a very different past'.

> It was a past full of affectively close and stable families, in which uncontrolled fertility produced large numbers of children within marriage (while strong morality inhibited their birth outside it), a past in which the population lived in large and complex households, set in stable communities and surrounded by large numbers of close and more distant relatives.
>
> (Anderson, 1983, p.2)

Anderson goes on to show that much of this picture is false. He does this from the evidence of a 2 per cent sample of all the communities appearing in the 1851 census of Great Britain, though he could, of course, have chosen another date.

As a way of getting into some of the issues discussed by Anderson, we shall look again at a census enumerator's book (CEB), but a little more closely than we did in Chapter 1. No family or community historian studying the nineteenth century (or early twentieth century in Ireland) can fail to draw on these magnificent documents at some time or another. (For a detailed critique and information on their availability see Volume 4, Chapter 3, and Collins and Pryce, 1993.) They are, however, not without their problems. If you are not familiar with them, it is worthwhile examining a page from one now (see Figure 2.1) using Exercise 2.1 as a guide.

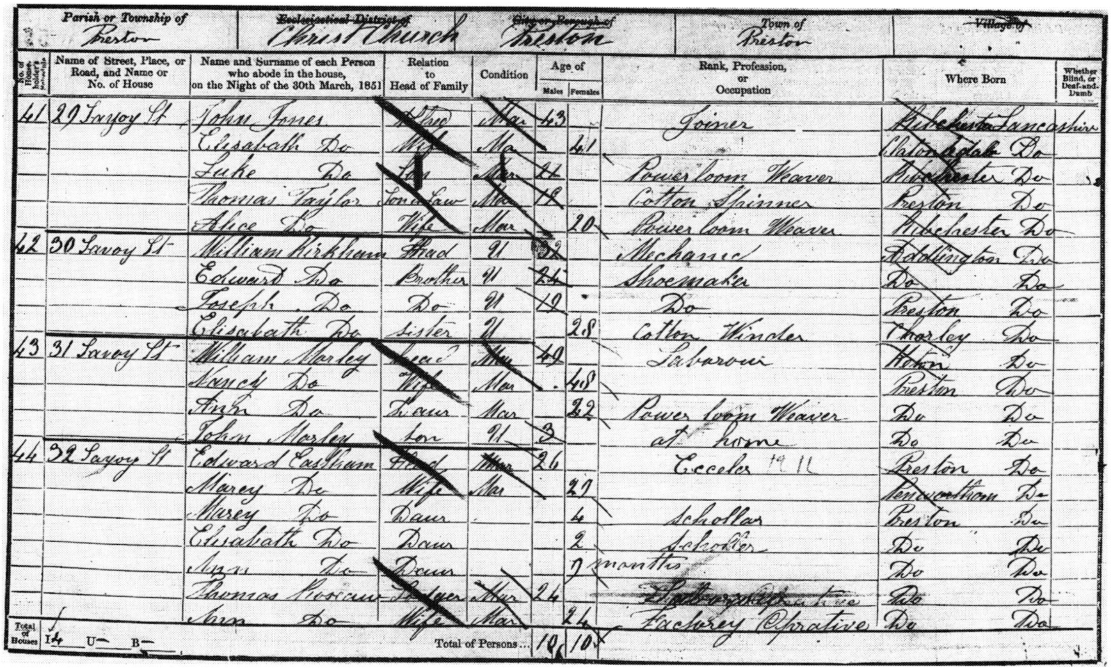

Parish or Township of Preston	Ecclesiastical District of Christ Church	City or Borough of Preston	Town of Preston	Village of					
No. of Householder's Schedule	Name of Street, Place, or Road, and Name or No. of House	Name and Surname of each Person who abode in the house, on the Night of the 30th March, 1851	Relation to Head of Family	Condition	Age of Males	Age of Females	Rank, Profession, or Occupation	Where Born	Whether Blind, or Deaf-and-Dumb
41	29 Savoy St	John Jones	Head	Mar	43		Joiner	Whalley Lancashire	
		Elisabeth Do	Wife	Mar		41		Clitheroe Do	
		Luke Do	Son	Mar	21		Power loom Weaver	Whalley Do	
		Thomas Taylor	Son in Law	Mar	18		Cotton Spinner	Preston Do	
		Alice Do	Wife	Mar		20	Power loom Weaver	Whalley Do	
42	30 Savoy St	William Kirkham	Head	U	32		Mechanic	Waddington Do	
		Edward Do	Brother	U	24		Shoemaker	Do Do	
		Joseph Do	Do	U	19		Do	Preston Do	
		Elisabath Do	Sister	U		28	Cotton Winder	Chorley Do	
43	31 Savoy St	William Marley	Head	Mar	49		Labourer	Walton Do	
		Nancy Do	Wife	Mar		48		Preston Do	
		Ann Do	Daur	Mar		22	Power loom Weaver	Do Do	
		John Marley	Son	U	3		at home	Do Do	
44	32 Savoy St	Edward Eastham	Head	Mar	26		Eccles [illegible]	Preston Do	
		Marey Do	Wife	Mar		27		Penwortham Do	
		Marey Do	Daur			4	Schollar	Preston Do	
		Elisabath Do	Daur			2	Schollar	Do Do	
		Ann Do	Daur			7 months		Do Do	
		Thomas Horrocks	Lodger	Mar	24		Factory Operative	Do Do	
		Ann Do	Wife	Mar		24	Factorey Oprative	Do Do	
Total of Houses	4 U— B—			Total of Persons	10	10			

Figure 2.1 Extract from an 1851 census enumerator's book for Preston (Lancashire) (Source: Public Record Office)

EXERCISE 2.1

1 What do you think the horizontal lines represent?

2 Do you detect any possible ambiguity in the 'Relation to Head of Family' column? For a clue look at the inhabitants of 32 Savoy Street.

3 What do you think is given in the column headed 'Condition'?

4 In the column headed 'Rank, Profession, or Occupation', almost all the lines are filled. Do you notice anything about the adults not blessed with an entry?

5 Who do you think made the oblique strokes across some of the entries, and why?

6 What do you think the letters 'I', 'U' and 'B' stand for, near the bottom left-hand corner of the CEB?

Answers/comments p.179.

The first myth Michael Anderson sought to explode was the extent of geographical mobility in mid-nineteenth-century Britain. If you thought this was likely to be small (no cars, buses, few trains, expensive to travel by coach and wagon), you may be surprised to learn that he found less than half the population in 1851 living in the place of their birth. Already by age 15 some 40 per cent had moved from their birthplace and one-sixth had done so by the time they were two years of age (Anderson, 1983, p.3).

EXERCISE 2.2

Take a look at Figure 2.1 again. Of the people listed there, how many had moved from their birthplace?

Answer p.180.

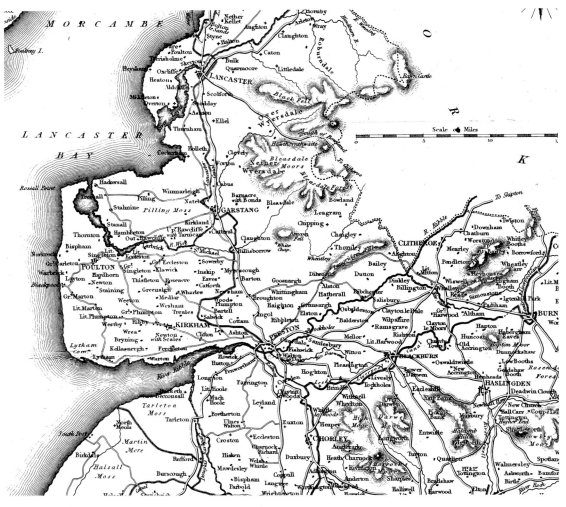

Figure 2.2 Preston district, 1831 (Source: Lewis, 1831)

EXERCISE 2.3

Examine the map in Figure 2.2 and locate the birthplaces of the nine people living in Preston in 1851 (in Figure 2.1) but not born there. When you have done this, draw straight lines from these to what you estimate to be the centre of Preston. Measure these lines and, using the scale given on the map, calculate the distances between Preston and each birthplace. To help set you on the right track, we believe the distance from Ribchester to Preston is 1 1/8 inches. The scale of this map is seven miles to the inch. So the distance from Ribchester to Preston – as the crow flies – is just under eight miles. What was the average (mean) distance travelled by the nine migrants shown in Figure 2.2, from their birthplaces to Preston?

Answers/comments p.180.

We turn now to another topic for which information can be gleaned from the census enumerators' books: the size and composition of the family and the household. Anderson states the following:

> *Preliminary estimates from my own work on the mid-nineteenth century suggest a mean household size of 4.6, with a mean conjugal group of 3.7. Some 19 per cent of urban households*

32

contained relatives and 27 per cent of households in rural areas; there were 0.3 relatives on average per household and 8 per cent contained three or more generations.

(Anderson, 1983, p.3)

Incidentally, Anderson notes that over the eighteenth century the size and complexity of households seems to have risen a little. This is not what 'popular', even 'social scientific' thinking would have led us to expect. For until the work of Laslett and Anderson appeared it was thought that in pre-industrial societies not only were households large and complex by modern standards, but it was the process of industrialization itself which *reduced* that size and complexity. This is an important issue to which we shall return.

_____ *EXERCISE 2.4* _____

Let us return to Figure 2.1. For the purposes of this exercise we will assume that the people living in 32 Savoy Street form a household, though it seems probable that more members of it appeared on the next page of the return (why? – because there is no long line across the page; see the answer to question 1 of Exercise 2.1 for the explanation of this line). We therefore have four households, showing an interesting mix. (Note: in this exercise we are following Anderson in using 'conjugal' as synonymous with 'nuclear' family, i.e. parents and their own co-resident children. As you will see later, 'conjugal' is also sometimes used to refer just to the married couple.)

1   What is the mean household size?

2   How many conjugal family *households* are there?

3   How many conjugal *families* are there?

4   What is the mean conjugal family size?

5   How many complex (i.e. non-conjugal) households are there?

6   We suggest that the households at Nos 31 and 32 Savoy Street pose problems of interpretation as regards familial relationships. What do you think?

7   What would you say about the degree of social homogeneity of this group of households?

8   What does Figure 2.1 tell us about the number of women in paid employment?

Answers/comments p.180.

In completing Exercise 2.4 you may again have been struck by the similarity of your findings as to mean household and conjugal group size and that of Anderson for the country as a whole (see the quotation on pp.32–3 above). Taken together with the answer to Exercise 2.2 and Anderson's findings for the country as a whole concerning the proportion of the population enumerated in 1851 at a place other than their birthplace, one begins to wonder whether there was very little variation across the country, whether we are dealing with a couple of chance happenings, or whether this is a case of 'the meaningless mean'.

_____ *QUESTION FOR RESEARCH* _____

These are early days yet. Nevertheless, you may already have become interested in the question of the size and composition of families and households. Should you decide to work on nineteenth-century England, Wales or Scotland or early twentieth-century Ireland, you should first check on the accessibility of the CEBs for the period and area you have chosen to explore – and by accessibility we mean not only their physical existence, but also their legibility. You will probably only have access to the originals on microfilm (transcripts are another matter) and some are notoriously difficult to read. A check on this at an early stage is well worthwhile. Don't give up immediately – it is surprising how initial illegibility disappears after an hour or so. But don't waste your time battling with an impossible script. Find another district!

Assuming the basic source passes muster, you need to focus on a researchable topic. This will almost certainly involve some sort of measurement and the presentation of your findings in tables, graphs or diagrams (see Volume 4, Chapter 11 for advice on this). As to the topic itself, although we know now that the mean household or family size was small, it is worth going behind the averages to calculate their size and composition in terms of:

occupation of household head

age of head

nationality of head

geographical area

date (i.e. of census)

If you have information about the size and composition of your family over time you could explore these questions longitudinally. (This is done rather rudimentarily in Chapter 3 below.) If you know other people who have similar information (members of your local family history or historical society perhaps?) you could pool your data and produce a more representative study.

The sources so far have been documentary, especially that rich resource the CEBs. Another useful source lies in people's memories. These too lead us into the past, though in a different way from the nineteenth-century records and to a more recent period. They also have their strengths and weaknesses, and are worth exploring as another way of linking specific cases with more general findings.

Here, then, is an exercise on tapping people's memories to provide a further link with Anderson's findings.

EXERCISE 2.5

For your own family or some other family in which you are interested, discover from two people's memories (a) the size and composition of their household at two particular points in time earlier in the twentieth century, and (b) at what ages they themselves and their own children (if any) married and how long the marriage lasted.

Having done that, compare your findings with those discussed by Anderson in the comments above and in the short summary in Chapter 1, pp.24–5 (also elaborated in his 1983 article). Anderson notes, for example, the greater life expectancy (and hence duration of marriage) in recent years compared to the past, and the somewhat smaller household groups in the mid to late twentieth century (if only because of parents' completing their families earlier in life compared to the mid-nineteenth-century parents). How do your findings fit with these trends?

Finally, note down any advantages or problems you encountered with this method (i.e. trying to tap people's memories).

Note on methods: In choosing people to interview, interpret 'earlier in the century' in whatever sense is practicable, provided you make some attempt to go beyond what you know from your own first-hand observation. Asking people over sixty would take you back to a childhood in the 1930s and 1940s, but later dates are interesting too.

Consulting older people can be done in various ways: a passing conversation with a relative or friend already in your own home; telephoning or writing to family members further away; or extended interviews with notebook or tape-recorder. For this preliminary exercise, short informal questioning would suffice. Even a brief face-to-face conversation or an informal chat on the phone are forms of interviewing – a basic method in much social research. Despite the limitations, you will still learn something not only about the answers to your specific questions but also about some of the costs and benefits of trying to draw on people's memories. If you have more experience of this method already (or more time), you may prefer more formal interviewing and recording (see below pp.122–5 and Volume 4, Chapter 7). Whichever route you follow, try to get something from at least two people (at a later stage you could extend your endeavours to as many more as you wish or have time for, and conduct more systematic investigations).

Comment p.181.

You looked at the size and composition of mid-nineteenth-century households in Exercise 2.4. So your own findings from this century can supplement that earlier work, and link to Anderson's conclusions (pp.24–5 above and 1983) about changes in the size and composition of households over the last two centuries.

On the related question of the position of children, Anderson points to the interesting contrast between the modern (well, 1979) family, in which almost all 17 year-olds were living in a parent's household, and the mid-nineteenth-century pattern where roughly 10 per cent of children 'at all ages from birth to early teens were separated from their parents' (1983, p.10). This too could form the basis of further research for a particular family or locality (such as the detailed project on the child population in two small areas of Birmingham in 1851 by Dyer, 1991).

The complexities of using oral sources are considered more fully in Chapter 4 (also in Volume 4, Chapter 7), but it is worth reflecting immediately on some of their strengths and limitations. On the one hand you may have found out further information about a family, and put it in a wider perspective by relating it to Anderson's work. You may also have been drawn to think further about his findings. But you will doubtless have encountered problems too. Such an exercise is extremely time-consuming. It can also be difficult to discover 'hard' figures about household size, certainly in a comprehensive or systematic form. People forget or mis-remember, mix up names and dates, deliver what they think the interviewer wants, or are affected by hindsight.

Some positive points come out of this. For example, 'facts' and how they are defined are complex. The size of 'the household' is not always an easily measurable or indeed a permanent thing. It *looks* hard and fast enough in the CEBs, and certainly the aim was to achieve consistency, but the final results rested on the judgement both of those making the returns and of the enumerator – and interpretations could vary. With oral methods you can sometimes question participants directly and get a feel for such complications as *who* exactly are members of the same household, and how permanently they have to live there to count (surely more than just one census night?).

So any method that relies on personal memory has both advantages and problems. Memory changes and is influenced by more recent experiences, both happy and painful: it is not just a mechanical technique for information transmission! It is often less reliable on numbers or dates than information written close to the time and can cover only a limited period. But against this, oral methods are strong on tapping experiences and feelings of a personal kind. Even if memories can never just be equated with 'the bare facts' (can any source?) they do provide some hold on evidence which may be inaccessible through other methods.

The final exercise moves away from questions about household structure to some research on interactions within the family, as reported in Lynn Jamieson's article 'Theories of family development and the experience of being brought up' (1987). This opens by explaining some influential theories about interconnected changes in family life that occurred during the late nineteenth and early twentieth centuries, among them the emergence of 'the family' as a separate unit – a kind of 'haven in the heartless world' – characterized by intense emotional relationships within it.

How true is this theory? And does it apply in your case?

Jamieson's own conclusion was based on oral accounts recorded in the 1970s from men and women who grew up in urban Scotland in the early 1900s. Here is a brief extract about how she explored the 'extent of emotional intensity' by looking at the parent/child relationship in terms of the ways parents intervened in their children's time:

> Among my respondents many parents, working-class and middle-class, did not spend much of their free time with their children. Time spent on children was predominantly on their physical care or helping with their formal education. The pattern of activity and interaction between the overwhelming majority of working-class mothers and their children suggests that mother's priority was good housekeeping, not her children as such. Indeed, for mothers of both classes time spent with children was rarely classifiable as involvement with children as an end in itself. Only two respondents remember their mother as ever taking part in their imaginative play. Rather, time spent together involved accompanying or assisting mother on her business or leisure, or receiving explicit instruction from her. The prevailing view of a good mother I received from working-class respondents was that of a busy mother who excelled at housekeeping – making jam and potted meat in addition to routine high standards of cleaning and cooking. The typical division of labour between middle-class mistresses and the servants suggests that they too shared the same set of priorities, since they were more prepared to delegate child care than cooking.
>
> The following quotations capture something of the quality of parent/child relationships for most respondents:
>
>> 'I don't know if you know the golden rule, "Children should be seen and not heard". You were not to talk back to elders. You never joined in at the tea table. You were never allowed at the tea table if there were visitors. Children were kept apart.' (Angus, born 1902; father: tailor);
>>
>> 'We spent a good deal of time with the maid ... I don't remember getting a lot of attention from my parents. I really can't remember my mother ever, you know, taking me in her arms or anything like that but we were happy somehow or other.' (Catherine, born 1902; father: commercial traveller)
>
> Deference was a feature of the majority of children's relationships with their parents. In working-class households, 'good behaviour' meant obedient service and was expected well beyond school-age years – fetching and carrying on demand, performing required domestic tasks and handing over any earnings including those from part-time and casual work. Although less universal, unquestioning obedience was similarly expected in many middle-class homes; in either case, asking questions of authority was 'giving cheek'. While some children feared or even hated their parents as a result, the majority clearly did regard them with affection. The style of parenting which appeals to the traditional legitimacy of parental authority does not exclude affection between parents and children. But the emphasis in the relationship is on the beneficence of the parent, not the marvel of the child.
>
> 'The boss that you love' was not the only image of parents among my respondents. Some talked of their parents as kindly strangers who had little impact on their lives. This was particularly true of middle-class fathers whose occupations meant they were seldom at home: 'he was just the man who came to the house for weekends' (Elizabeth, born 1897, father: commercial traveller). Others expressed intense feelings for their self-sacrificing mother who starved and slaved to protect them from the worst of their circumstances: 'I always wanted to help my mother.

Her and me were very close' (Tilly, born 1890, father: brass finisher). But in any of these cases, the types of relationships respondents generally had with their parents do not match an image of child-centred families in which mothers, if not parents, cherish spending time with the children as a valuable and rewarding end in itself and, hence, strive to make time and space for their family over other concerns. Certainly, the majority of respondents grew up in a household with a full-time or near full-time mother/housewife who was the acknowledged orchestrator of material, financial and organizational dimensions of family life, whether her domestic work for the family involved daily toil or more lofty supervision. But 'mother', I suggest, even if also the most loved in the household, was not necessarily at the heart of the specific complex of feeling and meaning commonly assumed by authors and recently referred to as familism.

(Jamieson, 1987, pp.599–600)

_____ *EXERCISE 2.6* _____

First, read through the extract above. Then, using the same methods as in Exercise 2.5, discover from two people what they remember of (a) how much time their parents spent with them as children, and (b) what kind of relations they had with either parent (close affection, deference, obedience, or what?).

Having done that, compare your findings with Jamieson's conclusion that, at least for the families she studied, there was *not* in fact the great 'emotional intensity' you would have expected if the general theories were true.

Comments p.181.

What point have you reached after going through these various practical exercises? As we said earlier, these are early days. As you progress through this and later volumes in the series you will come across other sources to be exploited, other techniques to be employed, other hypotheses to be tested – and new ways of presenting your findings. The experience you have gained thus far will be essential for using other sources too. Equally important, you have been engaging in the characteristically scholarly tactics of examining the evidence so as to link particular cases with the more general patterns discussed in the wider literature on the history of the family.

Section 2 shows how you can build on such tactics to plan and follow through more sustained research projects.

2   RESEARCH STRATEGIES

As you know, a central feature of this and the later volumes is to help you complete a research project in family or community history. So far you have looked briefly at some current issues in family history and related them to specific cases by carrying out practical exercises on a selection of primary sources. But, as with most researchers, you will not want to stop at that. Like them, you will be considering how to put these elements together in some sustained piece of research.

Crucial to this enterprise is the research strategy you adopt, since this will dictate how you go about your work from start to finish. Just as there are many ways to skin a cat, so there are numerous research strategies you may choose. Here we are going to isolate two models. They are not the only ones by any means and they are certainly not as distinct from each other as we, for pedagogic reasons, will make them here. If we seem a little overbearing in urging you to think about the strategic element of your research at as early a stage as possible, we hope you will forgive us. The reason is that we are very conscious that we are mostly directing ourselves to researchers with limited time and resources. And we believe that if you conduct your research with a clear strategy in mind – at all times! – your chances of success will be immeasurably increased.

But rather than starting off in the manner of many 'research methods' courses with abstract philosophical disquisitions, let us move to some examples, pausing only to point out the basic principles of any research strategy.

Schema A: Principles of research strategy

1 Connect *particular examples* with debates about *general issues.*

2 Reach some better *understanding* of patterns, actions or events in the real world.

3 *Investigate the evidence* and *present conclusions* (which sometimes lead to *further questions*).

2.1 THE HYPOTHESIS TESTING STRATEGY

To show this strategy in action we will take one piece of research through the seven stages we suggest you follow.

Stage 1: Topic of interest   For the sake of this illustration we are assuming that you are interested in the history of the family. You want to know how families operated in the past, particularly families that belonged to the culture and the times experienced by your own family. This 'topic of interest' is virtually limitless, opening up vast areas of experience, stretching across the globe for families living in the United Kingdom and Ireland today. Let us assume, again for the sake of illustration, that you would like to know something more about how families in England functioned during the nineteenth century in those parts of England that were affected by rapid industrialization and urbanization. This was the experience of a branch of Michael Drake's family, the Goodaires. During the period 1841–1891 the small villages and hamlets of the woollen cloth-producing areas of the West Riding of Yorkshire like Rastrick, where they lived, witnessed massive population growth and industrial change. From the occupations reported in the census (see Chapter 3, section 2), we see the Goodaire family closely involved in the industrial scene: cotton piecer, woollen twister, railway wagon inspector, wire drawer. You will also notice that the different branches of the wider family appeared to be closely in touch with each other: in two cases one member lived next door to another; another was apprenticed to and lived with his uncle; in changing occupations, two branches of the wider family came together as manufacturing chemists. We have, then, a clear case of kin (what English people call their 'relatives') doing things together, or for each other. How common was such a situation?

Stage 2: Articulate problem   How can we show the importance of kin? Michael Anderson has suggested four different ways. First, one can use literary evidence to show how much contact there was between members of one conjugal (nuclear) family and their relatives. This would include shared leisure activities (e.g. sport, drinking, gossiping, parties, weddings, funerals, baby minding, attendance on the sick). Unfortunately, as Anderson points out, 'there is no way of measuring for the population as a whole the extent of these contacts or their importance in comparison with relationships with neighbours, workmates, friends and so on' (Anderson, 1971, pp.62–3).

Despite this lack of quantitative precision it is still worthwhile seeking out letters (see section 3 below), diaries and reports which might indicate the extent of relationships between kin. Sometimes these do provide quantifiable information, as Anderson shows in relation to a report on a cholera epidemic which hit a working-class area of Manchester in 1832 (Gaulter, 1833). By categorizing the contacts into 'assistance', 'visiting', 'conversed with or transitory', 'trade (including child-nursing)', he was able to show that, in this particular case, 'most of the kin contacts involved positive assistance' (Anderson, 1971, p.64).

A second way of finding out the importance of kin is to search the literature for positive explicit statements on the subject. Anderson, for example, cites the custom of naming children after uncles and aunts. A glance at the Goodaire family tree (see Chapter 3, Figure 3.1) reveals the same first names repeated generation after generation. The Benjamin Goodaire we come across in the 1841 census (see Table 3.6) named his eldest son John Heaton presumably after his father-in-law; a daughter was named Esther, his mother-in-law's name. Joseph Goodaire (1840–1925) named one of his daughters Sarah Jane, the name of one of his sisters. There is also evidence of kin being employed by 'better off' relatives. The interpretation of such evidence does, however, pose very considerable problems. Novelists, Anderson concludes, do not provide much reliable evidence, since they 'generally portray family bonds as strong' (Anderson, 1971, p.65). On this last point Oliver MacDonagh's (1991) *Jane Austen: real and imagined worlds* is very interesting. He seeks 'to draw attention to the illumination of English history, in the quarter-century 1792–1817, which her novels may provide … [and] to try to illuminate the novels themselves, by historians' evaluations of the period' (p.ix). Thus, for example, in a chapter on families he sets Jane Austen's own family relationships – revealed in correspondence – against those of the Musgroves, Elliots and Crofts in her novel *Persuasion*. At one point he writes how the Austen family – the whole complex of brothers and sisters and their relations – was 'seen as a corporate enterprise' (p.125), a point illustrated 'most dramatically' when one of them went bankrupt.

A third indicator was to see how many households contained co-residing kin (i.e. relatives of the nuclear family unit). Anderson found 23 per cent in Preston in 1851. As Table 2.1 shows, this was comparable with other communities (both rural and urban) at that time. This, however, is well above what Laslett found in his study of one hundred communities in the period 1574–1821 (Laslett and Wall, 1972), and above that experienced in England and Wales in the more recent past.

Table 2.1   Percentage of households including relatives beyond the nuclear core: various communities, 1574–1966

Communities	Percentage kin
100 communities (1574–1821)	10.1
Ashford (Kent, 1851)	21.0
Preston (Lancs, 1851)	23.0
York (1851)	21.6
Rural[1] (1851)	27.0
Swansea (1960 approx.)	10.0–13.0
England and Wales (1966)	c.10.00

[1] These were agricultural villages in Lancashire where many of the migrants to Preston had been born.

Source: Drake (1974) p.75

These figures suggest that the nineteenth century was a high point for extended families, at least in England. We shall return to this in Chapter 3.

We come now to the fourth indicator of the importance of kin, namely whether or not people chose to live close to their relatives. Young and Wilmott (1957, p.20) noted in their study of 1950s Bethnal Green that 'the couples who chose to live with their parents are the exception. Most people do not want to live with them, they want to live near them'. Anderson decided that the only way to assess the importance of residential kinship behaviour was to look both at co-residence and propinquity (living nearby). Co-residence, though much easier to measure, is not by itself enough, for, as he noted, 'co-residence of married children with parents may … turn out to be related above all to the balance between supply and demand for housing suitable for young married couples' (Anderson in Wrigley, 1972, p.57). It may, therefore, be an indication not of a positive desire to be with kin but of *having* to be.

So we have now 'articulated our problem' in a form which we believe will allow us to make at least a stab at solving it. In so doing we have examined various alternative ways of proceeding, none of which turned out to be wholly satisfactory. What do we do next?

Stage 3: Formulate hypothesis   Formulating hypotheses involves what is known as the hypothetico-deductive method, which starts with the notion that *deduction is a process of particularizing from the general* and uses hypotheses drawn from an existing body of theory. Thus one starts with a theory, or explanation, which one wishes to challenge, refine or confirm. The hypothesis is a *prediction* and a *testable* aspect of the relevant body of theory.

Like the man who found he'd been speaking prose all his life, you will probably discover that you are a theoretician. As children we very soon realize how certain behaviour is likely to lead to certain consequences. Smile at one's grandma and she'll give you a sweet. The theory here (articulated by many a parent!) is that grandparents 'spoil' their grandchildren. Various hypotheses can be devised to test this theory, e.g. that if the child is left with a grandparent it will stay up 'past his or her bedtime' or that when children return from a visit to grandparents 'one can do nothing with them'.

Think about the theories that guide your everyday life and devise hypotheses that can be used to test them.

In the situation we are considering, the theory concerns family relationships. It suggests that relatives (i.e. kin) played a supportive role and that this was important in meeting the everyday problems of living, particularly in periods of rapid change like nineteenth-century Britain. In colloquial terms this theory explains how people coped in often difficult times. If this explanation is broadly correct, it should be possible to set up tests that would confirm or refute it. One such is the test of propinquity, for if it is true, we would expect relatives to make positive efforts to live close to each other.

Our hypothesis can, therefore, be formulated thus: *That the residences of sons (living outside the parental home) and those of their parents are closer to each other than would be found if such persons were not making a positive effort to ensure this.*

Stage 4: Devise test   One of the tests Anderson devised was to examine the residence patterns of kin in a small area of Preston containing in 1851 some 1,703 houses or 16 per cent of the houses in the town. Using a large-scale Ordnance Survey map of the area he numbered each of the houses. The object of the test was to discover whether the distance between the houses of persons who were known to be related to each other was closer than the distance between randomly selected pairs of people who were not known to be related to each other. If it was, then one would have some evidence to suggest that kin were making positive efforts to live close to each other. One couldn't be certain of this, but in the absence of literary evidence this would be the strongest indication possible.

Stage 5: Collect data   Note that this stage comes quite late in the research process. In real life it may come first, with the other stages then being fitted to it. This is not quite so heretical as purists might assert, for if you have a cache of promising data (e.g. a collection of letters such as those discussed in section 3 below, a diary, some family business records, a report on some aspect of community life), then going through the various stages outlined here will help you exploit it to the full. This will be so because considering these stages in a systematic manner will sensitize you to the context of the data cache, make you think about what aspects of family or community life it will help you to understand better, and then indicate a route that your subsequent research can follow.

For his research exercise Anderson used the census enumerators' books for the 1851 and 1861 censuses of Preston. He began by putting the name of each individual on a card and then attempted to relate them to each other, building up in this way a series of family histories. This process – known as *nominal record linkage* – has now reached the stage where computers can be used to do the linking automatically. It involves, as you can imagine, the creation of definite rules to determine whether or not two people are related. There is little point in giving Anderson's rules, since considerable advances have been made since he wrote, though there is still some dispute as to the best procedures (Schürer, 1993). Suffice it to say that he managed to 'identify positively 80 households containing someone definitely related to a person traced in another household', twenty-four of them being married sons.

Stage 6: Test   How does one know if the behaviour of these twenty-four sons represented a positive attempt to live close to their relatives? Anderson proceeded as follows:

o   First, he found that 127 sons aged five years and over in 1851 disappeared from those co-residing families that could be traced in the 1861 census.

o   Second, he estimated, from a mortality table, that eleven of these would have died.

o   Third, he estimated that, on the basis of the proportions married in each age group of the population as a whole, 50–55 of the 116 who survived to 1861 would have been married.

o   Fourth, as the area searched contained 1,703 houses or 16 per cent of the 11,000 or so houses in Preston at the time, then had the surviving married sons been scattered randomly throughout the town, and none had left it (highly unlikely), one would have expected to find between seven and nine in the area searched. In fact, as already noted, twenty-four were found and nine of these lived within one hundred yards of their parents.

Stage 7: Result   It would appear that this exercise confirms that relatives did play an important part in family life, since something of the order of three times as many sons were found in the searched area than would have been expected if no positive efforts to live close had been made. But, as Anderson noted, the confirmation is not watertight: 'Sons would seek homes near their work and friends and also would be more likely to know about housing vacancies in the local area' (Anderson, 1971, p.59). On this last point, however, a study by Dennis Mills which sought to replicate Anderson's, though in a Cambridgeshire village and using different sources and methods, came up with the same result. Relatives lived closer to each other than expected if they had distributed themselves randomly (Mills, 1978). Since the village was quite small, one would imagine that living near work and friends and knowledge of housing vacancies would not be a factor.

―――――――――――――――― **QUESTION FOR RESEARCH** ――――――――――――――――

This is a simplified summary of part of Michael Anderson's study. Anyone wishing to replicate it on its original scale would need to read his book and master the techniques he used. You may, however, think of other ways of testing the same hypothesis, perhaps using oral history methods – in which case you would start from individual families rather than localities.

2.2   THE QUESTIONING SOURCES STRATEGY

Testing hypotheses is a common strategy and has the advantage of providing a clearly demarcated and circumscribed path to guide your research. It also makes replication easier. For example, as with a scientific experiment, one could follow Anderson step by step, asking the same questions, using the same sources, but in a different place or different time.

It is not the only possible approach, however. Another common strategy in social and historical research involves spiralling – or iteration – between sources and questions. This is also known as the 'humanistic strategy', and often emphasizes interpretation and 'understanding' rather than the precise 'testing' of a hypothesis.

You have already met one example of this strategy: Jamieson's (1987) research which draws on oral accounts from people who grew up in urban Scotland in the early 1920s (see the extract in section 1 above). Let us look more closely at this example, once again under sequential stages. This time, however, the stages overlap, and we have to go back- and forwards between them before reaching the final outcome.

Stage 1: General topic or problem   How did the 'modern' family develop and what changes has it gone through to reach its present state? This is certainly an interesting, but also extremely broad, question. How could it be tackled?

A two-step approach is needed. One is to turn this general interest into more specific, researchable questions, partly through discovering what else is known on the topic and what are the currently debated questions. The other, *extremely important* approach is to find what sources are available, and allow the questions to be partly moulded by them. These two steps usually overlap.

Stage 2: What kinds of sources?   So what about our specific example? Lynn Jamieson's interests in the development of the family were clearly influenced by the sources to which she had access – or, in this case, had herself created. She had been inspired by Paul Thompson's suggestions on oral history in *The voice of the past: oral history* (1978) and had conducted a series of interviews in the 1970s which were structured by his detailed guide. These provided a rich source of data on people's lives, including their memories of early childhood and youth. Although this interview guide had not originally been drawn up to answer the precise questions followed up in Jamieson's doctoral thesis and later article, her recorded interviews contained a great deal of information about growing up earlier this century. She thus had a source which could be mined for information about the earlier development of the family.

Stage 3: Exploring researchable issues through wider reading, etc.   A concurrent step always has to be that of translating one's inevitably vague initial interest into something more direct and researchable. What proved useful for Jamieson's research was the wider literature on the history of the family and the debates pursued there. Much of it focused on the changes in the British family said to have taken place in the nineteenth and early twentieth centuries, especially the increasing tendency of family household members around this period to regard themselves as a distinct and bounded unit, separated from the 'outside' world. So could these theories be related to Jamieson's sources?

Stage 4: Back- and forwards: problem, sources, limited questions   Making further progress depends not just on reading the general literature but also translating it into more specific questions. It also demands further exploration of the available sources to see which (if any) aspects of the questions could really be investigated through those sources – in this case Jamieson's oral accounts.

'The development of the modern family' could not be investigated by just one person – not for *all* of Britain or *all* periods within the late nineteenth and early twentieth centuries! Putting a limit on the locality and time span was one essential step – in this case the limit was families growing up in urban Scotland in the early 1900s. Even that proved too large. Jamieson in fact focused on a smallish number of people born between 1886 and 1910 who were still living when she conducted her interviews in the 1970s: sixty-four working-class and twenty-three middle-class men and women.

As we have already noted, oral sources tend to be stronger on remembered experience than on precise numbers or dates. Reasonably enough, then, Jamieson concentrated on people's views and experiences in her assessment of what she calls 'the classical account' of changes in the family in the late nineteenth and early twentieth centuries. This is summarized in Schema B (based on Jamieson, 1987, p.591).

Schema B: The 'classical account' of changes in family life in the late nineteenth and early twentieth centuries

o   Family household members increasingly come to have a sense of themselves as a distinctive and sacrosanct unit, 'the family', which is separated from the wider social world.

o   Emotional relationships within the family household become very intense.

o   Gender divisions become more acute, with the sharp demarcation between a housewife/mother role and an earner/father role.

o   Respect for the individual is increased: loyalty to oneself may take precedence over loyalty to the family.

Jamieson's sources were thus the records from her semi-structured interviews on growing up and people's experience of family life in the early 1900s. But, like many sources, they were not originally compiled for assessing the precise theories just listed. Another step involved bringing together the theories and the sources into questions that both made sense and could be investigated through the sources available: i.e. the oral accounts.

You have already met one example (pp.36–7) that explored 'emotional intensity within the family' in the light of interview evidence about the time parents (and specially mothers) spent with their children and the nature of the relations between them. Similarly, the question about whether the family was regarded as a separate 'unit' was re-expressed as how far parents tried to restrict their children's activities to the confines of the family, e.g. parental prohibitions, incitements and suggestions about when and where children should spend time etc.

The interviews did not provide a full picture. As Jamieson (1987, p.598) admits, 'unfortunately, it is not possible to speak to the parents directly and to assess how self-conscious they were about their role as parents and builders of family boundaries'. It also seems that there were differences between working- and middle-class families. The sources thus turned out to be less than comprehensive, while also suggesting further questions that could be added if similar interviews were being conducted specifically to explore the topic. Still, the general impression given was that there was no evidence of clear barriers between the family and the wider social scene: 'The leisure time of many children is neither home centred nor family centred, and parental restrictions on it often foster neither' (Jamieson, 1987, p.598).

Stage 5: Looking at comparable cases and/or wider patterns or theories   One feature of this style of research is the constant process of moving backwards and forwards between,
on the one hand, particular sources and what they tell us, and, on the other, more general
patterns or theories. Besides her reference to the 'classic' theories, Jamieson was also able to
draw on other comparative evidence, for example findings on women's work elsewhere, to give
a wider perspective to her conclusions about her own respondents' experience of gender
divisions in the home.

Stage 6: Interpreting the sources and their evidence   Interpreting and consulting the
sources is continuous in this kind of research, in contrast to hypothesis testing where it is mostly
confined to one particular step. This process is particularly worth highlighting for two reasons.
First, it is often the most time-consuming part of the research, and so needs to be taken seriously.
Second, we need to note the word 'interpret'. Sources are not transparent information but require
the exercise of judgement in their interpretation. As you saw earlier, the sources in any given case
may or may not be able to give full answers to the questions you are exploring. Furthermore they
are likely to be deficient in at least some respects. One quality of a competent researcher is to be
open and self-aware about such problems. In our example here, certain limitations will already
be apparent: the restricted selection of respondents; the problems inherent in memory and
hindsight; the unclear nature of some questions; and the absence of definitive testing that can
often be undertaken in quantitatively based hypotheses.

It is important therefore that the limitations of any source are made explicit. Jamieson
frankly admits:

> *It is only fair to note ... the limitations of such data and mine in particular ... Experiential
> accounts are individuals' memories of one slice of the life-cycle. A more thorough exploration of
> quality of family life could involve a picture gathered from several participants in each family
> household at all stages of the individual life course and family life-cycle. Moreover, the kinds of
> questions that I ask of these particular data are sometimes a compromise between what my
> reading of authors suggest that I should ask and what my knowledge of the data tells me I can ask.*
>
> (Jamieson, 1987, p.593)

Jamieson also adds her assessment of the *value* of her sources – a judgement we are the more
inclined to accept given that she has obviously also taken account of their limitations:

> *The interviews contain many details of family life, particularly bearing on the parent/child
> relationship ... Sociologists of contemporary family life generally construct a picture by inter-
> viewing parents with dependent children. A (remembered) child's view has the virtue of giving a
> different perspective and, if oral rather than documentary evidence of the generation round 1900
> is sought, it is all we have to go on. My respondents' parents were all dead. By now, many of the
> respondents will have died too.*
>
> (Jamieson, 1987, p.593)

Stage 7: Presenting and assessing the conclusions – and further questions

What do you think Jamieson's sources led her to conclude about the 'classic' account of the
history of the family?

You will already have guessed that Jamieson's final conclusions on the basis of her evidence were
that 'the portfolio of supposedly interconnected changes ... in "the classical account" was absent
in the experience of my respondents' (1987, p.604). She thus presents as the central finding of her
research the doubt it casts on certain general theories about changes within families in the late
nineteenth and early twentieth centuries.

She goes on, however, to examine the implications and uncertainties of this conclusion. She took only a limited area, period and set of respondents. So do her conclusions apply elsewhere? Are the postulated changes in the 'classical' account real enough but in fact for a later period? As with many research projects of this kind, Jamieson ends by pointing to the incomplete but suggestive nature of her own limited findings, and uses this to call for further empirical investigation of the questions that she has raised, and their relation to the theories.

In this strategy, therefore, there is more emphasis on to-ing and fro-ing between the various 'stages', and on 'understanding' and 'questioning' rather than definitive testing. Even more so than in the hypothetico-deductive model, it often generates further questions.

QUESTIONS FOR RESEARCH

Are there any questions here that you could follow up?

Clearly Jamieson's own study, for all its limitations, would be too large for someone with only limited time and resources: each of her eighty-seven or so interviews took many hours. But, as you perhaps discovered earlier (Exercise 2.6), you could certainly follow up some of her questions on a smaller scale and for a different period or area. If you do, you will no doubt find that you too will be modifying the precise questions (hopefully making them more exact) and reformulating the relationship that they have to wider issues in the light of your particular sources. These might include written sources (locally available autobiographies, say) or existing audio sources, as well as, or instead of, interviews directed by yourself (further comments on sources can be found in Volume 4).

Irrespective of the scale or detailed content, what remains the same is the basic *structure* of such research. 'Questioning sources' is central, and in two senses: the sources are *questioned* ('What …' or 'how …') and the sources themselves raise questions for us, often making us reformulate the questions we started with.

It should not be assumed that this strategy is only suitable for oral sources, 'experiential' questions, or twentieth-century research. Let us look at a further example from a different period and sources: Michael Anderson's well-known (1971) book on family structure in nineteenth-century Lancashire (which contained the hypothesis you were testing earlier). Perhaps surprisingly, the overall research that led to the book's publication followed a similar structure to that just discussed.

First of all, it started not from a clear hypothesis, but almost by accident:

> *During a discussion over dinner about the relationship between industrialisation and family structure a chance remark made me suddenly aware of a paradox. All the sociological literature that I had read implied that industrialisation … disrupted pre-existing wider kinship systems. The historical writings to which this remark drew my attention stressed that pre-industrial family patterns in Britain, at least among the poorer sections of the population, were predominantly of a nuclear kind. By contrast, the writers on family patterns in modern 'traditional' working class communities were adamant that kinship relationships in such communities were well developed. It thus, superficially at least, appeared that modernisation in Britain had increased not decreased kinship cohesion. Why, I asked myself, should this have been so?*
>
> (Anderson, 1971, p.1)

Anderson goes on to describe how he started following up this central question – also expressed as 'What did industrialisation do to kinship in Britain?' (p.4). He read further, looking at both theoretical analyses and existing kinship studies, commenting ruefully – in words that recur time and time again in research – that 'as soon as I started a more detailed investigation, the issues, predictably, became less clear cut' (p.1). He also checked whether data were available to start answering the question. His answer was yes: in the quantitative material in the CEBs, supplemented by a mass of more qualitative documentary material, including contemporary novels. Covering everything was impossible, so Anderson limited himself largely to mid-nineteenth-century Lancashire and, within that, to the class of labourers and small shopkeepers with particular emphasis on Preston where he took a one in ten sample from the census of all occupied private residences. To introduce some comparison he took samples from surrounding villages and (based on reports by the Poor Law Commissioners) from that part of rural Ireland from which many of the migrants had come.

Anderson's research took on new insights as he recast his earlier questions in the light of the data. He found it more intelligible to move away from earlier assumptions that envisaged one single 'pre-industrial' stage or industrialization as a kind of irresistible force, towards an interpretation that conveyed a greater appreciation of people's diverse and complex reactions to pressures for social change (Anderson, 1971, p.7). He turned instead to explaining how people tried to control their own life chances and achieve their own goals – hence to the role of kinship. Basically he concluded that the explanation for the importance of kinship in Victorian England was the need to rely on family and kin in the precarious circumstances of rapid industrialization and migration.

> For the young and healthy, day-to-day life could largely continue independently of any family or kinship relationship. However, for most of the population critical life situations of one kind or another were common: ... distress resulting from sickness, death, and unemployment, the problems of old age and those resulting from a housing shortage, the difficulties of finding good employment, and the special problems of working mothers and of immigrants needing advice and shelter in a strange community.
>
> (Anderson, 1971, p.171)

Though both neighbours and other agencies provided some assistance, these both had their drawbacks: 'kin did, indeed, probably provide the main source of aid' (p.171).

This, then, formed the background for the final answer to Anderson's question. This was that in the period of industrialization, at least in nineteenth-century Lancashire, there was both a need for wider kinship links and the resources to exploit these. This presented a contrast, on the one hand, to some earlier periods (great problems but limited resources), and on the other to the modern situation where – according to the surmise with which Anderson ends his book – 'kinship is again weakened but now, by contrast, because the problems are reduced, resources are so much increased, and ready alternatives are open to all' (p.179).

His conclusion represents more than just factual findings about nineteenth-century Preston. Like many studies following this research model, it also suggests new insights and questions, new ways of looking at the subject. It is not surprising that he ends by pointing to opportunities for further research.

This example, even more than Jamieson's study, is obviously far too extensive for any one person to undertake without many years of research time. But whatever your own timescale, you could develop some research interests through a similar strategy – as long as you limit your scope and find manageable sources to question and to be questioned by.

_____ *EXERCISE 2.7* _____

Spend a few moments summarizing the main stages shared by Jamieson's and Anderson's overall research strategy.

Comments p.181.

2.3   RESEARCH STRATEGIES: A SUMMARY

Let us end this section by summarizing what is common to the hypothesis testing and questioning sources strategies. One outline was given on p.38. Below is a more elaborate checklist.

Schema C: Key stages in research

1   Think about a *topic, problem* or *source*.

2   Locate and assess *available sources and methods* (especially important, for if it turns out that appropriate sources and methods are not available, you may need to abandon the topic and start again).

3   Consider the specific *issue* (question, debate, generalization or usual assumption) you could explore through these sources and methods.

4   Translate the issue into *a limited researchable question/hypothesis/topic*.

5   Pursue *investigation and/or testing of evidence,* with available methods and sources, *refining the question* etc. if appropriate.

6   *Relate results back to (4)* (your specific question, hypothesis, etc.) and *compare or contrast* with any similar studies you can find.

7   Close circle by *presenting results and relating them back to (3)* (the issue, etc.): how far does your work support or challenge received views? How far has it changed your own original views? What further questions are now raised?

Note: further advice on sources, methods and modes of presentation is given in Volume 4. Information about issues, theories, debates, comparative cases, together with illustrative examples, can be found throughout Volumes 1–3.

3   STARTING WITH A SOURCE: THE LETTERS OF JOSEPH AND REBECCA HARTLEY

by Michael Drake

As noted on p.40 above, many pieces of research start with a source. Here I shall outline how one source can be subjected to the hypothesis testing strategy. Note that the same stages are used here as outlined in section 2.1, though in a different order, i.e. Stage 5 becomes Stage 1. In Chapter 5 you will find in finished form a piece of research which also started with a particular source but was conducted more in tune with the questioning sources strategy.

3.1   COLLECT DATA

The twenty-seven surviving letters of Joseph and Rebecca Hartley have been in my family's possession for over 100 years. Joseph Hartley was my great-grandmother's brother. He emigrated to the United States in 1858 from Brighouse in the West Riding of Yorkshire and died in

Figure 2.3 Photograph of Joseph Hartley: the photo is a tintype in a union case; a US stamp has been stuck on the back of the photo (original size 2 x 1¾ inches; 51 x 44 mm.)

Lockport, which is in upper New York State on the Erie canal, in 1876. My father always alleged that the letters had been kept as evidence of a relationship just in case Joseph or his descendants 'made good'. For good measure I published them all in 1964!

The caption to Figure 2.3 states that the photograph is of Joseph Hartley. Photographs, however, should be treated as seriously as any source (see Volume 4, Chapter 6). So can I be sure that the photograph *is* of Joseph Hartley? There is no direct evidence. What of circumstantial evidence? First, it came from the Drake family 'archives'. Second, Joseph did send his 'likeness': a letter of 12 September 1858 from him to his 'Hant and cusin' says that 'sister Hannah … wanted me to send my likeness and I have sent it by A man of the name of Richard driver of Bradford'. Third, the photograph is a tintype, an early process introduced in 1851 and widely used until after the Second World War. Fourth, the photograph is carried in a union case (see Figure 2.3), first produced in the USA (hence the name): few were sold after the 1880s. Fifth, on the back of the photograph is a US stamp. This had, by law, to be affixed on the back of all photographs as a form of taxation. Sixth, in a letter of 29 December 1858, Joseph writes: 'you wanted to now wich nicktie i had on * i had got on that plad scarf and my blue wascote'. Joseph is certainly wearing a waistcoat in the photograph. But is his scarf a plaid one? That is the question!

3.2   TOPIC OF INTEREST

It was my father's comment that gave me a topic of interest: the American dream. Nineteenth-century America was widely regarded as the 'land of opportunity' where one could move from 'rags to riches', from log cabin to White House. Hundreds of millions of people shared that dream, and in the nineteenth and early twentieth centuries tens of millions, mainly from Europe, but also from other parts of the world, immigrated to the USA in an attempt to realize it: Joseph and Rebecca were among them. Here there is much of interest to the family historian. What were the family circumstances of those who emigrated? Were the older sons and daughters more likely to migrate than the younger? Were better-off families more likely to be involved in the emigration process than the poorer? Were emigrants more likely to travel as individuals, as nuclear families, or with members of the extended family? Did families (or family members) on the whole do better through emigrating than those who stayed at home? What contacts were kept up? Were cash or other goods more likely to flow from the emigrant to his or her family in the 'mother' country or vice-versa?

3.3   ARTICULATE PROBLEM

You can't, of course, do everything at once, so I focused on the question of whether Joseph and Rebecca realized the 'American dream'. How too can their letters help us to understand more of the experience of the millions who crossed the Atlantic, no doubt with similar hopes? Relatively few sets of private letters like these have survived (for others see Erickson, 1972) and one wonders, therefore, just how typical their authors were of emigrants generally. That apart, one must begin by subjecting the letters to a critical assessment, for much is riding on them. Here there is not space to consider all the aspects (see Volume 4, Chapter 2, for a fuller treatment of how to assess primary sources). We know about their date, their origin, and the category of source (private letters), but we must also see whether they can serve our purpose by asking three questions of them.

HOW CLOSE WERE JOSEPH AND REBECCA TO THE EVENTS DESCRIBED?

Much of what Joseph and Rebecca wrote concerned events which they participated in and reported on quite soon after they occurred. This would apply to virtually the whole of the first letter written by Joseph on his arrival in America. I print this in its entirety below, partly to make this point clear and partly to give you the flavour of the letters. Note that neither Joseph nor Rebecca used punctuation marks. To make the text easier to read I have inserted an asterisk between what I take to be sentences.

First surviving letter from Joseph Hartley

Madina June 9 1858

Dear Hant and cusen

I Write those few lines to you Hopeing to find you in good health as it leavs me at presant * we got into liverpool on the wensday forenoon and whent on bord on the thirsday and we did not set sail untill the tusday following * we had a very good passage

but i was sick most part of the way * we landed safe in new york on the twenty seventh af may and we whent to the manchester house and got our diner and it was the first good diner we had since we left home and we staid in new york untill about seven o clock and then the train was due and we got in for albony and we got there about five o clock in the morning and we had to Cros the river in a steamboat and wate there untill 12 o clock at noon and we got into the cars for madina and we arived there on sunday the 29 of may and there was plenty of Jhon Buls to meet us but gorge Hartley and william shapard was not theare * they had gone to buflo a few weekes before * work is very bad hear at preseant and the wages is lower but they think they will get up by and by and i got work on they monday and i am living with Henery Dawson and i think i shall like this cuntary very well after a bit but i am not working at my own trade i am stone paving but i am thinking of going into the Qurey in a day or too * you must give my kind love to my father and mother and sisters and brothers and Mary webster and Eliza Hibetson and missis dunel and missis holms * you must tell Joseph Warinton when he drects he must drecet madina orlens county state of new york north amarica and you must Drect the same * so no more at preseant from your affectionate
son Joseph Hartley

Sometimes what Joseph writes is a matter of speculation, although, as in the following example written in the early days of the American Civil War, it tells us something of his mood at the time of writing:

Lockport August 27 1861
*… I think we shall all have to go for soulds [soldiers] befoo long * they ar goin to prees them to go and if they do I shall stand to go too * this countree is about plade out now * I think this is about the worst summer thay have ad in America this long tin and ther is no sines on it ben any beteter at I see …*

But comments such as this are rare. The letters stick very closely to the people (mostly relatives) whom he asks about, or whom he meets in America, his job, his wages, the prices he pays, his prospects, his returning to England, or not returning.

HOW COMPETENT ARE JOSEPH AND REBECCA AT UNDERSTANDING AND DESCRIBING THE MATTERS APPEARING IN THE LETTERS?

As noted above, these letters stick fairly closely to the concerns of the immediate family and locality. One assumes this is an area Joseph and Rebecca know well and therefore what they write on it inspires confidence. Here are some examples:

Madin [Medina] September 12 1858
*… you want to now how provision ar * thay are A lettle cheaper here * egs ar ten cents per dosen and butter 14 cents per pound * flower is 5 Dollar and a harf per brel * clothing is very dear but bootes and shes is very cheaper …*

Madina April + 15 + 1859
*… I have not deum any work sentes lest November nor I doent now wen I shall do any amore * when I do any more I hope it will never be in the quary …*

Lockport NY 21 October 1860
*… we have garate times hear now * they are electing a presedant * we have [clubs] there is one called the wide awakes and i have joined them and whe have a grand prade every few nights with oil Cloth sutes and torch lights and baners * the wide awakes goes for lincoln and the demcrates goes for duglas and i tell you we have grate fun * i wish you Could just see us once …*

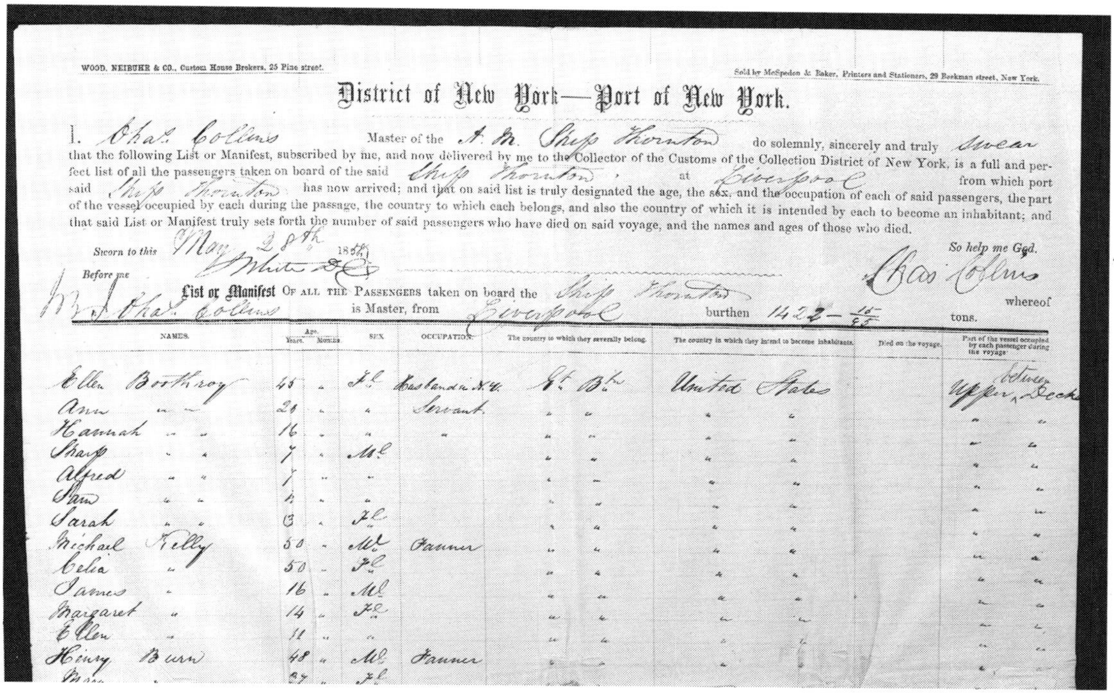

WOOD, NEIBUHR & CO., Custom House Brokers, 25 Pine street.

Sold by McSpedon & Baker, Printers and Stationers, 29 Beekman street, New York.

District of New York—Port of New York.

I, Chas. Collins Master of the A. M. Ship Thornton do solemnly, sincerely and truly swear that the following List or Manifest, subscribed by me, and now delivered by me to the Collector of the Customs of the Collection District of New York, is a full and perfect list of all the passengers taken on board of the said Ship Thornton at Liverpool from which port said Ship Thornton has now arrived; and that on said list is truly designated the age, the sex, and the occupation of each of said passengers, the part of the vessel occupied by each during the passage, the country to which each belongs, and also the country of which it is intended by each to become an inhabitant; and that said List or Manifest truly sets forth the number of said passengers who have died on said voyage, and the names and ages of those who died.

Sworn to this May 28th 1858 Before me J. White D.C.

So help me God. Chas. Collins

List or Manifest of all the Passengers taken on board the Ship Thornton whereof Chas. Collins is Master, from Liverpool burthen 1422 15/95 tons.

Names	Age Years	Age Months	Sex	Occupation	The country to which they severally belong	The country in which they intend to become inhabitants	Died on the voyage	Part of the vessel occupied by each passenger during the voyage
Ellen Boothroy	45	"	Fe	Husband in N.Y.	Gt. Bn	United States		Steerage Upper Deck
Ann "	20	"	"	Servant	" "	" "		" "
Hannah " "	16	"	"	"	" "	" "		" "
Sharp " "	7	"	Me		" "	" "		" "
Alfred " "	7	"	"		" "	" "		" "
Sam " "	4	"	"		" "	" "		" "
Sarah " "	3	"	Fe		" "	" "		" "
Michael Kelly	50	"	Me	Farmer	" "	" "		" "
Celia "	50	"	Fe		" "	" "		" "
James "	16	"	Me		" "	" "		" "
Margaret "	14	"	Fe		" "	" "		" "
Ellen "	11		"		" "	" "		" "
Henry Burn	48	"	Me	Farmer	" "	" "		" "
[illegible]	37		Fe					

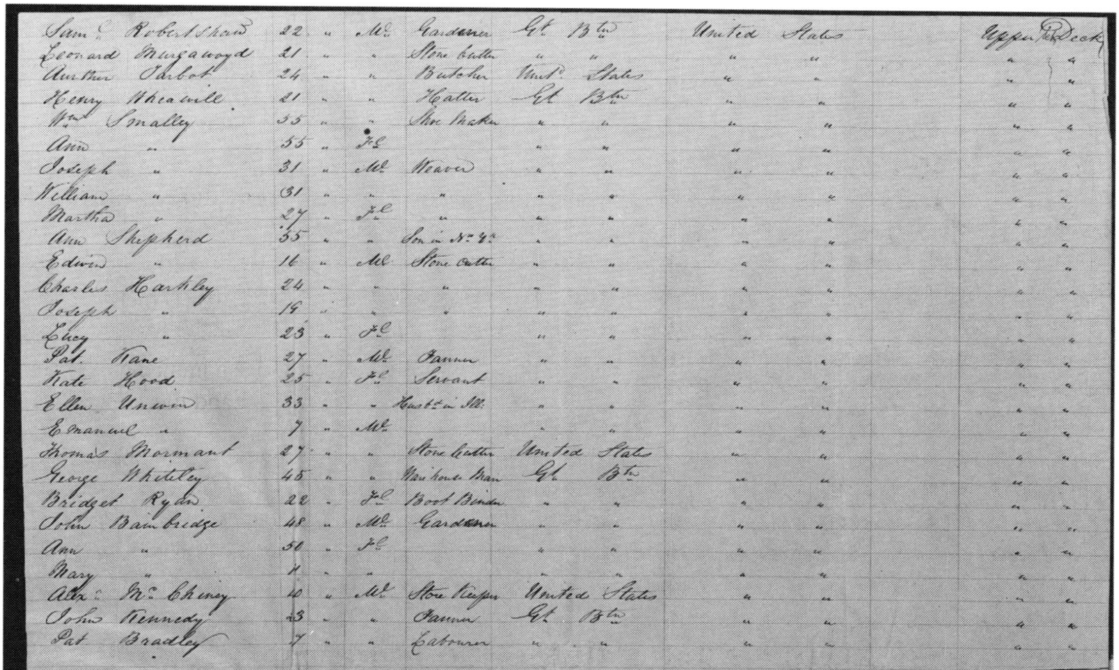

Saml Robertshaw	22	"	Me	Gardener	Gt. Bn	United States		Upper Deck
Leonard Murgatroyd	21		"	Stone Cutter	" "	" "		" "
Arthur Tarbot	24		"	Butcher	Unit. States	" "		" "
Henry Wheawill	21		"	Hatter	Gt. Bn	" "		" "
Wm Smalley	55		"	Shoe Maker	" "	" "		" "
Ann "	55	"	Fe		" "	" "		" "
Joseph "	31	"	Me	Weaver	" "	" "		" "
William "	31				" "	" "		" "
Martha "	27	"	Fe		" "	" "		" "
Ann Shepherd	55	"	"	Son in No. 4	" "	" "		" "
Edwin "	16	"	Me	Stone Cutter	" "	" "		" "
Charles Hartley	24		"		" "	" "		" "
Joseph "	19		"		" "	" "		" "
Lucy	23	"	Fe		" "	" "		" "
Pat. Kane	27	"	Me	Farmer	" "	" "		" "
Kate Hood	25	"	Fe	Servant	" "	" "		" "
Ellen Unwin	33	"		Husbd in Ill.	" "	" "		" "
Emanuel "	7	"	Me		" "	" "		" "
Thomas Mormant	27	"	"	Stone Cutter	United States	" "		" "
George Whiteley	45	"	"	Warehouse Man	Gt. Bn	" "		" "
Bridget Ryan	22	"	Fe	Boot Binder	" "	" "		" "
John Bainbridge	48	"	Me	Gardener	" "	" "		" "
Ann "	50	"	Fe		" "	" "		" "
Mary "	4		"		" "	" "		" "
Alex. McCheney	40	"	Me	Store Keeper	United States	" "		" "
John Kennedy	23		"	Farmer	Gt. Bn	" "		" "
Pat Bradley	17		"	Labourer	" "	" "		" "

Figure 2.4 Passenger list (extract) for AM Ship *Thornton* (arriving at port of New York, 28 May 1858) showing Joseph Hartley and companions (Source: National Archives and Records Administration, Washington DC)

HOW IMPARTIAL ARE JOSEPH AND REBECCA IN WHAT THEY SAY IN THEIR LETTERS?

Letters are notorious for what they omit, for putting a gloss on events; in other words, for distorting the record. The same applies to memoirs, diaries, company chairmen's reports, etc. In the case of these letters one assumes that much of the factual information as to prices, wages, topographical description, people met, is accurate. One could, in any case, check some of it. Joseph was, however, very homesick: he all but says as much on numerous occasions, and this could colour his observations:

Madin September 12 1858
… beth cliff wanted to know if I had forgot her but I shall never forget Brighouse wood nor none of them that live there.

Lockport November 28 1859
*… And I thought you ad forgot me *I roat a letter to you lest May and never receved any anser *I have been to the post ofice mooist every Day senes …*

This homesickness leads Joseph to ask some of his relatives to join him in America. One wonders if he paints too rosy a picture. In fact the reverse seems to have been the case. Of the two men who looked through prison bars, the one saw mud the other saw stars. Joseph often seems to belong to the former category, as for instance here:

Madin September 12 1858
*… you wanted to now if i was doing will but I am not doying as will as I expcted to do *ther is not much work and wages is louer …*

Lockport December 1 1863
*… I have a nise new hous and lott 1 acre and I have it paid for but I have had to work verey hard and be very saving *if I had not have ad it pade for I dont think I could now this warr time *Every thing is So very deer at this time it takes all a man Can Earn to live *as for mony we dont See any but paper mony…*

Lockport May 7th [1867/68]
*… Joseph is very lonesome without some of you with him *for I ham shure we would do all we could to make aney of you comfortable for we have nobody but poor Mother *I have no Father or brother to [s]peak too but if we put our trust in god he will comfort us *we wold lik to come and [see] you all but Joe thinks he can do better hear than in England *if Brother James wants to come and as not money to come with let us know and we will help him …*

In sum, I think a strong case can be made for these letters in terms of the writers' *closeness* to the events described; their *competence* in understanding and describing what they are writing about; and (perhaps) their *impartiality* in putting forward the case for America as the land of opportunity. We can then regard them as a test case for our investigation of the American dream.

3.4   FORMULATE HYPOTHESIS

Our hypothesis here is: *That there is evidence in the letters to suggest that at least some first generation immigrants were able to achieve some success in realizing 'the American dream'.*

3.5   DEVISE TEST

What are the criteria of 'success' in this context? I suggest three: health and wealth; social; psychological.

3.6 TEST

HEALTH AND WEALTH

We do not know why Rebecca went to the United States. The decision was hardly hers, for she appears to have left her native Cambridgeshire at the age of 14 with her father, mother and brother. The latter, incidentally, was drafted, or 'Prest' as Joseph sometimes put it, into the Union forces during the Civil War.

Lockport December 1 1863
*... my wife as a brother there *all she as *and she is freeting with thousands more for feor he should be kiled *we Expect him to be in the next battel that is Expected neor the Rapadom *he is in Meads army of the Potomac ...*

He was killed. Joseph escaped being drafted, though he constantly feared it.

Joseph travelled to the United States as a single man, but, as we have seen (Figure 2.4), he was accompanied by relatives and friends/acquaintances. His fortunes were mixed: 'work is very bad hear at preseant and the wages is lower' (9 June 1858); yet having arrived on Sunday 29 May he got work on the Monday.

Madina December 29th 1858
... we have bad times hear ... But I am 16 pund eavery nor I was when I left Home.

Lockport November 28 1859
*... the forst mun I Worked for this summer was William Worker *I work 19 days for A Dollar A day * But I never got my monny yet for it *and then I went of to Buffouly and thay was no work to be got there and *then I Keme bak to lockport and I got Work *I irde foe A month forst for 20 Dollars * And when that was oup he wanted me to stay A another month and I worked too month 20 dollars nd bord and I worked three month for 12 dollars a month and bord *And now I am goin on at six Dollars A month And bord and I shud have send you sum Monny But I can not get any yet ...*

Lockport May 3 1860
... there is beter times here now ...

Lockport August 27 1861
*... I am Working with the same man *yet I tould him last fall that I wood not board with him Any more but he did not want me to lev him *I had to take is noot for a hundred Dollars *that is twenty pound *And it was Dew to me 1 of July and he had not any monny then and now there is A nother hunder Dollars coming to me for this summers work * he wanted me to tak A naker of land for One hunder Dollars so I tought I woad And put A hous on it *then get Marred ... there his pretty hard times in America now But I think I can keep A wife ass chep as pai Board ...*

Lockport June 18 1866
... this is still a good country for anyone to work in although this warr as made every thing very high ... I was sorry it is not in our power to send you all something but my sickness as made me a grate loss ...

Lockport January 5 1868
*... the wages was very good last summer *I got 18 shillings for quarying *stonecutters had 20 to 24 shillinghs a day *Im geting 13 shillings per day this whinter... this is the land for a working man to make manney in if hee is stady and mindes is work ...*

Lockport Junary 1868
… All though a stranger to you all I feel it a dutay to take my pen to help my Joseph to hanswer your welcome letter … we have a family that came from Eyland [Elland near Brighouse] last July * they are very home sick but they have not done much work * when he came here he thought he was going to pick gold up in the road * it is not so * we have to work for what we have …

Lockport May 7 [1867–68]
… will you please tell Cousin Charley and James that Mr Whitmoor wants them to come for stone cutters are very scarce * for Joseph has to cut stone for he canot get aney men * Joe gets 20 shillings a day weet and dry * som as 24 shillings

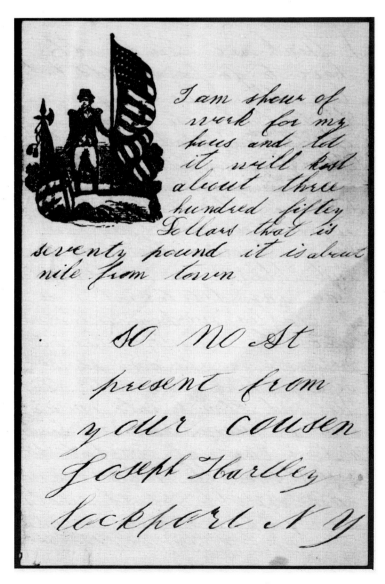

Figure 2.5 Letter from Joseph Hartley, 27 August 1861

Figure 2.6   Envelope containing Joseph Hartley's letter of 27 August 1861

Lockport April 18 [1870–71]
… we are all well at preasent and are doing very well although provishens are very dear but i think ther is not much difference for it seeames by the papers that things are dear in England … Joseph is very bissy in the querey

Lockport, January 22 [1876]
… Joe … is very sick and he is been growing worse ever since I wrote to you last … the Doktors here cannot do him aney good … he is so very week ∗ he was so bad befoure he quit woork that he had to ride horseback to the quarey for he was so short of breath that he could not walk ∗ I ham afraid that he will [not] live till Spring …

Lockport April 30 [1876]
I write with tears to let you know that your dear brother Joseph is dead ∗ he died April the 23 at 3 O Clock Sunday morning … he suffard a great deal ∗ befoure he died he laid on his back and i was so afraid he would choke but befoure he died he wanted to be turend on his side ∗ he died in a few minnets …

Lockport [Autumn 1876]
… if he could have live 3 or 4 years longer he could have left me moor Comfortable but I ham left alone know to look out for myself and Children I find it hard to get along sometime …

Lockport December 9 [?]
… i suppose you have heard of me getting Marred ∗ perhaps you will think it strange but if you knew my Sircomestances you would not blame very much ∗ I have 30 Acers of land 2 horses 2 colts 2 cows to take care of and i had no one to woork the land or to help me and i have 800 dollars to pay befower it is paid for ∗ i could not aford to pay a man to woork for me and cloth my Children and pay my depths [Joseph and Rebecca had four children: a girl, Lavina, born in 1862; a boy, Hulbert Willson, born in 1864; a girl, Liby, born in 1867; and a girl, Carie, born in 1869.]

I have quoted *in extenso* here in order to give you an outline of Joseph and Rebecca's circumstances in their own words. How much one quotes and how much one summarizes is a choice you must make in dealing with a topic like this and with this kind of source.

Joseph Hartley died at the age of 37. This was early by the standards of the time, though as a quarryman he was always at risk from chest complaints, especially in the winter when he sometimes got work indoors.

SOCIAL

Although health and income are two crucial elements, they are not the only criteria of success. Relationships in terms of how people fitted into the community they lived in, their activities outside work, also contribute to the quality of life. What do the letters tell us about this? Not a great deal. Was this because Joseph and Rebecca did not have much social life, didn't 'fit in', or simply felt it was not something worth writing about?

Joseph's first comment on reaching Medina was that there were 'plenty of Jhon Buls to meet us' (9 June 1858). He mentions the fourth of July celebrations several times, on the first occasion likening it to his local 'feast' back home, Rushbearing (12 September 1858). On another occasion he wrote that 'the yankees doo not think much of christmas … thay think more of 4 of July then any other day' (5 January 1868). His comment on his first Christmas hardly suggests he spent it in the bosom of the local community:

29 December 1858
*   I shood like to now what sote of a Christmis you have had * thay was A Mill birnt down in Medina on the Christmas day * that was all the Christmas we had.*

On the other hand he joined the Wide-Awakes, and he visited Niagara Falls to see Blondin walk across on a tight-rope. The Prince of Wales, he notes, was also in the crowd (28 November 1859). Joseph seems to have been a church-goer, noting that he went three 'times a day most every Sunday' (15 April 1859). Rebecca also comments on this church-going (more properly chapel-going as they appear to have been Wesleyan) noting that the minister was a very good preacher (9 September 1870/71). Joseph and Rebecca first met at a 'Suggar Party' – presumably the annual gathering of maple sugar in the woods (8 December 1872).

Joseph remarks in December 1863 that he had never voted and hadn't got naturalized. He hoped this would keep him off the draft. According to the 1865 census of Lockport, he was still an alien. But in the 1875 census he is listed as a naturalized citizen.

It was as he lay dying that Joseph and Rebecca's place in the community appears most clearly. Admittedly, one should be chary of the 'everybody loved him' type of remark, especially at such a time. But, as the extracts below indicate, some of the affection for him and his family did have practical outcomes:

April 30 [1876]
*… we lost a horse * I dare not tell Joe until we had another horse * the neibours have been very good * they have got another horse for us and it is going to have a colt * when he found out he cried for joy to think they had been so kind to him … he had A verry large funerl * 27 Carrages * every boddy respected him and done all that they could for him …*

[Autumn 1876]
*… every body that knew him had great respect for him for they all liked him * he allways ad kind word for every body * he had so meny friends calling to see him every day … the Neibours have been very kind to me * they come and cut my hay for me and then they come and cut my wheet for me * I have got 100 Bushells of wheet and 60 Bushells of barley and I have a nice crop of corn and potatoes * we have 2 pigs 2 cows 2 horses and 2 nice little colts and about 50 chickens …*

THE PSYCHOLOGICAL

From a series of comments scattered throughout the letters one can see Joseph and Rebecca coming to terms with their new environment. There is first the 'putting a brave face on it' comment: 'i think i shall like this cuntary very well after a bit' (9 June 1858). Then the talk of 'coming home if': 'I shud like to see better times in america befor I com hom' (29 December 1858); 'if I got stady work next summer I shall com hom I beleve next fall' (28 November 1859).

But already by 1860 Joseph's attitude has changed. Several times he remarks in similar vein to this:

May 3 1860
... if i live and all is well i shall Come home next fall but there is beter times here now than what there as been and if i was to Come back i should not want to stay for i should not like to work in the english Quereys aney more but i want to see you all very bad *but i am not as home sick as i was for Charles Hartley is liveing in lockport now and working with me ...

21 October 1860
... i am bound to make money before i come back to england agen *i am not going to come back as I left it ...

One of Joseph's reasons for not returning in 1863 was that he didn't 'like the sea as I should be sick all the way'. This may of course be reason enough, for he says in his first letter that he was 'sick most part of the way' during the thirty-two day voyage.

By the end of the 1860s there is another change in attitude. Now England comes under criticism: 'they say some poor people are starving in england' (6 March 1870) and 'I think England is a poor place for a man to get along * it seeams to me that you may work all your days and never have a house to hide your head' (18 April 1870/71). Then comes the final break with England, the articulated recognition of having passed from one set of loyalties to another:

8 December 1872
... I don't think we could live in England know *we are yankeys now *England is the place if you have plenty of money but America is the p[l]ace for a poor man to get a home *here is a home for every man if he is stedy ...

3.7   RESULT

We have followed Joseph and Rebecca Hartley as they struggled against loneliness, home sickness, unemployment, low wages, poor health, premature death, through to a modest prosperity and a seemingly valued place in the community. It is not quite a 'rags to riches' tale, but it fits into the idea of the United States as a land of opportunity, an idea both Joseph and Rebecca appear to endorse eventually. The hypothesis, then, appears at least partially confirmed.

This result could form the empirical core of an article intended for an academic audience interested in the processes of migration (see, for instance, Erickson, 1972). Or it could form the literary core of a publication enhanced by photographs, drawings, paintings, and facsimiles of letters and documents (see, for example, Gardiner, 1992). Alternatively it could be used as the introduction to the entire collection of letters. In each case the audience must be kept in mind at all times and addressed appropriately (see Volume 4, Chapter 10).

The Hartley letters focus our attention on issues of a wider relevance than nineteenth-century English migration to the United States. If, for instance, you are a member of a family that has migrated across national boundaries, for example from Ireland to England, Italy to Wales, Bangladesh to Scotland, then the Hartley experience might open up a line of questioning to illuminate your family's experience. Even migration within a single country might echo the Hartley experience. And if not, why not? One could also approach such letters as an aid to understanding the lives of working men and women, quite apart from the context of emigration.

From the letters we learn of the interests, concerns, hopes and fears of two people. They belonged to that vast – and mostly silent – majority of ordinary men and women. Because we have so little direct knowledge of their thoughts, such a cache of letters as the Hartleys produced is that much more important.

For example, we could incorporate some of the sentiments expressed in the letters into both of the studies discussed earlier in this chapter. As in the case of Anderson's propinquity study, there is concrete evidence of the role of kin: Joseph Hartley travelled to the United States with two cousins; his first letter (so far as we know) was to his 'Hant and cusen'; frequently Joseph refers to his relatives and their value to him; his wife Rebecca laments the absence of relatives. On the other hand we also have evidence of the help given by friends and neighbours. Joseph travelled not only with his cousins to the United States but with several acquaintances. He expected to be met by others. On his death his wife records, in both qualitative and quantitative terms, the help given to her and Joseph by their new neighbours.

The Hartley letters are also of interest in the context of Jamieson's study. She discusses the 'classical account' of family development, which emphasizes the increasing separation of the family from the wider world. In her (1987) article she seems to focus mainly on the nuclear family, for she questions the supposed 'weakening of the household's connectedness to neighbours and kin' (p.594), while herself saying little about the relationship with non-household relatives (kin). Here, surely, is a topic worthy of further investigation? In pursuing it one could draw both on the Hartley letters and the propinquity studies of Anderson and Mills.

EXERCISE 2.8

1 How would you use these letters in a project following the questioning sources strategy?

2 Of what significance is the change in the ordering of the stages in the Hartley case study as compared with the outline of the hypothesis testing strategy in section 2.1?

Comments p.181.

The understanding one gets from this kind of study and source is very different from that obtained, for example, from the study of residential propinquity. It is direct and immediate, not a matter of averages and probabilities. Both are necessary, since quite apart from what they tell us, both alert us to the possibilities of further enquiry. Thus the Hartley letters might lead us to more general studies of the process of migration; the Preston study on kinship might direct our attention towards more individual studies of particular sets of kin; while Jamieson's study from oral accounts of growing up in Scotland could be replicated by testing her findings in other places and at other times.

4 CONCLUSION

We started this chapter with some limbering up exercises designed to heighten your awareness of the potential of sources you may already have used, such as the CEBs and oral sources. You can scarcely do too much of this sort of thing. Every document you come across, every conversation or interview, is pregnant with possibilities. Ask yourself what is the significance of this date, that comment: is there more here than meets the eye; what sort of questions does this document – on its own or with others – help to answer?

Of course, such limbering up exercises do not constitute the game itself, essential though they are for success in that game. Although intellectual fitness is one essential, there is another – a strategy. We have suggested two you might follow. Inevitably they have much in common, sharing the same goals (to heighten our understanding) and often the same sources (documentary, oral, visual). But it would be best to keep them apart, especially if you are something of a beginner. No doubt top professional football teams can play different strategies at different parts of the game. That is part of their expertise. So competent and fluid are their movements that the strategies may not show. The same is true with history, as you will see when you come to the polished piece of historical writing in Chapter 5. This is something to aim for. Don't expect to succeed first time round. Keep exercising your skills. Practise one strategy, then the other. Rome wasn't built in a day!

REFERENCES AND FURTHER READING

Note: suggestions for further reading are indicated by an asterisk.

Anderson, M. (1971) *Family structure in nineteenth century Lancashire,* Cambridge, Cambridge University Press.

Anderson, M. (1972) 'The study of family structure' and 'Standard tabulation procedures for the census enumerators' books 1851–1891', in Wrigley (1972) pp.47–81, 134–45.

Anderson, M. (1983) 'What is new about the modern family?', Occasional Paper 31, *The family,* London, OPCS, pp. 2–16. Reprinted in Drake (1994).*

Braham, P. (ed.) (1993) *Using the past: audio-cassettes on sources and methods for family and community historians,* Milton Keynes, The Open University.

Collins, B. and Pryce, W.T.R. (1993) 'Census returns in England, Ireland, Scotland and Wales', audio-cassette 2A in Braham (1993).

Drake, M. (1964) 'We are Yankeys now', *New York History,* 45, 3, pp.222–64.

Drake, M. (1974) Unit 15 'Family and kinship' of D301 *Historical data and the social sciences,* Milton Keynes, The Open University.

Drake, M. (ed.) (1994) *Time, family and community: perspectives on family and community history,* Oxford, Blackwell in association with The Open University (Course Reader).

Dyer, J. (1991) 'The child population of Ladywood and Edgbaston 1851', *Local Population Studies,* 47, pp.30–8.

Erickson, C. (1972) *Invisible immigrants: the adaptation of English and Scottish immigrants in nineteenth-century America,* London, Weidenfeld & Nicolson.

Gardiner, J. (1992) *The world within: the Brontës at Haworth. A life in letters, diaries and writings,* London, Collins & Brown.

Gaulter, E. (1833) *The origin and progress of the malignant cholera in Manchester,* London, Longman.

Higgs, E. (1989) *Making sense of the census. The manuscript returns for England and Wales 1801–1901,* London, HMSO.*

Jamieson, L. (1983) *A case study in the development of the modern family: urban Scotland in the early twentieth century,* PhD thesis, University of Edinburgh.

Jamieson, L. (1987) 'Theories of family development and the experience of being brought up', *Sociology,* 21, pp. 591–607. Reprinted in Drake (1994).*

Laslett, P. and Wall, R. (eds) (1972) *Household and family in past time: comparative studies in the size and structure of the domestic group over the last three centuries in England, France, Serbia, Japan and Colonial North America with further materials from Western Europe,* Cambridge, Cambridge University Press.

Lewis, S. (1831) *Topographical dictionary of England,* London.

MacDonagh, O. (1991) *Jane Austen: real and imagined worlds,* New Haven and London, Yale University Press.

Mills, D.R. (1978) 'The residential propinquity of kin in a Cambridgeshire village, 1841', *Journal of Historical Geography,* 4, pp. 265–76.

Schürer, K. (1993) 'Nominal lists and nominal record linkage', audio-cassette 2B in Braham (1993).

Thompson, P. (1978) *The voice of the past: oral history,* Oxford, Oxford University Press (2nd edn 1988).*

Wrigley, E.A. (ed.) (1972) *Nineteenth-century society: essays in the use of quantitative methods for the study of social data,* Cambridge, Cambridge University Press.

Young, M. and Wilmott, P. (1957) *Family and kinship in East London,* London, Routledge and Kegan Paul.

PART II

SETTING YOUR FAMILY IN CONTEXT

❖ ❖ ❖

CHAPTER 3

YOUR FAMILY: TYPICAL OR NOT?

by Michael Drake

1 THE DEMOGRAPHIC EXPERIENCE: BIRTHS, MARRIAGES AND DEATHS

My mother, Florence Hilda Goodaire, was born in 1909. She had one sister, born four years later. Her mother died in 1917. Her father, who was 39 years old at the time, never re-married. Further information on parts of my family appears in Figure 3.1. Many of you will no doubt have much more detailed family trees than this. Yet no matter how sparse or rich they are, such trees are of consuming interest for the families concerned, just as they stand. But no family historian can deny that, except in rare circumstances, such information is not of riveting interest for anyone *outside* the family circle. But need this be the case? Can they tell us more? We have already tried to show how looking at your own family in the context of what we know about families in general, at various times in the past, can be enlightening (Chapter 2, section 1). Here I shall carry the process further by focusing on population change over the past couple of centuries. It should be said right away that there is much we do not know about this, especially at the local community level. I shall therefore be pointing out, in the course of this chapter, those areas of interest where you might make a contribution by undertaking a limited study.

For much of the past 200 years three ceremonies have stood at the centre of family life: baptism, marriage and burial. You are no doubt familiar with each, either from personal experience or from that of your friends and relations, or perhaps because you have produced a family tree. These ceremonies and the rites associated with them reveal much about the internal workings of the family and its relationship with the community or communities in which it is embedded. The ceremonies also constitute the building blocks of the demographic experience. Indeed, until the onset of civil registration (England and Wales 1837; Scotland 1855; Ireland 1845 – partially – and 1864) we are dependent upon the records of these ceremonies, kept by the clergy who conducted them, for what we know of that experience. Our exploration of the demographic experience of the United Kingdom and Ireland over the past 200 years begins by examining aspects of the three ceremonies.

1.1 BAPTISM AND BIRTH

What was happening to baptisms around 1800? As far as Ireland is concerned we know but little. Few registers of the Catholic majority have survived from as early as that, and even fewer give us the dates of both birth and baptism. Around 1800, a gap of a week or more between the two

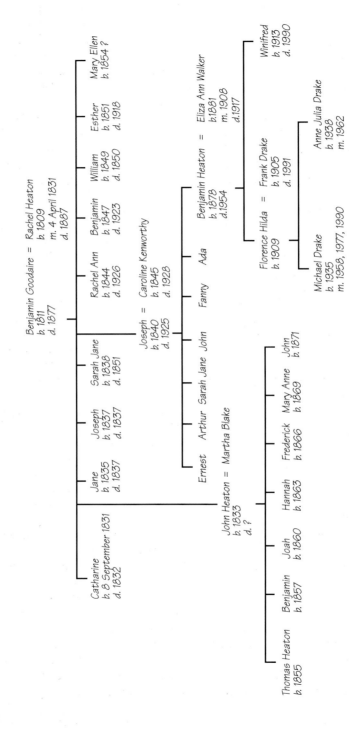

Figure 3.1   The Goodaire family tree, 1786–1990

events would have meant the death of quite a number of babies before baptism, so adversely affecting the calculations of birth rates based on the latter. Scotland too has few parish registers around 1800, though decidedly more than Ireland. From a few which give the requisite information it would appear that the number of babies baptized within a week of birth fell in the course of the eighteenth century: in Edinburgh, for example, 84.1 per cent were baptized within a week of birth in 1725, but only 29.0 per cent in 1795. It must be admitted that other registers do not show the same trend, suggesting, perhaps, that big cities were especially badly affected (Flinn, 1977, Table 4.6.1). Perhaps further research will provide a clearer picture.

But what of England and Wales? Work remains to be done on the registers of Wales (for availability see Williams and Watts-Williams, 1986). As for England, our knowledge is more complete. Put briefly, *one-third* of all children born around 1800 may not have appeared in a Church of England parish register (Wrigley and Schofield, 1981, p.135). It is hardly surprising that many family historians have found the early nineteenth century to be something of a black hole when it comes to constructing a family tree!

The reasons for this shortfall are various. First, the rapid expansion of population in the second half of the eighteenth century occurred most strikingly in areas not well served by the Church of England. There were, in other words, not enough clergy to cope. Second, the rise of nonconformity caused people to shift their allegiance away from the Church of England. Some 6 per cent of births and maybe more are therefore reckoned to have produced a baptism entry in one or other nonconformist register. A third reason, and possibly the more important, was that people were not in such a hurry to have their children baptized as had been the case previously. Why this was so remains a mystery. Was it because death rates were falling (though not by very much) in eighteenth-century England, so the danger of a child dying before baptism was less? Were the populations of the new industrial areas less observant of Christian ritual than their forebears in a more rural England? Was baptism becoming merely a social event? Or given the increase in pre-marital pregnancy, was there an element of embarrassment? Changes in theological teaching and practice may have played a role too. Whatever the reason, it would appear that overall by the end of the eighteenth century 'there was a median interval of about a month between birth and baptism, though with wide variation from parish to parish' (Wrigley and Schofield, 1981, p.96).

The effect of this on the registration system and, in turn, on any assessment of the level of fertility, could be considerable. As Wrigley and Schofield have pointed out (p.97), if one assumes that 'the infant mortality rate were 200 per 1000 live births and one half of all infant deaths occurred in the first month of life, one live birth in ten might be lost to the baptism register, if the delay between birth and baptism were one month'.

There have been numerous studies of the timing (or seasonality) of baptisms, several of which have appeared in *Local Population Studies*. These have revealed various patterns related to local festivals or fairs, the character of the local clergy, or the edicts of the Church of England (Bradley, 1970; McCallum, 1980; Doolittle, 1980; Cook, 1980; all reprinted in Drake, 1982). These patterns are an expression of people's attitudes towards the ceremony and an indication of the role it played in their lives. Ideally, of course, we would like written evidence of these attitudes and roles. But as is so often the case when trying to get at what ordinary men and women *thought*, we have to see what they *did* and then try to infer their thoughts from this.

A register that is particularly rich, over a not inconsiderable period, for ascertaining the changes that occurred in the birth–baptism interval is that of the rural Buckinghamshire parish of Iver. In Table 3.1 I give two systematic samples drawn from the register: i.e. every third entry for the years 1701–6 and every fifth entry for 1831–6 (for the technique of sampling see Volume 4, Chapter 8.) What is especially interesting about this register is that it not only gives the dates of birth and baptism, and does so over a long period, but it also gives the occupation of the father of the child being baptized. This allows us to pursue another line of enquiry, namely whether or not the birth–baptism interval varied according to socio-economic status. By using the entire register one could do quite a sophisticated analysis. Here, however, we will content ourselves by looking at the difference between labourers and the rest. See now if you can complete Exercise 3.1.

Table 3.1 Sample of births and baptisms in the parish of Iver (Bucks): (a) 1701–6 (one in three) and (b) 1831–6 (one in five)

1701–6	Date of Birth	Date of Baptism	Sex	Father's occupation
1701	Mch 18	Apr 5	f	Maltster
	Apr 4	Apr 21	m	Labourer
	May 11	May 17	m	Maltster
	May 9	May 23	m	Farmer
	May ?	Jun 18	m	Paper-maker
	Jun 3	Jun 27	m	Labourer
	Aug 3	Aug 10	f	Labourer
	Oct 25	Oct 27	m	Labourer
	Nov 12	Nov 24	f	Labourer
1702	Jan 15	Jan 17	f	Labourer
	Feb 8	Feb 8	f	Labourer
	Feb ?	Feb 22	f	Labourer
	Mch 1	Mch 13	f	Carpenter
	Mch 29	Apr 18	m	Farmer
	Apr 17	May 1	f	Farmer
	May 27	Jun 7	f	Maltster
	Jun 23	Jun 28	m	Labourer
	Sep 2	Sep 12	m	Farmer
	Sep 23	Oct 9	m	Shoemaker
	Oct 27	Nov 14	f	Victualler
	Nov 19	Nov 22	m	?
1703	Jan 17	Jan 29	m	Farmer
	Feb 17	Feb 28	m	Labourer
	Mch 2	Mch 7	m	Shepherd
	Mch 1	Apr 5	m	Farmer
	Apr 15	Apr 30	f	Farmer
	May 16	May 22	f	Farmer
	Jul 23	Jul 26	m	Labourer
	Aug 15	Aug 20	f	Farmer
	Oct 14	Oct 15	f	Farmer
	Oct 13	Oct 24	m	Hoopshaver
	Oct 24	Nov 7	m	Labourer
1704	Jan 11	Jan 11	m	Labourer
	Feb 6	Feb 6	m	Labourer
	Mch 1	Mch 24	m	Farmer
	Mch 4	Apr 2	m	Shepherd
	Apr 6	Apr 22	m	Gentleman
	May 18	May 19	f	Gardener
	Jun 28	Jul 12	f	Yeoman
	Jul 31	Aug 19	f	Labourer
	Oct 12	Oct 22	m	Labourer
	Dec 4	Dec 24	m	Labourer
1705	Jan 4	Jan 21	m	Labourer
	Feb 21	Mch 7	f	Minister
	Apr 16	Apr 16	m	Fisherman
	Apr 16	May 2	f	Farmer
	Apr 24	May 12	m	Victualler
	Jun 21	Jun 21	f	Stranger
	Jul 11	Jul 12	m	Paper-maker
	Jul 28	Jul 29	m	Steward
	Nov 5	Nov 18	m	Victualler
	Nov 28	Dec 14	f	Labourer
1706	Jan 5	Jan 7	f	Labourer
	Jan 10	Jan 11	f	Labourer
	Jan 22	Feb 4	m	Labourer
	Feb 16	Feb 17	m	Labourer
	Feb 6	Mch 1	f	Smith

1831–6	Date of Birth	Date of Baptism	Sex	Father's occupation
1831	Mch 1	Mch 27	m	Farmer
	Mch 27	Apr 17	m	Labourer
	Apr 10	May 29	f	Tailor
	Nov 25 (1830)	Jul 23	m	Esquire
	Jul 27	Sep 4	m	Gardener
	Sep 1	Sep 25	f	Labourer
	Oct 11	Oct 12	f	Farmer
	Nov 16	Dec 11	f	Coachman
1832	Jan 18	Jan 19	f	Labourer
	Dec 20 (1831)	Feb 5	f	Labourer
	Jan 25	Feb 26	m	Labourer
	Feb 26	Mch 25	f	Labourer
	Apr 5	Apr 29	f	Labourer
	Apr 21	May 20	f	Haberdasher
	Jun 12	Jul 8	m	Labourer
	Jul 14	Aug 5	m	Labourer
	Jun 27	Aug 12	m	Labourer
	Aug 24	Aug 24	m	Baker
	Aug 19	Sep 23	m	Labourer
	Oct 16	Nov 11	f	Thongmaker
	Nov 2	Dec 2	f	Labourer
	Nov 18	Dec 30	m	Paper-maker
1833	Feb 7	Mch 3	f	Labourer
	Nov 17 (1832)	Apr 9	m	Miller
	Apr 21	May 27	f	Lt Gov of Island of St Vincent
	Jun 18	Jun 27	m	Blacksmith
	Jul 19	Aug 18	f	Ship's Steward
	Sep 5	Sep 22	m	Carpenter
	Sep 18	Oct 13	f	Labourer
	Oct 25	Nov 17	f	Domestic
	Oct 21	Dec 1	m	Shoemaker
	Nov 22	Dec 15	m	Labourer
1834	Jan 16	Jan 16	m	Labourer
	Mch 2	Mch 2	f	Labourer
	Dec 27 (1833)	Mch 30	m	Farmer
	Mch 19	Apr 27	m	Paper-maker
	Apr 3	May 4	f	Sawyer
	May 2	May 12	f	Labourer
	May 5	Jun 1	f	Labourer
	May 6	Jul 6	f	Miller
	May 7	Aug 17	m	Labourer
	Sep 14	Oct 12	m	Labourer
	Oct 5	Nov 2	f	Labourer
	Jan 17 (1831)	Nov 30	f	Labourer
	Dec 13	Dec 22	m	Labourer
1835	?	Feb 13	m	Labourer
	Jan 14	Mch 22	m	Labourer
	Mch 19	Apr 12	m	Labourer
	May 31 (1834)	May 17	m	Labourer
	May 9	May 24	m	Labourer
	?	Jun 14	f	Labourer
	Sep 24 (1834)	Aug 8	m	Gentleman
	Aug 8	Sep 6	m	Labourer
	Oct 2	Oct 25	f	Miller
	Nov 4	Nov 29	f	Labourer
1836	?	Jan 10	f	Farmer
	Aug 11 (1835)	Jan 17	f	Labourer
	Nov 29 (1835)	Feb 26	m	Labourer

Source: Iver Parish Register, Buckinghamshire County Records Office, Aylesbury

_____ *EXERCISE 3.1* _____

1   What is the median birth–baptism interval for children of (i) labourers and (ii) non-labourers in the years:

(a)   1701–6;

(b)   1831–6?

Note: The median is the middle value in the series. You should make lists of the birth–baptism intervals for labourers and non-labourers from Table 3.1 and put them in order from the lowest number of days to the highest (i.e. 0, 0, 0, 1, 1 ... 16, 17, etc.). (Note: ignore incomplete entries.) The number appearing mid-way between the top and bottom of the list is the median. See Volume 4, Chapter 8 for this and other measures of central tendency.

How would you interpret your findings?

2   Using the perpetual calendar (Table 3.2), find the days of the week on which baptisms occurred in:

(a)   1701–6 (Julian calendar);

(b)   1831–6 (Gregorian calendar).

How would you interpret your findings?

3   Suppose the implications of the birth–baptism interval interest you. How would you organize a project using the hypothesis testing strategy? Use the stages suggested in section 2.1 of Chapter 2: topic of interest; articulate problem; formulate hypothesis; devise test; collect data; test; result. A sentence or so for each should suffice.

Answers/comments p.182.

The Church of England appears to have improved its registration system after 1820 or thereabouts, so that the shortfall between births and the number of baptisms appearing in its registers was never so high as in the first decade of the century. The need to rely on these registers – at least in England and Wales – was coming to an end. In 1837 the Registration Act, passed in the previous year, came into operation. This transferred the responsibility for registering births, marriages and deaths from the Church of England to a state official, the Registrar General. The new system was not accepted by all in its early years, especially not by certain members of the clergy; some people also thought – mistakenly – that by baptizing their children, they had also registered their birth (Ambler, 1987); prosecutions occurred only if people refused to give the required information to the local registrar (not until 1874 was the 'onus of registration placed on the informant, e.g. parents of a child, occupier of a house, nearest relative in the case of a death, etc.'); and as in the early days registrars were paid so much per entry, fictitious entries were encouraged (Nissell, 1987, pp.21–6).

As tens of thousands of family historians have discovered, civil registration in England and Wales, after these initial teething troubles, did come to cover the overwhelming bulk of the population. The Registrar General believed, for example, that whereas 6.5 per cent of births were not registered in the years 1841–50, the figure had fallen to 1.8 per cent by 1861–70 (Registrar General, 1875, p.5). All this is not intended to suggest that after 1837 the Church of England parish registers are useless for research purposes. They help us check the Registrar General's returns (incomplete as these were in the early years) and on occasion they contain more information than the civil registration certificates.

Table 3.2 Perpetual calendar[1]

Year				Century											
				Julian Calendar								Gregorian Calendar			
				0 700 1400	100 800 1500[3]	200 900 1600	300 1000 1700[4]	400 1100	500 1200	600 1300	1500[2]	1600 2000	1700 2100	1800 2200	1900 2300
0				DC	ED	FE	GF	AG	BA	CE	...	BA	C	E	G
1	29	57	85	B	C	D	E	F	G	A	F	G	B	D	F
2	30	58	86	A	B	C	D	E	F	G	E	F	A	C	E
3	31	59	87	G	A	B	C	D	E	F	D	E	G	B	D
4	32	60	88	FE	GF	AG	BA	CB	DC	ED	CB	DC	FE	AG	CB
5	33	61	89	D	E	F	G	A	B	C	A	B	D	F	A
6	34	62	90	C	D	E	F	G	A	B	G	A	C	E	G
7	35	63	91	B	C	D	E	F	G	A	F	G	B	D	F
8	36	64	92	AG	BA	CB	DC	ED	FE	GF	ED	FE	AG	CB	ED
9	37	65	93	F	G	A	B	C	D	E	C	D	F	A	C
10	38	66	94	E	F	G	A	B	C	D	B	C	E	G	B
11	39	67	95	D	E	F	G	A	B	C	A	B	D	F	A
12	40	68	96	CB	DC	ED	FE	GF	AG	BA	GF	AG	CB	ED	GF
13	41	69	97	A	B	C	D	E	F	G	E	F	A	C	E
14	42	70	98	G	A	B	C	D	E	F	D	E	G	B	D
15	43	71	99	F	G	A	B	C	D	E	C	D	F	A	C
16	44	72		ED	FE	GF	AG	BA	CB	DC	...	CB	ED	GF	BA
17	45	73		C	D	E	F	G	A	B	...	A	C	E	G
18	46	74		B	C	D	E	F	G	A	...	G	B	D	F
19	47	75		A	B	C	D	E	F	G	...	F	A	C	E
20	48	76		GF	AG	BA	CB	DC	ED	FE	...	ED	GF	BA	DC
21	49	77		E	F	G	A	B	C	D	...	C	E	G	B
22	50	78		D	E	F	G	A	B	C	...	B	D	F	A
23	51	79		C	D	E	F	G	A	B	...	A	C	E	G
24	52	80		BA	CB	DC	ED	FE	GF	AG	...	GF	BA	DC	FE
25	53	81		G	A	B	C	D	E	F	...	E	G	B	D
26	54	82		F	G	A	B	C	D	E	C	D	F	A	C
27	55	83		E	F	G	A	B	C	D	B	C	E	G	B
28	56	84		DC	ED	FE	GF	AG	BA	CB	AG	BA	DC	FE	AG

dominical letter

January, October				A	B	C	D	E	F	G
February, March, November				D	E	F	G	A	B	C
April, July				G	A	B	C	D	E	F
May				B	C	D	E	F	G	A
June				E	F	G	A	B	C	D
August				C	D	E	F	G	A	B
September, December				F	G	A	B	C	D	E
1	8	15	22	29	Sunday	Saturday	Friday	Thursday	Wednesday	Tuesday	Monday
2	9	16	23	30	Monday	Sunday	Saturday	Friday	Thursday	Wednesday	Tuesday
3	10	17	24	31	Tuesday	Monday	Sunday	Saturday	Friday	Thursday	Wednesday
4	11	18	25		Wednesday	Tuesday	Monday	Sunday	Saturday	Friday	Thursday
5	12	19	26		Thursday	Wednesday	Tuesday	Monday	Sunday	Saturday	Friday
6	13	20	27		Friday	Thursday	Wednesday	Tuesday	Monday	Sunday	Saturday
7	14	21	28		Saturday	Friday	Thursday	Wednesday	Tuesday	Monday	Sunday

[1] This perpetual calendar provides a means of finding the day of the week for any date in a wide range of years. In the calendar given here, to find the day of the week for any Gregorian or Julian date, first find the proper dominical letter for the year in the upper table. Leap years have two dominical letters, the first applicable in January and February, the second in the remaining months (note that in the Gregorian calendar only those century years — 1600, 1700, 1800, etc. — that are divisible by 400 are leap years). Then find the same dominical letter in the lower table, in whichever column it appears opposite the month in question. The days then fall as given in the lowest section of the column.
[2] On and after 1582. October 15 only.
[3] On and before 1582. October 4 only.
[4] 1752 E January, February. D March to 2 September. A 14 September to December; 1753 onwards use Gregorian calendar.
Example: what day of the week was 29 August 1982? Scan the top rows to find the century. You will find '1900' at the extreme right of the table. Look down the four left-hand columns to find the particular year. You will find '82' towards the bottom ot the third column from the left of the table. Now scan along the row which begins with '82' and down the column headed '1900'. Where the two meet you will find the dominical letter, i.e. 'C'. Now go to the bottom part of the table. On the extreme left you will find the months of the year. Find 'August'. Move along this row till you find the dominical letter 'C'. It is in the first column. Go back to the left of the table where you will find the days of the month and locate '29'. It is at the top of the fifth column of figures from the left. Now scan along the row headed '29' and down the column in which you have found the 'C'. Where the two meet you will find the day on which 29 August 1982 fell, i.e. Sunday.
Note: if you use the Gregorian calendar with parish records for dates earlier than 1752, you will encounter some difficulties, as the Julian calendar was used for dating registers up to 1752. We have extended the range of the Julian calendar by adding 1600 and 1700 to the columns headed 200 and 300 respectively. For 1752 there are three dominical letters: E for January and February; D for March to 2 September; and A for 14 September to December. (In 1752 the eleven days between 3 and 13 September were omitted.) The dominical letters for 1753 and subsequent years are found in the Gregorian calendar.
Source: *Encyclopedia Britannica*, 15th edn, 1974, *Micropedia*, vol. II, p.455

—————————————————————— *EXERCISE 3.2* ——————————————————————

Before we see what can be gleaned from the registers (civil and ecclesiastical) and the associated population censuses about the levels of fertility over the last two centuries, take another look at Figure 3.1. What does it suggest happened to the fertility level of this one branch of the Goodaire family over the past two hundred years?

Answer/comment p.183.

FERTILITY TRENDS 1800–1990

Figure 3.2 shows what is called the crude birth rate for the period 1800–1990. Ideally the crude birth rate is calculated by taking the number of births in any one year, dividing this by the estimated total population in the middle of the same year, and multiplying the outcome by one thousand. The rate is expressed as 'so many births per thousand population'.

Figure 3.2 is based, for the most part, on returns made by the Registrars General of the various countries. Scotland together with England and Wales appear to track each other closely. The Irish figures are, however, way out of line, being very considerably lower in the 1860s, when the experience of the different countries can first be compared, and somewhat above since the 1940s. Ireland's lower rates could be due to the under-registration of births, low marriage rates (see Figure 3.2), a late age at marriage, or a different age distribution. Apart from the first of these factors, each could influence the crude birth rate. This measure of fertility suffers from the fact that it relates births to the total population, whereas, of course, the births are produced by women in a relatively narrow age range (say 15–44 years) who, until recently, were almost always married. Because the crude rate takes no account of the sex ratio, age composition and marital status of the population, it reflects differences in them, as well as in fertility. As a result, demographers have spent a great deal of time refining their measures of fertility, mortality and nuptiality. Unfortunately most family and community historians are unlikely to be able to adopt these refined rates, either because the data are not available to them, or the calculations are too sophisticated. Two somewhat more refined rates do, however, satisfy the requirement of greater accuracy and accessibility: the general fertility rate and the child/woman ratio. The former relates the number of births to the number of women aged 15–44. The latter relates the number of children under 1 year of age (or, alternatively, 0–4 years) to the number of women aged 15–44 years. (For details see Volume 4, Chapter 8.)

Before leaving this section it will pay us to return to Figure 3.1 and the Goodaire family tree. Whilst the experience of the nineteenth- and twentieth-century members of this family bear out what we know in crude terms, i.e. there was a sharp fall in fertility, it does not do so in detail. After all, Rachel Goodaire had eleven children we know about, or more than five times as many as her great-granddaughter, born just one hundred years later. Yet the crude birth rate did not show such a major shift over the same period. Also, looking at the behaviour of the rate in the middle decades of the nineteenth century, one would not expect her son Joseph to have had only about half the number of children (six in all) that she had. The answer to these and other discrepancies lies in the fact that here we are dealing with an individual family's experience. The crude birth rate, the general fertility rate and the child/woman ratio or any other measure reflect the *average* experience of the community, or region or class, to which they refer. And at any one time the fertility experience of individual families varied widely. Thus in the 1870s, when birth control was barely practised, the number of children a woman might have, varied according to her age at marriage, her health, whether or not she was widowed whilst still in the fertile age group, whether she breast-fed her babies and for how long, and so on. You must therefore take account of this when looking at the fertility experience of your own family within the context of fertility generally at the time and place in which they lived.

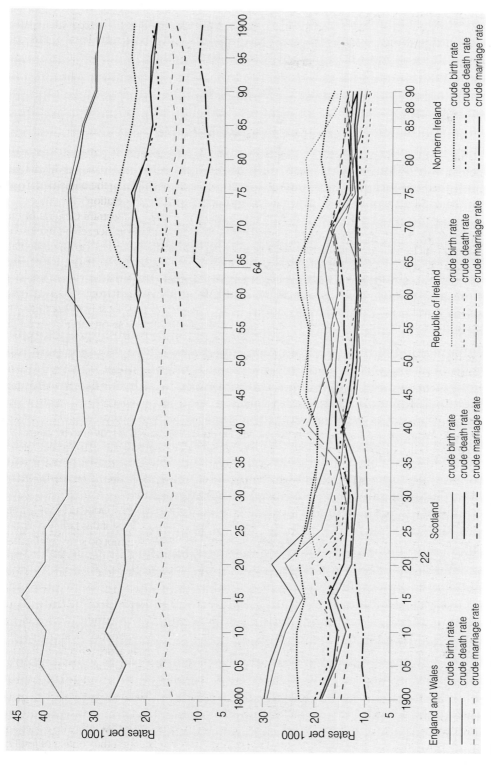

Figure 3.2 Births, deaths and marriages per 1000 population in England and Wales, Scotland, the Republic of Ireland, and Northern Ireland, 1800–1990 (Source: Mitchell, 1992, pp.90–111)

BIRTHS OUTSIDE MARRIAGE AND PRE-MARITAL CONCEPTIONS

A topic that has interested historians for some time has been the incidence of births produced or conceived outside marriage. It would appear that throughout Europe such births varied, as a proportion of total births, quite considerably over time.

In England the percentage of all births occurring outside marriage rose from a low point of 3 per cent in the 1660s to a high of 6 per cent in the 1860s. It hovered around there to the end of the century and then fell to a low point in the 1950s. Beginning in the 1970s, however, there has been a marked and continuous rise to unprecedented levels. This marks a completely new attitude towards marriage, indicated too in an equally dramatic rise in the number of divorces (Phillips, 1991).

A matter worthy of further exploration is the considerable variation in the number of births outside marriage amongst 'new' Britons. As Figure 3.3 shows, such births occur hardly at all to mothers born in Pakistan/Bangladesh, India or East Africa. Nor over the ten years 1976–86 was there any change, upwards or downwards. This contrasts with the doubling in the number of illegitimate births for women born in the UK. This suggests that the aforementioned women were not taking on the habits of women in the 'host' community. The startling feature of the graph is the high and relatively constant number of illegitimate births to women born in the Caribbean, at around 50 per cent of all births.

The causes of these differences between people, over time and between communities, is worthy of further study because it reflects important attitudinal differences – or *mentalités* as they are often now called. With the setting up of the General Register in Britain and Ireland, the basic statistical information is available, though given the delicate nature of the subject in Victorian times – indeed up to the 1960s – this has to be interpreted with caution. There is also a considerable amount of literary evidence, from official or quasi-official reports to newspaper accounts and novels.

Another interesting example of sexual mores can be discovered, on occasion, by combining the information from baptism and marriage registers. The technique is simple enough, though time-consuming. Find a marriage register at your local library or record office and put the entries in it onto cards or sheets of paper, with one entry for each card. How many years you cover will

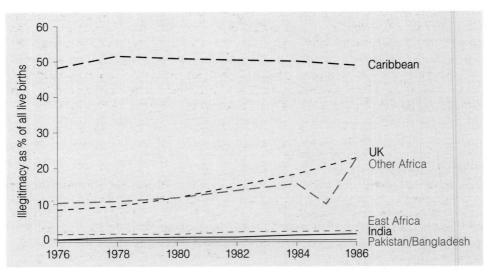

Figure 3.3   Births outside marriage to women born in various countries who had their children in England and Wales, 1976–86 (Source: Diamond and Clark, 1989, p.195)

depend on the number of entries per year and on the hypothesis you wish to test. Turn to the baptism register which encompasses *all* your marriage entries and for three years after the last marriage entry. Take one card at a time and search through the baptism register to see if you can match a marriage to one or more baptisms. Baptisms which take place less than nine months after the marriage of the parents of the child being baptized can be presumed to be the result of pre-marital conception.

EXERCISE 3.3

What problems do you think might arise in matching entries from a marriage and a baptism register?

Answer/comment p.183.

Taking England in the years 1660–1920, which of the following statements do you think is true?

1   That when the age at marriage was relatively early, the proportion of births outside marriage was relatively low.

2   That a shift to a later age at marriage brought a rise in the proportion of births outside marriage.

3   That the number of pre-marital conceptions was higher when the age at marriage was relatively late.

The answer is that none of the statements is true. Since this seems to run counter to common sense, what is the explanation? Although sexual intercourse outside marriage was condemned by the religious establishment (on moral grounds) and by the secular establishment (fearing the financial burdens associated with bastardy), what seems to have determined its incidence was the state of the economy. In the late eighteenth and early nineteenth centuries proto-industrialization (cottage-based industry) meant that people could marry earlier. The shackles that had previously tied the population to a relatively late age at marriage were loosened. It was no longer a case of waiting for someone to retire or die before you could marry. Sexual activity rose, reflected mainly in pre-marital conceptions – accounting for perhaps 40 per cent of all first births (Hair, 1966, 1970) – but also in illegitimate births, i.e. those that occurred because for one reason or another a marriage did not take place. In the late nineteenth century the age at marriage rose, but the proportion of births outside marriage fell. Sexual deprivation, as indicated by later marriage, did not result in rising illegitimacy (Laslett and Oosterveen, 1973, p.257).

QUESTION FOR RESEARCH

What happened to pre-marital conceptions in the second half of the nineteenth and first two decades of the twentieth centuries? Work on what lies behind the statistics remains to be done, as it does on the years since 1960. Between 1980 and 1990 in England and Wales the percentage of conceptions outside marriage rose from 27.3 per cent to 43.3 per cent (Office of Population Censuses and Surveys, 1992, p.3). Births outside marriage also rose rapidly – from 12.8 per cent of total live births in 1981 to 30.2 per cent in 1991 (OPCS, p.2). Are the explanations we gave for the nineteenth century still applicable? Or are we dealing with something quite new?

IMPACT OF BIRTH CONTROL

One of the great mysteries of recent demographic history is the question of what caused birth control to begin to be widely accepted in the closing years of the nineteenth century. Somewhere here there is an answer waiting to be questioned, but so far it has eluded researchers. Plenty of plausible suggestions have been put forward (Woods, 1987; Haines, 1989; Garrett, 1990). For instance, children were a valuable resource in most pre-industrial societies and continued to be so during the early years of industrialization, especially in Britain (Levine, 1987). They could not only contribute to family income from an early age; they were also a possible means of providing for aged parents in the period before state pensions. Changes in technology and the advent of schooling reduced the earning potential of young children and the state took over some of the burdens associated with sickness and old age though not significantly until after the Second World War. Children therefore became less of an 'investment good': that is, investing in children brought smaller and smaller returns, materially speaking. Rising expectations also made children a more expensive 'consumption good': it cost more to feed, clothe, educate and entertain them as standards rose and choice increased.

It seemed, therefore, only rational to restrict the number of children one had. Although common sense (not, it must be admitted, always the best research aid) would suggest there is something in these suggestions, the matter does seem to be more complicated. For one thing the onset of the fall in fertility brought about by birth control within marriage was remarkably uniform (dating from the last decades of the nineteenth century) across a wide range of societies and cultures, from industrial England to peasant Hungary. We also know very little about how detailed information about birth control was acquired. That it did not depend on mechanical devices seems to be fairly well established, since 'withdrawal (*coitus interruptus*) was almost as popular in Britain as the sheath (or condom), each of these methods being adopted at some time by nearly half the users' amongst men and women married between 1930 and 1960 (Rowntree and Pierce, 1961, pp.99, 127).

QUESTION FOR RESEARCH

Now is the time for family and community historians to examine this topic. This is largely because of a disenchantment with the large-scale studies. The Princeton Fertility Decline Project, for example, has been described as 'one of the most elaborate, well organized projects ever designed by demographers to investigate a problem of comparative interest … the historic fertility decline in Europe' (Lynch, 1992, p.71) (for a summary of the findings see Coale and Watkins, 1986); yet critics of the project (e.g. Levine, 1986, and Tilly, 1986) have argued that because 'the authors have not worked with *local-level data*, they are unable to offer substantive explanations of the aggregate trends they find' (Lynch, 1992, p.71). If correlating one set of figures with another at a macro level hasn't provided the answers we seek, how can more qualitative work at the local and family level be carried out? Oral historical methods would seem to be one answer (see Chapter 4 below and Volume 4). For in this context disenchantment has also set in with the use of 'rigid, questionnaire based research that fails to listen to people whom it purports to be trying to understand' (Lynch, 1992, p.72; see also Seccombe, 1990). And oral history, since its early days, has eschewed this kind of approach.

If oral history is the method adopted here, perhaps one should use a questioning sources strategy (see Chapter 2, section 2.2).

1.2   MARRIAGE

Marriage was central to the demographic experience – until recently. Prior to the Industrial Revolution, its timing, as already noted, often depended upon 'dead men's shoes'. Economic growth, being comparatively modest, did not provide many new openings with a sufficient income to support a family. Hence the need to wait for the death or retirement of the people in such employment before entering upon matrimony. Once in marriage, children followed, so long as the couple were physiologically capable of having them, at least down to the late nineteenth century. And once children had arrived the unfortunate demise of one or other marriage partner led to a relatively speedy re-marriage, especially in the case of men (see below).

Marriage was also of major legal significance, crucial for matters of inheritance and access to poor relief, for example. Until civil marriage was introduced in 1837 the ceremony had to be performed by a clergyman, overwhelmingly one belonging to the Church of England, Wales or Scotland, though in Ireland the Catholic clergy could solemnize weddings for members of their faith. As for the choice offered by the advent of civil marriage, it produced dramatically varying effects in different parts of England and Wales after 1837 (Anderson, 1975 and 1979; Floud and Thane, 1979).

What do you make of this quotation?

Only a local historian, for example, could explain why during the mushroom growth of Pontypridd incoming migrants first turned to chapel marriage, so that in 1880 there were no registry office weddings there at all, although in neighbouring Merthyr Tydfil there were 487, but only four years later [they] were using the registry office for over 27 per cent of their weddings.

(Anderson, 1975, p.76, footnote 13)

NUPTIALITY TRENDS 1800–1990

Figure 3.2 suggests that there was comparatively little change in crude marriage rates over the period considered here, until the last decade or so. But this says as much about the crudity of the measure as it does about marriage. To get closer to the phenomenon itself we need to examine other aspects, such as age at marriage, proportions married in different age groups, divorce, and the extent of re-marriage.

AGE AT MARRIAGE

The median age at marriage for spinsters in England and Wales over the last 150 years is given in Table 3.3. It was relatively steady at just over 23 years until 1881, rose to over 24 years to the 1930s, then fell to just below 23 years in the 1940s and 1950s and to just below 22 years in the 1960s and 1970s. Since then there has been a sharp rise. However, as co-habiting before marriage is more the norm, the age at marriage does not reflect economic and social change in the way it did in the past, nor, since the late nineteenth century, has it had the same importance for the level of fertility.

Table 3.3 Median age at marriage for spinsters in England and Wales, 1851–1991

Date	Age	Date	Age	Date	Age
1851	23.4	1901	24.0	1951	22.6
1861	23.3	1911	24.5	1961	21.6
1871	23.1	1921	24.2	1971	21.4
1881	23.2	1931	24.2	1981	21.9
1891	23.7	1941	22.9	1991	24.5

Source: for 1851–1981, Nissel (1987) p.154; for 1991 (March–September) OPCS (1992) p.72

As with the crude birth rate, however, this figure for age at marriage is a national aggregate. As an average figure it tells us little about the range of ages, or of the differences between people living in different communities or belonging to different social or ethnic groupings.

To see how typical your own family's experience is, it is necessary to look further than the marriage certificate. To illustrate this, turn back to Figure 3.1. You will see that the Benjamin Goodaire born in 1811 married Rachel Heaton in 1831. He was therefore 20 years of age; his bride was 22. His grandson Benjamin married in 1908, aged 30; and his bride, in turn, was 27. Although there is strong evidence that the age at marriage was earlier in the 1830s than in the 1900s, we would be unwise to conclude that Benjamin the elder and his bride Rachel were marrying at an earlier age than their peers, whilst his grandson Benjamin and his wife Elizabeth were marrying somewhat later. The answer is to find out the proportions marrying in each age group in the community concerned. Such information from 1838 onwards is available for many parts of England and Wales, as it is for Scotland from 1855 and Ireland from 1864 in the reports of the respective Registrars General.

EXERCISE 3.4

The relatively early marriage of Benjamin the elder and Rachel (see Figure 3.1) may have been for a common enough reason already discussed. What is it?

Answer/comment p.183.

CHOICE OF PARTNERS

Who marries whom? This question can be examined in a number of ways. First, there is the question of age. Were men usually older than their brides when both were entering their first marriage? Did this age relationship vary in different parts of the United Kingdom and Ireland, between urban and rural communities, between one time and another? (For some indications that it did, see Pearce and Mills, 1986, pp.63–6.) The answers to these questions in other countries and at other times show considerable diversity, a diversity which reflects differences in social and economic circumstances.

There is also the question of social class. To what extent does this show itself in the choice of marriage partner? Was marriage a vehicle for social mobility? (See Volume 3, Chapter 5.)

Re-marriage is another factor worth considering. How common it was can be discovered from the Registrar General's returns for each registration district beginning in England and Wales in 1837. From the 1851 census onwards the population is categorized by *civil* condition (i.e. whether people were single, married, widowed or divorced) in five-year age groups for the registration counties. Civil registration began in Scotland in 1855 and for that year only the marriage certificate contains 'present' and 'usual' place of residence, the marital status of the parties to the marriage, the number of the marriage (if re-marrying) and the number of children by any former marriage. A pilot study of part of Glasgow revealed that in 1855 the overwhelming majority of re-marriages were second – as opposed to third or fourth, etc. Widowers married over a wider age range than widows, the latter being confined to ages under 45 years. Widowers who re-married had twice as many live children at the time they did so than did widows. Looking at England and Wales by county in 1851, it would appear, as the pilot study suggested, that widows and spinsters operated in the same marriage market. Thus in areas where the marriage rate for spinsters was high, so it was for widows and vice-versa (Drake, 1981). It would appear that re-marriage tracked marriage in the same way that births outside marriage tracked those within it.

WEDDING SEASONALITY

What month of the year or day of the week people got married might be considered a personal matter with little social or economic significance. In fact now the likelihood of having good weather on 'the day' would appear to be the most important single determinant of when people marry. Take a look at Table 3.4. This shows the number and percentage of the annual total of marriages for each month in 1978, for England and Wales on the one hand and New Zealand on the other. You will detect quite a marked seasonality. Thus in England, September, the most popular month, had three times as many marriages as January, the least popular one. The three most popular months accounted for 35 per cent of all marriages. Wanting to test the hypothesis that weather was a factor in determining when marriage took place, I chose another society, with similar cultural characteristics and a similar annual weather pattern. This was so that I could isolate the weather factor and keep all other factors constant. I chose New Zealand and compared the number of marriages month by month – after taking account of the fact that the countries are in different hemispheres. Table 3.4 shows my calculations. First of all I ranked the marriages, giving number 1 to the month with the largest number of marriages and 12 to the month with the least. To take account of the seasons being reversed, July in New Zealand was equated with January in England and Wales, August with February, and so on. If there was a perfect correlation between the two series then the same numbers should appear against each pair of months. As you will see, they do so for the first couple of months: July is the least popular month for marriages in New Zealand; January the least popular in England and Wales. August is the second least popular month for marriages in New Zealand; February the second least popular month in England and Wales. Then the symmetry breaks down somewhat. However, the correlation between the two series is pretty high at 0.76 (I have used here the correlation coefficient Spearman's Rho). There seems to be something in my hypothesis.

The dominance in England and Wales of the quarter comprising the months of July, August and September is a feature of the present century, the 1890s being the last decade (since civil registration began) when there were more marriages in the *final* quarter of the year than any other. In the 1840s some 23.9 per cent of marriages occurred in the months of July, August and September. By the 1930s this had risen to 32 per cent and by 1978 to 35.4 per cent (Registrar General, 1949, p.7 and Table 3).

Table 3.4 Monthly marriages in New Zealand and England and Wales, 1978

	Jan	Feb	March	April	May	June	July	Aug	Sept	Oct	Nov	Dec	Total
(a) New Zealand	1 903	2 215	2 615	1 798	1 740	1 575	1 288	1 512	1 632	1 977	2 017	2 154	22 426
England and Wales	15 075	19 460	36 439	29 359	26 499	33 706	43 436	40 048	46 991	29 165	22 595	25 485	368 258
(b) New Zealand	8.49	9.88	11.66	8.02	7.76	7.02	5.74	6.74	7.28	8.81	9.00	9.60	100
England and Wales	4.09	5.28	9.89	7.97	7.20	9.15	11.79	10.87	12.76	7.92	6.14	6.92	100
(c) New Zealand	5	2	1	7	8	10	12	11	9	6	4	3	
England and Wales	12	11	4	6	8	5	2	3	1	7	10	9	
	July	Aug	Sept	Oct	Nov	Dec	Jan	Feb	March	April	May	June	
(d) New Zealand	12	11	9	5	4	3	6	2	1	7	8	10	
England and Wales	12	11	4	6	8	5	2	3	1	7	10	9	
	Jan	Feb	March	April	May	June	July	Aug	Sept	Oct	Nov	Dec	

Key: (a) = absolute figures; (b) = percentages; (c) = rank order; (d) = rank order lagged by six months

Source: New Zealand Government (1978); OPCS (1979)

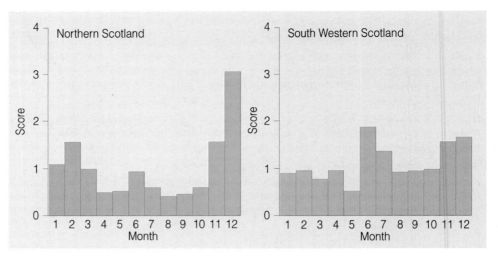

Figure 3.4 Actual as against 'expected' marriages per month in northern and south-western Scotland, 1856–65 (Source: Registrar General of Births, Deaths and Marriages in Scotland, 1856–66)
Note: A score of 1 indicates an 'actual' number of marriages in line with the 'expected' number; a score of 2 = twice as many; 3 = three times as many, etc.; scores between 0 and 1 indicate the extent to which the actual number of marriages was less than the 'expected' number.

But what of the past? Most continental statistical offices in nineteenth-century Europe gave monthly totals of marriages. Here only Scotland did so. Ireland, together with England and Wales up to 1947, gave only quarterly totals. This, unfortunately, blunts the picture of variability across the year and makes comparative studies more difficult.

However, let us turn to the one country which did give monthly totals. Do we find variations there over the year, and between different places? Figure 3.4 shows that in Scotland this was the case. In northern Scotland in 1856–65, for instance, December had three times the expected number of marriages – expected, that is, if all months had the same number of marriages (allowing for the different number of days per month). This contrasts with south-western Scotland, where there was very little variation from month to month. How can we explain these differences? What influence did weather have? Are there particular local economic and social circumstances that account for the variation? For example, in England for an earlier period marriage peaks were associated with the ending of annual contracts of employment on the farms. These in turn varied according to whether the area was dominated by arable or pastural farming. In the former, contracts ended after the grain harvest, i.e. in the autumn; in the latter, they ended in late spring to early summer after the calving and lambing season (see Kussmaul, 1990, and Edwards, 1977). Once a pattern has been 'found', local literary sources should then be investigated for evidence of this type.

As noted above, the Irish Registrar General only produced quarterly totals of marriages. He did, however, do so for Catholic and non-Catholic marriages separately – quite an unusual practice. Figure 3.5 shows these for one year, 1879.

To all intents and purposes the histogram shows little variation in the number of non-Catholic marriages from quarter to quarter, apart from a slight rise over the year. By contrast the Catholic marriages peaked in the first quarter. A first reaction would be that this reflected a difference in religious observance. However, Lent, which occurs in the first quarter, is a period when marriages were discouraged by the Catholic Church. Probably, therefore, there were other factors at play. Take, for instance, the information in Figure 3.6: eastern Ireland seems to show a non-Catholic

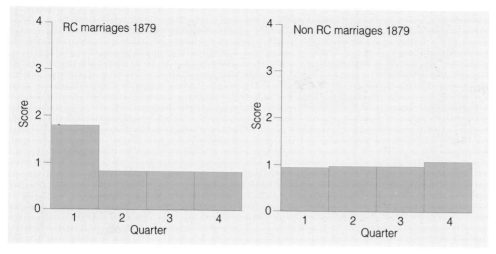

Figure 3.5 Actual as against 'expected' marriages per quarter in Ireland, according to whether the celebrants were Catholic or non-Catholic, 1879

pattern of marriage, whilst western Ireland shows a Catholic one. It is true that there were more Protestants in eastern Ireland than in the west, but would this account for all the difference?

Figure 3.6 also shows the situation in County Mayo and – going down to a smaller area still – a very pronounced peak in the first quarter in Swineford (also in County Mayo).

Could this perhaps be due to some economic factor? What we know about this area is that there was a good deal of seasonal migration to England and Scotland. Each year around March the able-bodied men travelled to work on Scottish, Welsh and English farms, or as navvies on the roads, railways and building sites. They returned in November after the potato harvests and when the weather (the weather again!) reduced building activity. Thus if you wanted people to come to your wedding, the end of one year and the beginning of the next would seem to be the best time.

This question does, however, need further research both in the qualitative literature (memoirs, diaries, newspapers, journals, novels, etc. and oral recall) and the quantitative. Marriage registers, of course, would supply the latter, and breaking down the number of marriages by months or even days and weeks for the first quarter of the year would tell us more. The pattern noted above seems to have persisted in the west of Ireland until the 1920s, after which the swing to the summer months began (Brody, 1973, pp.20–5, 34–5).

_____ **QUESTION FOR RESEARCH** _____

It is a relatively simple task to count the actual number of marriages per month in a church or chapel register and then to set these (for ease of comparison) against the expected number – as shown in Figures 3.4–3.6 (for method see Volume 4, Chapter 8). You could then seek an explanation for whatever monthly variation occurred by deriving various hypotheses from the theory that religious observance was overriding, or that the economic circumstances of the community were the key variable, or that in seeking to explain change over time (as in the case of the west of Ireland from the 1830s to 1960s) there is evidence of 'the decline of community life and the weakening of the social system which was nourished by it' (Brody, 1973, p.36). For possible sources see Volume 4.

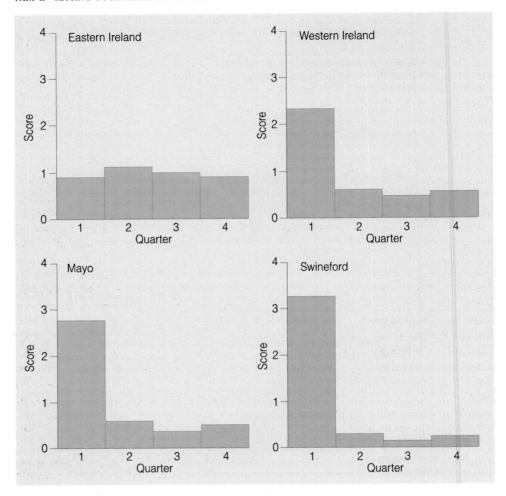

Figure 3.6 Actual as against 'expected' marriages per quarter in eastern and western Ireland, Co. Mayo and Swineford (Co. Mayo), 1871–80

Returning to the Scottish experience, we can benefit from work done by the Scottish Registrar General in 1862. He discovered that there were virtually no marriages in Scotland on a Saturday. He also discovered that the most favoured day by far was New Year's Eve. In fact some 5 per cent of all marriages took place on this one day, over eighteen times as many as would be expected had the marriages been distributed evenly across the year. So what happened when New Year's Eve fell on a Saturday as it did in 1859? Instead of the 1,055 *expected* marriages, only 59 took place. And those marriages were, for the most part, not of natives of Scotland! Here is what the Registrar General of Scotland had to say, by way of explanation:

> *At present we flatter ourselves that the days of superstition have passed away. It is not so, however, with the Scottish people, as these registers avouch. No Scotchman will begin any kind of work on a Saturday if he can possibly avoid it, because he has the superstitious belief that he will never live to finish it. For the same reason no Scotchman will marry on a Saturday; it is with him an 'unlucky day', and he dreads that one or other of the parties to the marriage will not live out the year, or if they outlive the year, that they will leave no family.*

(Registrar General of Scotland, 1866, pp.413–5)

Scotland's Registrar General talks here of 'superstition' relating to Saturday. Can you think of any similar beliefs that had such a profound effect on behaviour? If so, how would you go about investigating them?

It has been said that historical demographers might pay more attention to hypothesis-generating studies than to hypothesis-testing ones, on the grounds that 'much of the new demographic historical research is working with problems where few earlier investigations have been made' (Gaunt, 1978, p.72) and where, therefore, there are few general propositions to test.

What do you think?

THE RELEVANCE OF THE MALTHUSIAN EXPLANATION

We have looked at marriage in a variety of ways: its incidence over time; re-marriage; the age at marriage; and the time of year in which it took place. We have seen various patterns emerging; so marriage, in all its manifestations, would not appear to be a haphazard occurrence. But is it possible to find one overarching explanation – or theory, as social scientists would call it – that would account for *all* these variations? Malthus (1766–1834), the greatest of English demographers, is better known for his depressing conclusion that man (sic) was, in general, doomed to a life of misery because his propensity to reproduce himself was greater than his ability to support – essentially feed – his offspring. For, as Malthus put it, whilst the reproductive side tended to grow according to a geometrical ratio (1, 2, 4, 8, 16, etc.), the productive side only managed an arithmetical one (1, 2, 3, 4, 5, etc.). Since man needed food to survive, the two ratios had obviously to be brought in balance. At first Malthus thought this was done primarily via what he called the *positive* check, i.e. starvation and disease brought about or exacerbated by starvation. Later he placed more emphasis on what he called the *preventive* check. By this Malthus meant man's recognition that too many children would lead to pressure on resources. Since birth control was not practised within marriage and since most births occurred within marriage, the only effective check on too rapid a growth of population was delayed marriage. Marriage, then, according to Malthus, was inextricably linked with economic circumstances.

We do not have space here to test Malthus's ideas in all the communities in which your family might have resided over the past couple of centuries (for example, the Indian sub-continent, Africa, the Caribbean, or most of Europe). What we can do is to take the Malthusian ideas of positive and preventive checks at a general level, give an example of their working out, and then suggest you examine in the same way your own family histories, within the contexts of the actual communities inhabited by them.

It has been suggested (Wrigley and Schofield, 1981) that most, if not all, societies in which birth control within marriage was not practised, can be divided into two groups. The first are called 'high pressure societies' and cover most non-European societies until relatively recently. Here, marriage is early – by which is meant at puberty or within a few years of it – and is universal. This results in high levels of fertility. Malthus's *preventive* check, in other words, is weak and consequently the *positive* check is the main determinant of population change, i.e. mortality is high. The population is constantly pressing against resources (hence the 'high pressure' metaphor). The second type of society has a 'low pressure' system. Here marriage is late, rarely before 21 for women or 25 for men, and lifetime celibacy is high, i.e. up to one-third of men and women never marrying or having offspring. In these societies the 'preventive' check is the main determinant of population change. Fertility is low or modest, as is mortality. Those who do get married do so only when a job capable of sustaining a family is available. The very close tie between job prospects and entry into marriage has recently been demonstrated for the Lancashire town of Bolton in the 1840s (Southall, 1991).

How does this apply in practice? Let us take Ireland's demographic history in the nineteenth century by way of an example. Put crudely, one might see this as a classic shift from a 'high pressure' to a 'low pressure' situation. Although our evidence is scattered and of a mostly qualitative nature, Ireland probably entered the nineteenth century with a rapidly expanding population, due in large part to a relatively early age at marriage by western European standards. Exactly how low has been the subject of considerable controversy, but the mean age at first marriage for men seems to have been in the mid twenties and for women in the early twenties. These early ages came about largely because increasing numbers of the population were prepared to live almost entirely on potatoes (14 pounds a day for the average labourer). Potatoes sufficient for a family could be grown on a tiny plot, since their yield per acre was high, while buoyant demand from England for Irish grain encouraged landlords to provide these tiny plots almost for the asking, since labour was needed for expanding the area under grain (for an up-to-date summary see Macafee, 1987, and Collins, 1991). All went well (if that is the right way to put it) for a time, though failures of the potato harvest did lead to minor or localized famines during the first half of the century. Then came one of the worst Malthusian crises ever experienced in this part of Europe: the Irish famine of 1847–9. We shall never know exactly how many died or fled as a direct result of the famine, possibly 2 million from a population of 7–8 million. The effect was traumatic (see Figure 3.7) and had an immediate and lasting impact on Ireland's demographic history. From a situation of early and all but universal marriage, we find that by 1911, 27.3 per cent of males aged 45–54 were unmarried, as were 24.9 per cent of females. The proportions rose even higher in the 1930s and 1940s. In 1851, in the immediate aftermath of the famine, but obviously reflecting the experience of the previous half century, only 12.6 per cent of men and 12.1 per cent of women aged 45–54 were unmarried. Because we believe life-long celibacy to have been on the increase in the first half of the century, these proportions were likely to have been lower still in the early 1800s (Mokyr and O'Grada, 1984; Morgan and Macafee, 1984; Fitzpatrick, 1987, p.168).

As a footnote in a chapter rather top-heavy with statistics, it is interesting to note how wide of the mark 'informed' public opinion could be without them. Thus *The Times* on 18 June 1851 estimated that the population of Ireland was not 'much over 8,000,000'. On 4 July 1851, however, it had to report the 'painful but authentic communication … that the population of Ireland is at this moment very little more than six millions and a half'. The report continued: 'it appears that the aggregate population of these islands [i.e. the United Kingdom and Ireland] is only about half a million more than it was ten years ago, and that instead of increasing at the rate of a thousand a day, *as is generally supposed* [my italics] we have only increased at the rate of a thousand a week' (*The Times*, 18 June 1851, p.5b, and 4 July 1851, p.4d).

Was this shift from a high pressure to a low pressure system a reaction to the shock of the Great Famine of 1847–9? No doubt that had an effect, but, in Malthusian terms, it would appear that access to land was the key determinant of change. Even before the famine this had become more and more difficult to come by, not least because the collapse in grain prices after the end of the Napoleonic Wars made it less attractive for landowners to grow grain, though initially, of course, attempts were made to counter falling prices by raising output. There was also a shift to animal husbandry, which required less labour. Meanwhile 'informed opinion' was becoming more aware of the dangers of a rapidly growing, semi-pauperized population (not least, of course, from the potential rise in poor relief costs). The rate of population growth was falling: possibly down from between 1.5 and 2.0 per cent per annum in the years 1790 to 1820, to 0.8 per cent in the period 1821–41 (Collins, 1991, p.4). After the famine various land laws 'gave' the holdings to the peasantry, which increasingly moved away from a diet dominated by potatoes and, more importantly, sought to pass on the holding to a single heir. Access to land was dramatically reduced, and since Ireland did not have an industrial revolution, apart from in limited areas that were to be found especially in the north of the country, the only alternatives were emigration or (if one stayed) late marriage and probably life-long celibacy (Connell, 1968; Harris, 1972). That Ireland in the late nineteenth century had the highest rates of emigration of all

Figure 3.7   The Irish potato famine: starving peasants at the workhouse gate, 1846–7 (Source: Mansell Collection)

western and north European countries, as well as the highest rates of life-long celibacy, are indications of the extent of the change in demographic behaviour between 1800 and 1900. There may be other explanations of Ireland's demographic experience. For instance, it has been suggested that increased celibacy was not because the Irish could not get an income sufficient to maintain a family; rather they *chose* permanent celibacy because they could live comfortably without marrying (Guinnane, 1991).

QUESTION FOR RESEARCH

You may care to test some hypotheses based on the theory of Malthus. For instance, if Malthusian theory is correct we would expect age at marriage for both men and women to vary significantly (otherwise it would not have much effect on fertility) according to occupation. If you can find a parish or civil register which gives both age at marriage and occupation of the groom, you could test the following hypotheses:

That the age at marriage of men in industrial occupations in the years … in … was earlier than that of men in non-industrial occupations, as predicted by Malthus's theory …

That changes in the age at first marriage of woman in the years … in … were too small to affect fertility, contrary to Malthus's theory …

That the brides of industrial workers were not sufficiently younger than those married to non-industrial workers in the years … in … to affect fertility significantly, contrary to Malthus's theory …

1.3 BURIAL AND DEATH

As with births and marriages, we start our look at deaths in something of a statistical dark age. The estimates of Wrigley and Schofield (1981) suggest that the Church of England did not bury, and therefore did not register the deaths of, some 30 per cent of the population of England and Wales in the 1810s. This percentage had been reduced to some 10 per cent by the 1830s. Some of the deficit is no doubt to be accounted for by burials in nonconformist graveyards. Others would appear to have been buried privately in the growing number of private cemeteries, a much cheaper procedure (Krause, 1958). The situation improved up to the onset of civil registration in 1837, and, it is generally thought, was not a problem from shortly afterwards.

MORTALITY TRENDS 1800–1990

Prior to the onset of civil registration we have the highly sophisticated calculations of Wrigley and Schofield (1981) on which to base our estimates of mortality for England. For Ireland, Scotland and Wales our estimates are much less soundly based. The pattern revealed for England should not, therefore, be taken as representative of these other countries.

Figure 3.2 indicates a crude death rate for England of 27 per thousand population at the beginning of the nineteenth century. (For methods of calculating this and other rates see Volume 4.) By the 1840s – and the introduction of civil registration – this had fallen to around 22 per one thousand, a level that was to be maintained to the 1870s. It then fell consistently to the current 11 per thousand. The initial fall seems to have been the product of some improvement in medical provision (most notably vaccination against smallpox), though a better and more regular diet seems to be of chief importance. That crude rates remained relatively unchanged for about half a century was probably due to rapid urbanization. Conditions in the towns, especially the larger ones, posed a much higher risk of premature death than those in the countryside, principally due to polluted drinking water. Epidemics too spread more quickly and fiercely. After 1880 improved resistance to disease brought about by better living conditions (diet, housing, sanitation) and medical services (including, more than is sometimes recognized, preventive medicine) led to a long and continuing fall in mortality.

AGE AT DEATH

A glance back at Figure 3.1 is as good an entry point as any into this topic. Look at the children born to Rachel Heaton and Benjamin Goodaire. Rachel started her childbearing career in 1831 at the age of 21 and ended it (so far as we know) at the age of 44 in 1854. In that time she had eleven children. At the moment we do not know when John Heaton Goodaire died, though, as we shall see later, we know he reached adulthood and had a family of his own. Nor do we know what happened to the youngest child, Mary Ellen. What is interesting about the rest is that they either died early or reached a ripe old age. Thus of the nine members of the family for which we have age at death, three died within a year of being born, one before the age of 3 and another at the age of 12. Of the four who reached adulthood, the ages reached were 67, 76, 82 and 85 years. This age profile of death neatly exemplifies one of the classic and very consistent patterns of mortality, namely a high death rate at early ages, comparatively low mortality in the working ages, followed – inevitably! – by high mortality in old age. The graphs always have a 'U' form, though thankfully the left-hand upright of this letter has got shorter and shorter over time.

The greatest risk of all is in the first hours and days after birth. Until comparatively recently it remained high in the first year of life (for a discussion see Woods and Woodward, 1984; Woods et al., 1988–9; and Williams, 1992). Thus as Table 3.5 shows, the number of children who died before reaching their first birthday per one thousand live births did not change much between the early 1840s and the early 1900s. By 1921 it was down to double figures, though it did not reach single figures until the 1980s. The national totals hide, as they always do, very considerable local variations. And, of course, it is the local level that is of importance to the individual. Thus in 1951 the infant mortality rate in Merton and Morden was only 15 per thousand live births, whereas in Rochdale it was 47. The expectation of life at year one in 1950–2 was 66.2 years in Carlisle and 75.7 in Chigwell (Moser and Scott, 1961).

Table 3.5 Deaths of children under one year of age per 1,000 live births in England and Wales, Scotland, the Republic of Ireland, and Northern Ireland, 1840–1990

	England and Wales	Scotland	Ireland	Northern Ireland
1840–44	150			
1860–64	149	120	98[1]	
1880–84	142	119	98	
1900–04	143	122	101	
1920–24	77	92	69[2]	80[2]
1940–44	52	72	74	77
1960–64	21	26	29	27
1980–84	10.8	10.8	10.6	12.1
1990	7.9	7.7	8.2	7.4

[1] 1864 only
[2] 1922–24

Source: derived from Mitchell (1992) pp.116–23

SEASONALITY OF DEATH

With the fall in mortality at all ages, the fluctuations in the seasonality of death have become less extreme. Diseases have their own rhythms, and when in the mid nineteenth century infectious diseases accounted for one-third of all deaths (as against one-third of one per cent today!) the pattern of mortality over the year could show dramatic changes.

DEATH, WHERE IS THY STING?

The Victorians were obsessed by death. Earlier in the nineteenth century 'educated opinion', following the lead of Malthus, was equally obsessed by marriage or, to be more specific, by what it then saw as the recklessly early marriages of the labouring poor. These were regarded as a major social evil, putting up the poor rates through the swarms of children that resulted. In our own century births have dominated the discussion, at first because a rapidly falling birth rate from the beginning of the century raised the spectre of a declining population, with all that meant for power and influence in the world. More recently, since the Second World War, continuing high fertility in the so-called developing world has caused a comparable alarm, but this time because it seems to threaten the existence of life on this planet.

QUESTION FOR RESEARCH

In choosing an entrée into the study of death, you could do worse than focus on infant mortality (i.e. the number of deaths under one year of age per 1,000 live births). Often regarded as a sensitive indicator of the general mortality situation, this measure relates the number of deaths fairly closely to the *population at risk*. Some other indicators of mortality – often used by local historians – don't do this. For example, calculating, from a burial register, the proportion of deaths that fall in each ten- or twenty-year age group, or calculating the average age at death by adding up all the ages of those who died and dividing by the number that died, takes no account of the age distribution of the population. A falling birth rate, or high out-migration of young people in one community as compared with another, could produce very different average ages at death – even though age-specific mortality was the same. Another reason for focusing on infant mortality is that in this period contemporaries did too, so a researcher is more likely to come across local surveys, conducted for instance by Medical Officers of Health (see Volume 4, Chapter 4). Finally, the fight to reduce infant mortality was a heroic one in the second half of the nineteenth century and the first half of this century. It was a fight with setbacks and many local variations. Using the 'questioning sources' strategy to describe and analyse that fight at local level would be a worthwhile contribution to knowledge.

Of the three demographic variables, the literature on death is probably the most voluminous and accessible – not only in the physical sense of our being able to get hold of it, but also because it was written in a 'user-friendly' manner. The Victorians instigated a large number of enquiries into the causes of death with a view to ameliorating its sting. These can be found in a variety of sources (further discussed in Volume 4 but summarized for convenience here):

o   Annual reports of the Registrars General for England and Wales, Scotland and Ireland.

o   Reports from various statistical societies (see Cullen, 1975). These blossomed in the 1830s and were to be found in many towns (from London to Liverpool, Doncaster to Dublin). Their title is something of a misnomer, for though their journals contained various tables, these were perfectly straightforward, with much of the content being what today appears in social surveys.

o   Medical Officer of Health reports; local reports to the General Board of Health (1848–57) (see Pidduck, 1978); and reports of the Local Government Board (1869–1908) (see Thomas, 1979).

o   Periodicals such as the *Quarterly Review, The Edinburgh Review, The Westminster Review, Blackwoods Magazine* and *Frasers Magazine.*

o   Select committee reports from the Houses of Parliament.

This has been something of a romp through two hundred years of population history. It cannot be claimed to be a comprehensive account. Rather my aim has been to alert those of you living in the United Kingdom and Ireland today to a number of features which hopefully are of interest in their own right. At the same time I hope they may have given you some ideas as to how you might weave your own family's or community's history into some of the issues and patterns discussed here. Family history and local history can be studied for its own sake and there is, of course, nothing wrong in that. Here we are promoting another approach, one which seeks to locate the experience of your family or your community on a spectrum of experience. This is not to bury that experience, to make it but a single anonymous brick in a national structure. Quite the contrary: your studies should bring out the diversity that lies behind the national averages. Your findings should give a new meaning to the demographic, social, economic or political experiences that are played out on a local scene. As a result your explanations of those experiences, being closer to the ground, closer to the reality, could well bring out truths that lie hidden in the national averages.

2   FAMILY TYPES AND HOUSEHOLD STRUCTURES

2.1   THE LIFE AND TIMES OF JOHN HEATON GOODAIRE

To introduce this topic I return once again to a member of my own family, John Heaton Goodaire, born in 1833, died – I don't know when. We have already come across him in part of my family tree (Figure 3.1). He was the second of the eleven children of Benjamin and Rachel Goodaire. We have found him too in the census of 1841, in his birthplace, and then again in the censuses of 1851–91 (Table 3.6).

Table 3.6 Entries relating to John Heaton Goodaire and the families and households associated with him in the CEBs of Rastrick township, Parish of Halifax, and Hightown township in the Parish of Birstall (West Riding of Yorkshire), 1841–91

Name	Household position	Marital status	Age	Occupation	Place of birth
1841[1]					
John Heaton	Head	Married	55	Cloth dresser	Yorks.
Esther Heaton	Wife	Married	54		Liversedge, Yorks.
Benjamin Goodaire	Son in law	Married	30	Joiner	Rastrick, Yorks.
Rachel Goodaire	Daughter	Married	30		Liversedge, Yorks.
John Heaton Goodaire	Grandson	Unmarried	8		Liversedge, Yorks.
Sarah Jane Goodaire	Granddaughter	Unmarried	2		Liversedge, Yorks.
Joseph Goodaire	Grandson	Unmarried	4 months		Liversedge, Yorks.

[1] The information given here for 1841 is drawn partly from the 1841 census and partly from that of 1851. By 1851 the Benjamin Goodaire listed here was the head of his own household. His father-in-law had died but his mother-in-law was living with him. He had two more children aged 6 and 3 years.

Name	Household position	Marital status	Age	Occupation	Place of birth
1851					
Joseph Goodaire	Head	Married	40	Tailor employing two men	Rastrick, Yorks.
Ann Goodaire	Wife	Married	39		Furness Fell, Lancs.
James Goodaire	Son	Unmarried	10	Scholar	Rastrick, Yorks.
Elizabeth Goodaire	Daughter	Unmarried	11	Scholar	Rastrick, Yorks.
Rachel Goodaire	Daughter	Unmarried	5	Scholar	Rastrick, Yorks.
Elizabeth Myers	Mother in law	Widow	70	Dependant	Furness Fell, Lancs.
John H Goodaire	Nephew	Unmarried	17	Apprentice tailor	Liversedge, Yorks.

1861

Name	Household position	Marital status	Age	Occupation	Place of birth
John Blake	Head	Widower	60	Mechanic	Rastrick, Yorks.
John H Goodaire	Son in law	Married	27	Manufacturing chemist	Hightown, Yorks.
Martha Goodaire	Daughter	Married	27		Rastrick, Yorks.
Thomas H Goodaire	Grandson	Unmarried	6	Scholar	Rastrick, Yorks.
Benjamin Goodaire	Grandson	Unmarried	4	Scholar	Rastrick, Yorks.
Joe Goodaire	Grandson	Unmarried	1	Scholar	Rastrick, Yorks.

1871

Name	Household position	Marital status	Age	Occupation	Place of birth
John H Goodaire	Head	Married	37	Manufacturing chemist	Hightown, Yorks.
Martha Goodaire	Wife	Married	37		Rastrick, Yorks.
Thomas H Goodaire	Son	Unmarried	16	Cotton Piecer	Rastrick, Yorks.
Benjamin Goodaire	Son	Unmarried	14	Woollen twister	Rastrick, Yorks.
Joah Goodaire	Son	Unmarried	11	Scholar and cotton hand	Rastrick, Yorks.
Hannah Goodaire	Daughter	Unmarried	8		Rastrick, Yorks.
Frederick Goodaire	Son	Unmarried	5		Rastrick, Yorks.
Mary Ann Goodaire	Daughter	Unmarried	2		Rastrick, Yorks.
John Goodaire	Son	Unmarried	2 months		Rastrick, Yorks.

1881

Name	Household position	Marital status	Age	Occupation	Place of birth
John H Goodaire	Head	Married	47	Manufacturing chemist employing two men	Liversedge, Yorks.
Martha Goodaire	Wife	Married	47		Rastrick, Yorks.
Thomas H Goodaire	Son	Unmarried	26	Rly wagon inspector	Rastrick, Yorks.
Joah Goodaire	Son	Unmarried	21	Wiredrawer	Rastrick, Yorks.
Hannah Goodaire	Daughter	Unmarried	19		Rastrick, Yorks.
Fred Goodaire	Son	Unmarried	14	Printer compositor	Rastrick, Yorks.
John Goodaire	Son	Unmarried	10	Scholar	Rastrick, Yorks.

Name	Household position	Marital status	1891 Age	Occupation	Employer	Employee	Neither employer nor employed	Place of birth
John H Goodaire	Head	Married	57	Chemical Man. and Drysalters	—	—	X	Liversedge
Martha Goodaire	Wife	Married	57		—	—	—	Rastrick
Fred Goodaire	Son	Unmarried	25	Printer's compositor	—	X	—	Rastrick
John Goodaire	Son	Unmarried	20	Taylor	—	X	—	Rastrick
Mary Ellen Ogden	Servant	Unmarried	21	Domestic servant	—	—	—	Driffield

What do these census returns tell us of John Heaton Goodaire's household and family status over the 50 years from 1841 to 1891? In 1841 he was living with his parents, a sister and a brother in the household of his maternal grandfather. By 1851 he had left his family of origin and was living with that of his uncle, to whom, it would appear, he was apprenticed as a tailor. By 1861 he was married and had three children. As the eldest was 6 it would also appear that he married at quite an early age (20 or 21) for the time. He was now, however, living in his father-in-law's household. By 1871 John Heaton headed his own household whose other members were his wife and seven children. He still headed his own household in 1881, though he appears not to have had any more children, or if he did they seem to have died or left home. Of the children who were part of his household in 1871, two had gone by 1881. One, Benjamin, had not moved far. In 1881 he was living next door, working as a power loom cotton-weaver, married but with no children. Mary Ann, his daughter of two years in 1871, was no longer at home in 1881, and given her age could well have died. By 1891 John Heaton Goodaire still headed his own household and still described himself as a manufacturing chemist and drysalter. Rather curiously, however, he says he was neither an employer nor employed. He also had a living-in servant – a sign of affluence, perhaps, or that Hannah, his unmarried daughter of nineteen in 1871, was no longer at home and fulfilling that function. (For more on domestic service and the role played by relatives see Volume 3, Chapter 3.)

To close this section on John Heaton Goodaire, his kith and kin, I note that the uncle he was apprenticed to in 1851 was still living in Rastrick in 1871 and now, like his nephew, was a manufacturing chemist employing five labourers. John Heaton's father had also moved to Rastrick by 1871 and he too was a manufacturing chemist.

We see from these details that Michael Anderson's propinquity thesis – discussed above in Chapter 2, section 2 – would appear to be borne out, for members of various Goodaire families not only lived with each other in the same household, as John Heaton and his uncle did in 1851, or lived close together (one of John Heaton's sons lived as close as next door in 1881, and another did so in 1891), but the heads of several Goodaire households had entered the same occupation, that of manufacturing chemist.

To see how typical John Heaton's experience was, we now need to look at family types and household structures more generally. One should note at this point that it is difficult to keep the discussion of families and households separate from each other. This is because all families occupy households, but not all households are occupied solely by families, even if we include nuclear, extended and multiple families. Households may also contain servants, apprentices and lodgers. Nor should we forget that 'families' in the broadest sense also 'extend' beyond the single household.

2.2   CO-RESIDENT FAMILY TYPES

Co-resident family units are usually divided into three types. The first is the nuclear (simple, or conjugal) family unit. This consists of a couple (or single parent) and their children. The term conjugal is sometimes confined to a married couple with no offspring. The second is the extended family unit, i.e. a nuclear unit, together with kin-linked individuals. If such an individual is of a generation earlier than the nuclear family unit (e.g. married head's mother-in-law or father) the extension is said to be upward; if of a later generation (e.g. a grandchild or nephew) the extension is said to be downward; if he/she is of the same generation (e.g. brother, sister or cousin of the head of the nuclear unit or of the head's spouse) the extension is said to be sideways – of course, there can be combinations of these. The third type of co-resident family unit is the multiple or composite one and is made up of members of two or more nuclear family units linked by kinship or marriage. The same rules as to upward, downward and sideways linkages apply as with the extended family unit. Thus if the mother and father of the head live with him/her and his/her nuclear family, the extension is upward. If the head's married son lives with him/her, the extension is downwards. And if a married brother or sister lives with the head and his/her nuclear family, the extension is sideways (see Figure 3.8 and Table 3.7).

_____ *EXERCISE 3.5* _____

How, for instance, would you depict the family household of John Heaton Goodaire in 1841 using the kind of diagrams depicted in Figure 3.8? And how would you define the family household: nuclear, extended or multiple?

Answer/comment p.184.

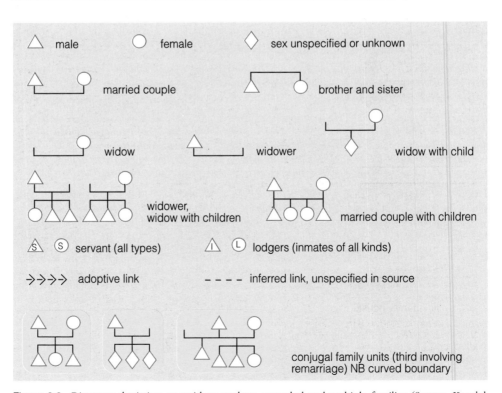

Figure 3.8 Diagrams depicting co-resident nuclear, extended and multiple families (Source: Knodel, 1979, pp.20–1)

Some twenty-five years ago Peter Laslett, after studying many communities in England from the mid seventeenth to the early nineteenth centuries, discovered that far more people seemed to be living in nuclear families than he and others had generally supposed. Extended family households were rare, and multiple ones virtually unknown. Subsequently he drew up a form for use in analysing household composition (Table 3.7). The summary figures in Table 3.8 for a range of

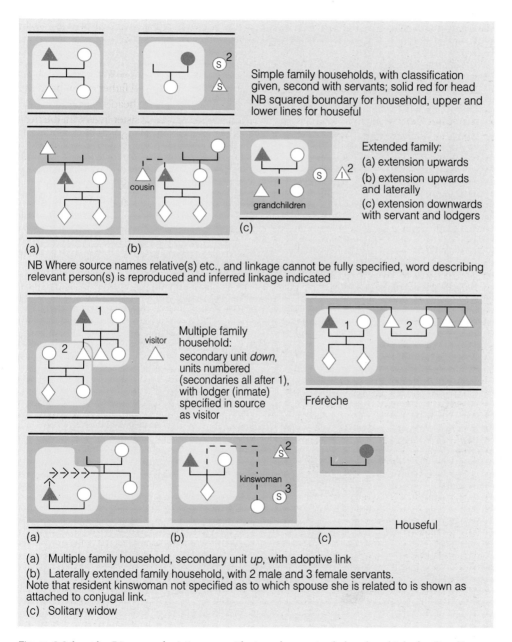

Figure 3.8 (cont.)   Diagrams depicting co-resident nuclear, extended and multiple families (Source: Knodel, 1979, pp.20–1)

Table 3.7 Household composition analysis form

Categories	Classes		Number of households	% of households
Solitaries (singletons in households)	1(a)	given as widowed		
	1(b)	given as non-married or of unknown marital status		
		sub total		
No family households (co-residents not constituting conjugal family units)	2(a)	co-resident siblings		
	2(b)	other co-resident relatives		
	2(c)	co-residents with no familial relationship given		
		sub total		
Simple family households (conjugal family units)	3(a)	married couples without children		
	3(b)	married couples with children		
	3(c)	widowers with children		
	3(d)	widows with children		
		sub total		
Extended family households (conjugal family units having kin-linked individuals)	4(a)	extension upwards (of which _____ fathers, _____ mothers)		
	4(b)	extension downwards (of which _____ grandchildren)		
	4(c)	extension sideways (of which _____ brothers, _____ sisters		
	4(d)	combinations of 4(a)–4(c), or any other form of extension		
		sub total		
Multiple family households (two or more kin-linked conjugal family units)	5(a)	households with secondary units disposed upwards from head (of which _____ also extended)		
	5(b)	households with secondary units disposed downwards from head (of which _____ also extended)		
	5(c)	households with secondary units disposed sideways from head, parent or parent-in-law of head, being present and not part of a cfu (of which _____ also extended)		
	5(d)	Frérèches, households with secondary units disposed sideways from head, parent or parent-in-law of head absent (of which _____ also extended)		
	5(e)	combinations of 5(a)–5(d) or any other multiple household arrangement (of which _____ also extended)		
		sub total		
Indeterminate		households whose kin-linkages are insufficient for classification in any of the above		
		sub total		
		Total		100%

Source: Knodel (1979) p.14

communities lend support to Laslett's earlier findings for an earlier period. Yet if we look at John Heaton Goodaire's experience we find that *for at least part of his life* he lived in extended family households. In fact he would seem to have started life in a multiple family unit (Table 3.6), one which would be entered in the 5(b) slot in Table 3.7.

Table 3.8 Kinship composition of households in Abergele, Denbighshire (1851); Elmdon, Essex (1861); Corofin Ennistymon, Co. Clare (1911); Ballinrobe, Co. Mayo (1911); Great Britain (1961 and 1987)

Place	Household type (%)				
	Solitary	No family	Simple	Extended	Multiple
Abergele	12.1	5.4	69.1	11.8	1.5
Elmdon	6.1	7.0	73.0	12.2	1.7
Corofin Ennistymon	5.5	—	50.9	43.6	—
Ballinrobe	16.0	—	60.0	24.0	—
Great Britain (1961)	11.0	5.0	80.0	3.0	
Great Britain (1987)	25.0	3.0	72.0	1.0	

Source: Schürer (1987) p.40; Laslett (1983) pp.518–19; Gibbon and Curtin (1978) p.451; *Social Trends 13* (1983) Table 2.2, p.36; *Social Trends 19* (1989) p.45.

EXERCISE 3.6

Examine the households in which John Heaton Goodaire lived according to the censuses of 1851–91 (Table 3.6). Then try to classify these households according to the categories given in Table 3.7. Again, you will find it helpful to construct diagrams of the type shown in Figure 3.8.

Answers/comments p.184.

QUESTION FOR RESEARCH

If you can get hold of data like that in Table 3.6, which, as we have seen, allowed me to trace some of the family units in which John Heaton Goodaire lived between 1841 and 1891, then you could do some life-cycle research (as discussed, for instance, in Hareven, 1991). You could, for instance, contact members of a family history society and ask if they could let you have this kind of material. Suppose you trace twenty individuals through six censuses, you could then enter the types of family unit in which they lived on to Table 3.7. Since you would be dealing with 120 households in all, you should be able to make some meaningful judgements about the life-cycle experience of individuals.

Was John Heaton Goodaire's experience atypical? Possibly, though there may be a way of squaring this circle. Lutz K. Berkner, taking his starting point in Laslett's findings, examined the Austrian community of Waldviertel in 1763. This was a peasant community, very different from industrial Rastrick a century or so later. Nevertheless, one of Berkner's findings may be relevant, for he discovered that although only 25 per cent of households contained any non-nuclear kin and could, therefore, be considered extended, if one controlled 'for the age of the head of the household, the extended family emerges as a normal phase in the developmental cycle of the peasant household' (Berkner, 1972, p.406). Thus, for example, when the male head of household was aged 18–27, some 60 per cent of households were extended. And even for male heads aged 28–37, the percentage was still as high as 45. Berkner is therefore suggesting that Austrian peasants, like John Heaton Goodaire a century later, did spend part of their lives in extended households. It is necessary, then, to look at households and their development over time, in order to get a true picture of the average person's life-time experience.

A further twist to the tale has come with the work of Steven Ruggles (1987). He begins by demonstrating in graphic form the notable rise and fall in the proportion of extended households in both England and America between 1750 and 1950 (Figure 3.9).

Figure 3.9 was based on 'twenty-seven separate studies of sixty-eight data sets drawn from localities and national samples in England and America between 1599 and 1984' (Ruggles, 1987, p.5). Ruggles concludes that, looking at all households, the proportion of extended ones in both countries was, at its peak, around 20 per cent. This is not very different from the 25 per cent found by Berkner, and therefore opens the possibility of a similar developmental cycle. Ruggles explains this rise to a peak in late Victorian England as the result of three forces: economic, demographic and cultural. Let's examine each in turn.

Ruggles agrees with the pre-Laslett view that in a pre-industrial society co-resident extended family units were desired principally because they were a means of *conserving* property, especially land. If land is divided amongst all offspring or all males then soon there is not enough for the resulting family of each to survive on (see the earlier discussion of Ireland on p.80). Marriage is then late and many do not marry at all, remaining in their childhood home. With

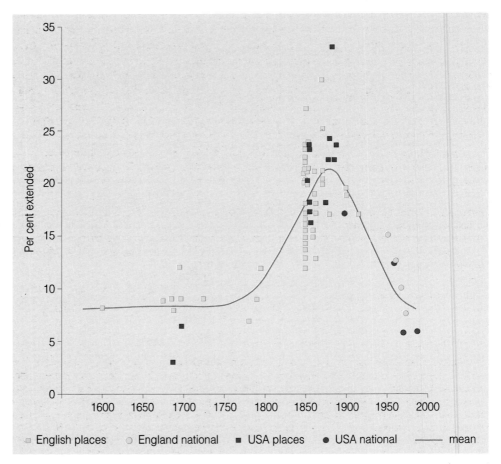

Figure 3.9 Percentage of households containing extended kin: England and America, 1600–1984 (Source: Ruggles, 1987, p.5)

industrialization a completely new situation arises. As argued by Anderson and others, co-resident extended family units are now necessary to cope with a *lack* of property. As thousands poured into the alien environments of the new industrial towns and villages, they needed the support of kin, simply in order to find their way around. Often, therefore, they would lodge with relatives or at the very least seek to live near them (see Chapter 2, section 2). Ruggles does not accept this, since he says co-resident extended family units were much more common amongst the relatively well-off than amongst the working class. Probably this was because members of such families were not prepared to set up house if this meant a fall in the standard of living to which they were accustomed.

Ruggles is more sympathetic, however, towards the demographic case for co-resident extended family units. In a situation of high fertility and high mortality the possibility of several generations living in the same household is reduced – people simply do not live long enough (Anderson, 1983). However, the nineteenth century brought falling mortality (see Figure 3.2) with a continued high, or relatively high, level of fertility. But though demographically the situation was more favourable for the formation of co-resident extended family units, was this enough? Ruggles thinks not, and believes that cultural factors were what determined their rise to a peak around 1900 and the sharp decline since (Figure 3.9).

Ruggles admits that arguing the case for cultural forces is more difficult than for economic or demographic forms, since they cannot be fitted into neat statistical boxes. Nevertheless, he concludes that Victorians did hold different views about the family to those of their forebears and their successors. They saw the family as a haven in a difficult world: 'The increased pace of urbanization, occupational and geographic mobility and the acceleration of economic and social change created unprecedented turmoil and a sense of uncertainty about the future' (Ruggles, 1987, p.132). In the course of his discussion Ruggles notes an interesting difference in the form of co-resident extended family units between different social groups. Table 3.9 brings this out quite clearly. By vertically extended, Ruggles means co-resident extended family units containing three or (rarely) more generations (categories 4(a) and 4(b) in Table 3.7). This situation was facilitated amongst the working class by their propensity to marry relatively early (at 24 for men and 22 for women in the Lancashire towns depicted in Table 3.9). This brought the generations closer together, extending the period three generations were likely to be alive at the same time (Anderson, 1983, p.8).

Table 3.9 Percentage of extended family members residing in 'vertical' and 'horizontal' families, Lancashire towns, 1871[1]

	Unskilled	Skilled	Bourgeois
Vertically extended families	67.9	58.0	27.0
Horizontally extended families	32.1	42.0	73.0
Total	100.0	100.0	100.0
N (100%)	254	390	448

[1] The Lancashire towns used by Ruggles were Turton, near Bolton, and Salford. Ruggles notes: 'The skilled category includes: weaver, finisher, piecer, carder, spinner, doubler, winder, tenter, cutter, cotton operative, bleacher, dyer and so on. The unskilled category includes: general labourer, outdoor labourer, porter, navvy, construction labourer, warehouse labourer, road labourer. For the bourgeoisie, occupation is just as poor an indicator of status as it is for the working class; it is very often difficult to distinguish large manufacturers from artisans. Thus, I distinguished the bourgeoisie on the basis of the presence of domestic servants. Servants whose occupation was apprentice or shop assistant, or who were employed by publicans or restaurateurs, could not determine inclusion of the family in the bourgeois category' (Ruggles, 1987, pp.35–6, footnote 8).

Source: Ruggles (1987) p.213

By horizontally extended, Ruggles means families composed of one or two generations, usually with unmarried adult siblings living with a married brother or sister (category 4(c) in Table 3.7). People in the middle class c.1871 married later (mean age for men 28, for women 24) than in the working class, and life-long celibacy rates were higher. This left a large number of unmarried adults to be accommodated. Ruggles suggests that people in the middle class had three options: they could live alone, but this was expensive; they could live with their parents, but late age at marriage meant a proportion of parents were dead before their children reached marriageable age; or they could live with a brother or sister. 'Most horizontally extended kin were between the ages of 15 and 34, and they usually resided with their older married siblings. Among the bourgeoisie, horizontal extension seems to have been a transitional phase between leaving the parental home and marriage' (Ruggles, 1987, p.213).

The Goodaire family shows examples of both vertically and horizontally extended families. It also shows – in the case of John Heaton's family in 1881 – three sons in employment and living in the parental home. Ten years earlier the census recorded that his father had four children living with him aged 14, 19, 23 and 26, all of whom were in employment (as milliner, silk winder, silk doubler, and engine fitter). One, a daughter, was married with a two-year-old son.

The proportion of households containing kin, i.e. relatives other than the nuclear family, remained remarkably stable between 1851 and 1951, though work remains to be done on the 1861–91 censuses. After 1891 there is something of a black hole, at least in England, Wales and Scotland, as, under the 100-year rule, there is no access to the CEBs, while the official reports do not give the requisite information. To return, however, to what we do know, co-resident extended family units formed 20.2 per cent of all households in 1851 and 15.0 per cent in 1951 (Wall, 1982, p.83). What had changed was the regional distribution. Whereas in 1951 it was the western part of Britain that had the most households with relatives (and this was also the case in 1961 and 1971), in 1851 such areas as Wales and south-west England had the lowest frequency. Admittedly, Scotland was high both in 1851 and 1951 (Wall, p.83).

Richard Wall notes that his figures pose two problems. Why was there apparently relatively little change in the proportion of households with relatives between 1851 and 1951; and why was there a precipitous fall thereafter? It may, of course, be that the 1951 figure is not an indicator of stability in the situation over 100 years, but the result of the desperate housing shortage in the immediate post-war years. As for the post-1951 changes, greater access to housing through rising incomes, increased life expectancy (adding to the households least likely to contain relatives), and a greater desire for privacy (e.g. a preference for one's own place rather than lodgings) could all play their part. The rise of mobile professionals – the social group least likely to share a household with relatives – may also have affected the situation (Wall, 1982, p.87).

--- *QUESTIONS FOR RESEARCH* ---

1 Take a look at the life-time experience of a member of your family, as regards the households he or she has lived in. Your own memories or those of your relatives should give you information for much of the present century, and probably you will find, like I did, information from the CEBs for the last century. Ask yourself:

(a) Was his or her household extended at any time?

(b) Was the extension vertical or horizontal?

(c) Can you trace a life-cycle element in the extended/nuclear situation, as was the case with John Heaton Goodaire?

(d) Were there any adult wage-earners (other than the parents) living in the parental home at any time?

(e) Does the nature of the extension (vertical or horizontal) fit the Ruggles' hypothesis, i.e. working class = vertical; bourgeois = horizontal?

(f)   If you have looked at your family in the post-war period, how far does their experience square with Wall's explanation of the fall in the proportion of families with relatives (kin)?

2   Ruggles (Table 3.9) gives us the percentage of co-resident vertically or horizontally extended families in two Lancashire towns in 1871. It would be interesting to test his findings in other places and for other dates. One could adopt either the hypothesis testing or the questioning sources strategy. Using the former, one might test such hypotheses as:

That the percentage of co-resident extended family units was higher in 1891 than in 1871.

That the percentage of horizontally extended family units increased amongst the bourgeoisie between 1871 and 1891 as opportunities for setting up independent households fell.

In both cases the CEBs provide the data (in Ireland the household returns for 1901 and 1911); Laslett's form (p.90 above) provides the test; Armstrong's categorization (1972, pp.198–224 and Volume 4) provides the means of distinguishing bourgeois occupations (Classes IV and V).

As for the questioning sources strategy, this involves an exploration of a wider range of sources. You could begin by accepting Ruggles' findings as presented in Figure 3.9 and Table 3.9. Where might you find sources that could put flesh on these statistical bones? Here are some possibilities (to be used with care, of course – see Volume 4):

(a)   Biographies of bourgeois family members, such as Lewis, G. (1987) *Somerville and Ross: the world of the Irish RM.*

(b)   Journals (quarterlies, monthlies) for articles on the financial pressures felt by the bourgeoisie.

(c)   Government reports on the economic situation.

(d)   Novels featuring middle-class life.

2.3   HOUSEHOLD STRUCTURES

As Table 3.10 shows, over the last three centuries the structure of households in Great Britain has changed quite dramatically.

Table 3.10   Percentage of household members by relationship to household head in England, England and Wales, and Great Britain, 1650–1970

	England 1650–1749	England 1750–1821	England and Wales 1851	Great Britain 1947	Great Britain 1970
Head	22	21	22	27	34
Spouse	14	16	15	22	24
Child	40	43	44	37	37
Relative	4	5	7	12	4
Servant	14	11	5	1	1
Attached lodger	6	5	8	2	—
Total	100	101	101	101	100
Mean household size	4.44	4.81	4.60	3.67	2.93

Sources of data: for England 1650–1821 from population listings held by the Cambridge Group for the History of Population and Social Structure; these cover eight communities for the period 1650–1749 and twenty for the period 1750–1821. The 1851 data is calculated from a one-sixteenth sample of CEBs provided by Michael Anderson. The 1947 figures are from Gray (1947). The 1970 data are from Barnes and Durant (1970).

Source: Wall (1989) p.370

As Richard Wall (1989) points out, the major change over the centuries has been the increase in the proportion of the household occupied by head and spouse at the expense of servants and lodgers: from about one-third to almost three-fifths.

The disappearance of domestic servants and lodgers is the most dramatic difference between present-day families in Britain and those of previous centuries. These two groups were to be found in a considerable number of households in nineteenth-century Britain, the numbers varying according to the community. Some years ago Carol Pearce examined three sets of communities in Kent: (a) the town of Ashford, an ancient market town serving an agricultural hinterland; (b) New Town, built on the outskirts of Ashford by the South East Railway Company in the late 1840s to house its employees in the railway works it had placed there; and (c) five agricultural villages to the south west of Ashford – Bethersden, Great Chart, Hothfield, Kingsnorth and Shadoxhurst. The mean household size of the three areas appears in Table 3.11.

The modest differences do mask some slight variations in the size of the component parts of the households. Ashford, for instance, had fewer children in the nuclear family: 19 for every 10 households as against 22 in New Town and 23 in the rural parishes. It did, however, have more extended kin per household (4 as against 1 in New Town, and 3 in the rural parishes per 10 households); and more lodgers (7 as against 5 in New Town and 3 in the rural parishes). As for servants, Ashford and the rural parishes had an average of 2 per 10 households, New Town 1.

Table 3.11 Composition of the average household in Ashford, New Town and five rural parishes in Kent in 1851

Mean number per 10 households	Ashford	New Town	Rural Parishes
Heads	10	10	10
Spouses	7	9	8
Children	19	22	23
Nuclear family	36	41	41
Kin	4	1	3
Lodgers	7	5	3
Domestic servants	2	1	2
Total	49	48	49

Source: unpublished paper by Carol Pearce; data described in Schürer and Anderson (1992)

That New Town should have more children, fewer non-nuclear resident kin and fewer domestic servants than either Ashford or the rural parishes is not difficult to explain, for its age and social composition (it consisted of young migrant railway workshop employees) might be expected to produce this result. Other differences – for example the greater number of children in the families living in the rural parishes as compared to Ashford – are more difficult to explain. The relatively high number of lodgers in Ashford also seems anomalous, especially as ten years later it had fallen to 3 per household, as it had in New Town.

Part, if not all, of the explanation here could be a definitional one. Some enumerators put lodgers into separate households, others counted them as boarders who lived, at least in part, with the main household. This came out particularly clearly in New Town in 1861, for at that census New Town was in two enumeration districts, the dividing line going through a row of terraced houses. One enumerator assigned all boarders and lodgers to separate lodging households, the other put them in the main household.

Table 3.12 Distribution of households by civil status of head in Ashford, New Town and five rural parishes in Kent in 1851 (percentages)

	Ashford	New Town	Rural parishes
Married and living with spouse	76.3	98.7	80.5
Widowers	4.3	1.2	7.2
Widows	9.2	0.6	6.6
Single males	5.7	0.6	3.8
Single females	4.2	—	2.0
Unspecified males	0.2	—	—
N	1028	176	559

Source: as for Table 3.11

The figure that stands out in Table 3.12 is the 98.7 per cent of New Town households headed by married couples, a figure one might expect in a community only four years old. Table 3.13 also has New Town showing up differently to either Ashford or the rural parishes when it comes to the percentage number of households with kin or with servants. The small proportion of kin can be accounted for by their being recent migrants to a brand new, highly specialized community – many were born 200 miles away in the cradle of the railway age, Northumberland and Durham. The smaller proportion of servants is explained by the households' being headed by manual workers.

Table 3.13 Percentage of households with kin, lodgers and domestic servants in Ashford, New Town and five rural parishes in Kent in 1851

	Kin	Lodgers	Servants
Ashford	21.0	17.5	16.9
New Town	9.8	28.2	9.8
Rural parishes	19.5	28.6	14.8

Source: as for Table 3.11

Finally, in Table 3.14 we see again how different New Town was, this time in the percentage of multi-generational households it contained.

Table 3.14 Distribution of households by number of generations in Ashford, New Town and five rural parishes in Kent in 1851 (percentages)

	Number of generations		
	1	2	3
Ashford	28.1	62.9	8.9
New Town	21.6	77.8	0.6
Rural parishes	21.3	67.5	11.2

Source: as for Table 3.11

2.4   CONCLUSION AND A WAY AHEAD

The size and composition of families and households reflects a variety of social, economic and ideological factors. A person's position in the life cycle is also reflected in the type of family or household he or she is likely to be a member of, at any given time. It is, of course, these fundamental aspects of family and wider social life that are important, so that the danger is avoided of 'treating household composition as something inherently important in itself' (Anderson, 1988, p.42). Nevertheless, *without the numbers* it is difficult to know what the researcher is seeking to explain.

QUESTION FOR RESEARCH

How should you begin to study the size, composition and behaviour of families and households? Here are my suggestions. First, if you have created a family tree and, as part of that exercise, have accumulated some CEB entries of the type presented earlier for the Goodaire family, then get them out and look at them. What sort of co-resident family units are they – nuclear or extended? What sort of kin are present – parents, parents-in-law, nephews, nieces, aunts, uncles, brothers, sisters or even more distant relatives? How old are they? Is there any evidence that members of the extended family are providing services for each other, like John Heaton Goodaire's uncle Joseph who appeared to have taken him on as an apprentice tailor? You should not be surprised to find a daughter or niece described as a domestic servant. Look too at the ages of the family and kin. Is there any evidence of the influence of the life cycle? And what about non-kin? Does your family inhabit a household with others? Are they lodgers, or boarders, or servants?

Second, when you have reflected on your own immediate family, look around at the community in which they live. What are neighbouring households like – very much the same, as was the case in the railway workshop community of New Town, or very different? Do you find any other families in the neighbourhood that seem related to yours (see Anderson's propinquity study in Chapter 2)?

Third, and this is where family and community historians join forces, carry out some analyses of the family and household structures of the community or communities occupied at one time by your families, or in ones you happen to be interested in. Use the household composition analysis form (Table 3.7) and the diagrams in Figure 3.8.

Fourth, if your family came to Britain or Ireland in the last hundred years or if, for some other reason, you cannot use the CEBs, draw on the memories of your living relatives to recreate the families and households of your more immediate past. Here an interesting line of enquiry would be to see how far the family and household structures created in this country mirrored those of the country from which your families came. Or if you are English but some of your ancestors were Scottish, Welsh or Irish, to what extent were their family and household structures different from the English?

Finally, seek out literary evidence that helps us understand what motivated families in the past to create the households they did. This is a much more difficult task, though not an impossible one. Joseph Hartley's letters, for instance (Chapter 2, section 3), indicate much about his relationship with kin. It would seem to have been a close one: his early letters were to his 'hant and cusen'. Memories, diaries, family and household manuals, novels, newspaper articles all discussed the family then – as they still do. Hunting the family is a game for all seasons.

REFERENCES AND FURTHER READING

Note: suggestions for further reading are indicated by an asterisk.

Ambler, R.W. (1987) 'Civil registration and baptism: popular perceptions of the 1836 Act for Registering Births, Deaths and Marriages', *Local Population Studies*, 39, pp.24–31.

Anderson, M. (1983) 'What is new about the modern family?', Occasional Paper 31, *The family*, London, OPCS, pp.2–16. Reprinted in Drake (1994).*

Anderson, M. (1985) 'The emergence of the modern life-cycle in Britain', *Social History*, 10, 1, pp.69–87.*

Anderson, M. (1988) 'Households, families and individuals; some preliminary results from the national sample from the 1851 census of Great Britain', *Continuity and Change*, 3, 3, pp.421–38.

Anderson, O. (1975) 'The incidence of civil marriage in Victorian England and Wales', *Past and Present*, 69, pp.50–87.

Anderson, O. (1979) 'A rejoinder', *Past and Present*, 84, pp.152–62.

Armstrong, A. (1972) 'The use of information about occupation', in Wrigley (1972) pp.191–310.

Barker, T. and Drake, M. (eds) (1982) *Population and society in Britain 1850–1980*, London, Batsford.*

Barnes, R. and Durant, M. (1970) *Pilot work on the general household survey*, Cambridge, Cambridge University Library, ref OP 1100 20 013(I).

Berkner, L. (1972) 'The stem family and the developmental cycle of the peasant household: an 18th century Austrian example', *American Historical Review*, 77, pp.398–418.

Berkner, L. (1975) 'The use and misuse of census data for the historical analysis of the family structure', *Journal of Interdisciplinary History*, 5, 4, pp.721–38.*

Bradley, L. (1970) 'An enquiry into seasonality in baptisms, marriages, and burials. Part 1: Introduction, methodology and marriages', *Local Population Studies*, 4, pp.21–40. Reprinted in Drake (1982) pp.1–13.

Brody, H. (1973) *Inishkillane: change and decline in the west of Ireland*, London, Allen Lane.

Coale, A.J. and Watkins, S.C. (eds) (1986) *The decline of fertility in Europe: the revised proceedings of a conference on the Princeton European Fertility Project*, Princeton, Princeton University Press.

Collins, B. (1991) 'The origins of Irish immigrants to Scotland in the nineteenth and twentieth centuries', in Devine, T.M. (ed.) *Irish immigrants and Scottish society in the nineteenth and twentieth centuries*, Edinburgh, John Donald.

Connell, K.H. (1968) 'Catholicism and marriage in the century after the famine', in *Irish peasant society: four historical essays*, Oxford, Clarendon Press.

Cook, M. (1980) 'Birth-baptism intervals in some Flintshire parishes', *Local Population Studies*, 24, pp.56–7. Reprinted in Drake (1982) pp.69–70.

Cullen, M.J. (1975) *The statistical movement in early Victorian Britain: the foundations of empirical social research*, Hassocks, Harvester Press.

Diamond, I. and Clark, S. (1989) 'Demographic patterns among Britain's ethnic groups', in Joshi (1989) pp.177–98.

Doolittle, I.G. (1980) 'Age at baptism: further evidence', *Local Population Studies*, 24, pp.52-5. Reprinted in Drake (1982) pp.65–8.

Drake, M. (1981) 'The re-marriage market in mid-nineteenth century Britain', in Dupaquier, J. *et al.*, *Marriage and remarriage in populations of the past*, London, Academic Press.

Drake, M. (ed.) (1982) *Population studies from parish registers*, Matlock, Local Population Studies.

Drake, M. (ed.) (1994) *Time, family and community: perspectives on family and community history*, Oxford, Blackwell in association with The Open University (Course Reader).[*]

Edwards, W.J. (1977) 'Marriage seasonality 1761–1810: an assessment of patterns in seventeen Shropshire parishes', *Local Population Studies*, 19, pp.23–7. Reprinted in Drake (1982) pp.14–18.

Fitzpatrick, D. (1987) 'The modernisation of the Irish female', in O'Flanagan *et al.* (1987) pp.162–80.

Flinn, M. (ed.) (1977) *Scottish population history from the 17th century to the 1930s*, Cambridge, Cambridge University Press.[*]

Floud, R. and Thane, P. (1979) 'Civil marriage in Victorian England and Wales', *Past and Present*, 84, pp.146–54.

Garrett, E.M. (1990) 'The trials of labour: motherhood versus employment in a nineteenth century textile centre', *Continuity and Change*, 5, 1, pp.121–54.

Gaunt, D. (1978) 'Household typology: problems, methods, results', in Åkerman, S. *et al.* (eds), *Chance and change: social and economic studies in historical demography in the Baltic area*, Odense, Odense University Press.

Gibbon, P. and Curtin, C. (1978) 'The stem family in Ireland', *Comparative Studies in Society and History*, 20, pp.429–53.

Gray, P.G. (1947) *The British household: based on an enquiry carried out in April 1947*, Cambridge, Cambridge University Library, ref: DP 1100 92 02(B).

Guinnane, T. (1991) 'Rethinking the western European marriage pattern: the decision to marry in Ireland at the turn of the twentieth century', *Journal of Family History*, 16, 1, pp.47–64.

Haines, M.R. (1989) 'Social class differentials during fertility decline: England and Wales revisited', *Population Studies*, 43, 2, pp.305–23.

Hair, P.E.H. (1966) 'Bridal pregnancy in rural England in earlier centuries', *Population Studies*, 20, 2, pp.233–43.

Hair, P.E.H. (1970) 'Bridal pregnancy in earlier rural England further examined', *Population Studies*, 24, 1, pp.59–70.

Hareven, T. (1991) 'The history of the family and the complexity of social change', *American Historical Review*, 96, 1, pp.95–124. Reprinted in an abridged form as 'Recent historical research on the family' in Drake (1994).

Harris, R. (1972) *Prejudice and tolerance in Ulster: a study of neighbours and 'strangers' in a border community*, Manchester, Manchester University Press.

Joshi, H. (ed.) (1989) *The changing population of Britain*, Oxford, Blackwell.[*]

Knodel, J. (1979) 'An exercise on household composition for use in courses on historical demography', *Local Population Studies*, 23, pp.10–23.

Krause, J.T. (1958) 'Changes in English fertility and mortality, 1781–1850', *Economic History Review*, second series, 11, 1, pp.52–70.

Kussmaul, A. (1990) *A general view of the rural economy of England 1538–1840*, Cambridge, Cambridge University Press.

Laslett, P. (1983) 'Family and household as work group and kin group: areas of traditional Europe compared', in Wall, R. (ed.) *Family forms in historic Europe*, Cambridge, Cambridge University Press.

Laslett, P. and Oosterveen, K. (1973) 'Long-term trends in bastardy in England: a study of the illegitimacy figures in the reports of the Registrar-General, 1561–1960', *Population Studies*, 27, 2, pp.255–84.

Levine, D. (1986) Review of Coale, A.J. and Watkins, S.C. (1986) in *Population and Development Review*, 12, 2, pp.335–40.

Levine, D. (1987) *Reproducing families: the political economy of English population history*, Cambridge, Cambridge University Press.*

Lewis, G. (1987) *Somerville and Ross: the world of the Irish RM*, Harmondsworth, Penguin.

Lynch, K.A. (1992) 'History and the pursuit of interdisciplinary research in the human sciences', in Karsten, P. and Modell, J., *Theory, method, and practice in social and cultural history*, New York and London, New York University Press.

Macafee, W. (1987) 'Pre-famine population in Ulster: evidence from the parish register of Killyman', in O'Flanagan *et al.* (1987) pp.142–61.

McCullum, D.M. (1980) 'Age at baptism: further evidence', *Local Population Studies*, 24, pp.490–51. Reprinted in Drake (1982) pp.62–4.

Mitchell, B.R. (1992) *International historical statistics Europe 1750-1988*, third edition, London, Macmillan.

Mokyr, J. and O'Grada, C. (1984) 'New developments in Irish population history 1700–1850', *Economic History Review*, xxxvii, 4, pp.473–88.

Morgan, V. and Macafee, W. (1984) 'Irish population in the pre-famine period: evidence from County Antrim', *Economic History Review*, xxxvii, 2, pp.182–96.

Moser, C.A. and Scott, W. (1961) *British towns: a statistical study of their social and economic differences*, London, Centre for Urban Studies.

New Zealand Government (Department of Statistics) *New Zealand vital statistics, 1978.*

Nissel, M. (1987) *People count: a history of the General Register Office*, London, HMSO.

O'Flanagan, P., Ferguson, P. and Whelan, K. (1987) *Rural Ireland 1600–1900: modernization and change*, Cork, Cork University Press.

OPCS (Office of Population Censuses and Surveys) (1979) *Marriage and divorce statistics*, London, HMSO.

OPCS (Office of Population Censuses and Surveys) (1992) *Population Trends*, 69, London, HMSO.

Pearce, C.A. and Mills, D.R. (1986) 'Researching in the Victorian censuses: a note on a computerized, annotated bibliography of publications based substantially on the census enumerators' books', *The Quarterly Journal of Social Affairs*, 2, 1, pp.55–68.

Phillips, R. (1991) *Untying the knot: a short history of divorce*, Cambridge, Cambridge University Press.

Pidduck, W. (1978) *Urban and rural social conditions in industrial Britain. The local reports to the General Board of Health, 1848–57. A complete listing and guide to the Harvester Press microfilm collection with an introduction by H.T. Smith*, Hassocks, Harvester Press.

Registrar General (1875) *Thirty-fifth annual report of the Registrar General of Births, Marriages and Deaths in England*, British Parliamentary Papers, xviii, pt. 1, p.5.

Registrar General (1949) *Statistical review of England and Wales for 1944*, London, HMSO.

Registrar General of Births, Deaths and Marriages in Scotland (1856–66) British Parliamentary Papers, 1856, xviii, p.15; 1857, iv, p.367; 1857–8, xxiii, p.233; 1859 session 1, xii, p.575; 1860, xxix, p.815; 1861, xviii, p.545; 1862, xviii, p.1; 1863, xiv, p.285; 1864, xvii, p.281; 1865, xiv, p.285; 1866, xix, p.317.

Registrar General of Marriages, Births and Deaths in Ireland (1884) *Supplement to Seventeenth Report containing decennial summaries for the years 1871–80*, British Parliamentary Papers, 1884, xx, p.983.

Registrar General of Scotland (1866) *Eighth detailed Annual Report of the Registrar General of Births, Deaths and Marriages in Scotland*, British Parliamentary Papers, 1866, xix, pp.365–640.

Rowntree, G. and Pierce, R.M. (1961) 'Birth control in Britain', Part 2, *Population Studies*, xv, 2, pp.121–60.

Ruggles, S. (1987) *Prolonged connections: the rise of the extended family in nineteenth century England and America*, Madison, University of Wisconsin Press.*

Schofield, R.S. (1972) 'Sampling in historical research', in Wrigley (1972), pp.146–90.

Schürer, K. (1987) 'Historical demography, social structure and the computer', in Denley, P. and Hopkin, D., *History and computing*, Manchester, Manchester University Press.

Schürer, K. and Anderson, S.J. with the assistance of Duncan, J.A. (1992) *A guide to historical datafiles held in machine-readable form*, London, Association for History and Computing.

Seccombe, W. (1990) 'Starting to stop: working class fertility decline in Britain', *Past and Present*, 126, pp.151–88.

Social Trends 13 (1983) London, HMSO.

Social Trends 19 (1989) London, HMSO.

Southall, H. (1991) 'The timing of marriage in mid-nineteenth century industrial communities', *Local Population Studies*, 47, pp.77–80.

Thomas, M. (1979) *Urban and rural social conditions in industrial Britain. Series two. The reports of the Local Government Board 1869–1908. A complete listing and guide to the Harvester microfiche collection*, Hassocks, Harvester Microform.

Tilly, C. (1986) Review of Coale, A.J. and Watkins, S.C. (1986) in *Population and Development Review*, 12, 2, pp.323–8.

Wall, R. (1982) 'Regional and temporal variations in the structure of the British household since 1851', in Barker and Drake (1982) pp.62–99.

Wall, R. (1989) 'Leaving home and living alone: an historical perspective', *Population Studies*, 43, pp.369–89.

Williams, C.J. and Watts-Williams, J. (1986) *Cofrestri Plwyf Cymru: Parish Registers of Wales*, Aberystwyth, National Library of Wales and Welsh County Archivist Group.

Williams, N. (1992) 'Death in season: class, environment and the mortality of infants in nineteenth century Sheffield', *Social History of Medicine*, 5, 1, pp.71–94.

Woods, R. (1987) 'Approaches to the fertility transition in Victorian England', *Population Studies*, 41, 2, pp.283–311.

Woods, R. (1992) *The population of Britain in the nineteenth century*, Basingstoke, Macmillan.[*]

Woods, R. and Woodward, J. (eds) (1984) *Urban disease and mortality in nineteenth century England*, London, Batsford.

Woods, R.I., Watterson, P.A. and Woodward, J.H. (1988–9) 'The causes of rapid infant mortality decline in England and Wales', *Population Studies*, part 1, 42, 3, pp.343–66; part 2, 43, 1, pp.113–32.

Wrigley, E.A. (ed.) (1972) *Nineteenth-century society: essays in the use of quantitative methods for the study of social data*, Cambridge, Cambridge University Press.

Wrigley, E.A. and Schofield, R.S. (1981) *The population history of England 1541–1871. A reconstruction*, London, Edward Arnold.[*]

CHAPTER 4

FAMILY RESOURCES AND EXPERIENCES

by Ruth Finnegan

This chapter moves on from the discussion of the demographic patterns of family life, and types of household, to some consideration of how families and their members actually function. How do they support themselves? Has this changed over time? What resources do families have, whether material (like shared income) or intangible (like family narratives and symbols)? And how do they feel about them and use them?

Do such questions represent a different emphasis from that of Chapter 3?

This chapter focuses particularly on active family strategies and experiences. This follows the lead of some recent scholars in family history who are now looking beyond formal structures to explore such processes as internal family dynamics, changing relationships between families, and the strategies or myths through which people and groups make their way in the world. Such studies extend the largely co-residential definition of the family (as household) that formed a main point of departure in Chapter 3. The emphasis here is on what people do – and feel – in their family lives rather than on household units as such.

As before, the aim is to put the experience of individual families into context, and to suggest questions for research.

1 DOMESTIC ECONOMIES AND FAMILY STRATEGIES

How do families support themselves? Let me lead into this question by starting again with a personal example, which can then be set in a wider perspective and perhaps compared with your own family.

One of my early memories is of my mother's stories of her excitement as a child when the wonderful parcels of clothes passed on from her rich Yorkshire cousins arrived in her home in Londonderry (Derry) in the north of Ireland. My mother's family were not well off, and her father much less financially successful than the Halifax manufacturing family from whom he had wooed his wife, Lucy Farrar. In the early years of the twentieth century, he was struggling (together with one younger brother) to carry on the family importing business; he was more interested in ornithology and the local folk museum, and was rather envious of the higher education and missionary careers of his other brothers. The small amount of money his wife (my grandmother) had from her father served only to pay for the occasional personal extras, but was supplemented by the hospitality and support of her husband's large extended family who lived nearby – my mother still talks of the huge gatherings and family feasts over Christmas.

My father's forebears, the Finnegans, seemed rather different. They had mixed fortunes and occupations, as is true of many families, but they traced at least one part of their origin to a line of Ulster farmers from the late eighteenth to mid-twentieth centuries, passing the family-run farm down through one son, then through his son, and so on down the generations. The sisters sometimes stayed on, unmarried, with their farmer brothers, or married nearby (often a cousin, it

Figure 4.1 Photograph of my mother, then Agnes Campbell, as a young child in Derry in 1908, with her mother, Lucy Farrar from Halifax (Source: Agnes Finnegan)

seems), while the non-inheriting sons turned to other occupations or – a common feature of the last century – emigration. My father's immediate family came from a younger-son branch who in successive generations took up shopkeeping, the Presbyterian ministry and, finally (starting from my paternal grandfather, John Finnegan, pictured in Figure 1.4 in Chapter 1) work in higher education.

My mother's own life spanned a period of great change. She grew up in the early decades of this century, took a degree at Queen's University Belfast, and married in 1930. She spent much of her married life bringing up five children, with the money allowance on which she ran the household coming from my father's university job in Derry. I think she would have liked to have pursued a profession herself, and certainly at one point got involved in local politics to the disapproval of some of her Protestant friends; later, she took up freelance writing and (later still) broadcasting. But she was also constrained by the local expectations of a middle-class wife's role, as well as by her own commitments to her growing children. Only after they grew up did she move into a salaried post as part-time and then full-time teacher, continuing this after she was widowed in 1964.

Can this brief personal history be linked to common family patterns in the nineteenth and twentieth centuries?

This is where we come back to the 'domestic economy' – a short-hand term for the economy of the individual household or, more broadly (as we shall see in due course), the processes by which a 'family' and its members support themselves. Researchers are now taking a keen interest in this topic, relating it both to the development of industrialization in its varied forms, and to other events on the national and international scene.

One set of changes noted by researchers has concerned the gradual change, particularly marked in the nineteenth century, from what could be called a 'home-based family economy' to a 'family wage economy'. In the former, the household was largely self-provisioning rather than relying primarily on cash, and often supported itself through a diversity of means, from local foraging or poaching to a series of concurrent tasks like farm work, local crafts, or other activities carried on at home. If (as often) this productive system was not sufficient to support the whole household, individual young people had to leave, to go into service for example, or emigrate. This certainly fits with the agricultural patterns of my father's forebears, and many others – think of the Arnisons (Chapter 1), of John Kerr's departure to the USA (Chapter 1) or of the Hartleys (Chapter 2). It also has some parallels with the 'proto-industrial' form of home industry where all family members worked productively in the home with an eye to making some money from selling. Among the eighteenth-century domestic 'clothiers' in Yorkshire, for example, Daniel Defoe's famous *Tour* describes 'the women and children … always busy carding, spinning, etc. so that no hands being unemployed, all can gain their bread, even from the youngest to the ancient; hardly any thing above four years old, but its hands are sufficient to it self' (Letter 8, in Rogers, 1971, p.493). Similarly, in Irish farming-weaving households the self-sufficient units of production 'with the farmer-weaver growing his own flax, his wife and children spinning it into linen yarn and he and the elder children taking it to sell in the local market' gradually developed a more industrial style as family labour was supplemented by temporary paid journeymen weavers or spinners (Collins, 1982, pp.130, 132 ff.)

The family wage economy, by contrast, is associated with the development of factory work. The period of industrialization was characterized increasingly by the separation of home and work, with the household being supported by wages earned by individuals *outside* the household. Thus my mid-nineteenth-century manufacturing relations from Yorkshire relied on a money income, as too did poorer families around them. There was not the same limit as in the home-based family economy on how many family members could contribute to the household: cash wages could be earned by men and women, whether adults or children, as in the case of the Goodaires (see Chapter 3, Table 3.6). And money – more easily than a family farm – could be divided between the remaining family on death rather than it all going to the first son. So my Yorkshire great-grandfather decreed in his will in 1894 that his residual cash was to be divided into fifteen, with two shares each for his five sons, and one each for his five daughters (hence my grandmother's small personal income).

Further changes took place that were mirrored in my mother's life. The earlier pattern meant that all active family members could contribute to household resources either through home-based work or, later, cash wages. But the ideal of the male wage-earner increasingly took over – the husband as financial supporter of the family, the woman as home-keeper, with the sons expected to leave to set up their own wage-supported households in their turn, complete with non-earning wife. As we shall see, this did not always match the practice: many women in poorer families did indeed go out to earn money for their family's upkeep. But the ideal of the asymmetrical family economy, with husband and wife having different roles, remained an influential one for many generations, supported in some respects by state policy (e.g. laws on pensions and national insurance) and by the role of trade unions in defining jobs along gender lines. It is still not without its influence, though it has been partially superseded again in recent decades by the growth of dual-earner families. Here wives and mothers, not just husbands and fathers, are in paid employment (though not always full-time) and contribute to the household upkeep. Sometimes we see multi-earner households, not least when adult children stay in the parental home in the absence of affordable housing elsewhere.

These changing patterns are summarized in Schema A. (For further discussion of these and similar trends, but not necessarily using the same terminology, see Levine, 1987; Young and Willmott, 1973; Tilly and Scott, 1978; Pahl, 1984.)

Schema A: Some forms of domestic economies in the nineteenth and twentieth centuries

- *Home-based family economy:* pre-industrial agriculture, proto-industrial home production.

- *Family wage economy:* multiple wage-earners, linked to industrialization.

- *Asymmetrical family economy:* one male wage-earner, woman at home – later nineteenth to twentieth centuries.

- *Dual (or multiple) earner family economy* with both male and female wage-earners – mid to late twentieth century.

How far does (a) my family history as outlined above and/or (b) any family or families you are studying fit with Schema A?

One basis for research could be to take some aspect of this model – perhaps turned into a hypothesis – and test out how far any families you are studying fit with these patterns. Since we do not know precisely how far local and personal experiences vary, information about those that do not fit could be as illuminating as those that do.

It will quickly appear that this schema – illuminating though it is to start from – can only provide a rough guide. The reality is, as often, more complex. The forms themselves may not be as incompatible as they look at first; they no doubt coexisted rather than one being ousted by another. Also in practice each sometimes included contrasting variants: some scholars, for example, emphasize the crucial differences between pre-industrial farming economies and the proto-industrial system (e.g. Collins, 1982). Furthermore, summary sequential lists like the above can give the misleading impression that there was some static or homogeneous pre-industrial state, whereas in fact even if the home-based economy was the norm before industrialization, there were also many cases of paid labour outside the household. A full understanding also needs to relate these family cases to wider economic structures and changes, e.g. in demography (see Chapter 3 above, also Levine, 1987) or work patterns (see Volume 3, and Hudson and Lee, 1990). Equally important, there are many cases where families or individuals carved out their own strategies. We also need to take into account the effects of legislation on, say, pensions or compulsory schooling, or of historic events such as the Irish famine, the massive number of male deaths in the 1914–18 war, the depression in the 1930s, or the effects on family economies during and following both world wars. There are also, no doubt, differences related to variables such as locality or class – as you will see in the Katharine Buildings example in Chapter 5.

These variations can themselves provide a stimulus for research. Take, for example, Holley's (1981) study of domestic economies among workers in two factory-dominated Victorian communities in south-east Scotland: Penicuik in 1851 and Walkerburn in 1881. Looking at Schema A, you might expect these to fall under the broad 'family wage economy' heading. In fact Holley found that the situation was more complicated, for there were two contrasting forms. He relates information from factory wage books to the CEBs to delineate two distinct forms of family strategy, of skilled as against unskilled wage-earners. In 'the respectable family economy of the skilled workers', the larger wages earned by the men meant the family could essentially depend on the father's earnings: an asymmetrical family economy, in fact. There could be a difficult patch when the children were young, but the wages were still enough for the father's work to support his family. In the unskilled case, however, things were different. The male wages were smaller, so other family members had to find paid work to support the struggling family, especially at the vulnerable low point of the early domestic cycle (with young children). This was not so easy, for in these particular local economies opportunities for female paid work were limited. Unlike the more stable skilled-worker families, these multiple-earning families of the labouring poor therefore moved at specific points in the family cycle to places where work was more easily available (such movements being traceable through the birthplaces of both the labourers themselves and their co-resident children), and they stayed less continuously in their factory jobs. This was the 'disreputable family economy of the unskilled'.

Two implications of this study are particularly worth noting. First, it provides another interesting model for further investigation. Holley argues that the two strategies sketched out here are

> *not isolated and local phenomena, but … part of a broader change in family forms. Thus the strategy of the lower paid workers to employ as many of their family as they could, however unrespectable it appeared to upper strata observers, was in fact part of a well established culture with its antecedents in the earlier period of domestic outwork … [adapted to the new system in which] the various family members went to work in places outside the home and were often paid individually.*

(Holley, 1981, p.66)

Can similar strategies be found elsewhere? Here is a topic for further research. Indeed there may be yet further variants, related to the conditions of particular places or periods – a second point to notice. It cannot be assumed that a particular situation applies everywhere; it is necessary to elaborate and qualify the models in the light of locally based investigations. We could consider, for example, Wall's (1986) detailed analysis of family economic strategies in the parish of Colyton in south-west England, based mainly on the 1851 census. He demonstrates the flexibility of domestic economies, interrelated with patterns of local recruitment into the labour force, status, stages in the life cycle, or the relation between specific occupations and residence (more sons than daughters leaving the parental home among labourers and craftsmen, for instance – unlike farmers). The different patterns of work for girls and boys were significant too, as was the work – paid and otherwise – performed by women (all too often underestimated in the census returns). As Wall points out, the strategies were modified according to the needs and fortunes of individual families – the 'adaptive family economy' as he calls it – and built on a combination between wage labour and home-based industry rather than just the one or the other.

I think also of the other economic strategies followed in that same town, Derry, where my mother was inhibited, by the expectations of her middle-class background and the nature of my

Figure 4.2 W.J. Little's shirt and collar factory, Spencer Road, Londonderry, in the 1930s (Source: Bigger and McDonald, 1990)

father's job, from finding paid work in the 1930s onwards, but where women from the poorer families worked in large numbers in the shirt factories (like that shown in Figure 4.2).

It can be useful, too, to stand back from the detailed findings to think about the approach that Holley, Wall and other recent writers take. Did you notice that they talk not of static household structure but of changing strategies adopted by families at different stages? This is no accident, for an interest in processes, in families' active strategies and in the changing conditions of different points in the domestic life cycle has been the hallmark of many recent studies (e.g. Tilly and Scott, 1978; Pahl, 1984; Roberts, 1993; Hareven, 1991).

In considering such cases we need to take account not just of money wages but of all the resources used by the family to support itself. Contrary to what is sometimes assumed, home-based production was not all ended by industrialization. Women in particular continued with productive work run from the home, like laundering, sewing, child-care, or small-scale home trading, paid for sometimes in money, sometimes in kind (see Pennington and Westover, 1989). Taking in lodgers was another source of income. I remember too my mother's description of their shortage of money as a child, but, as she added, 'Father was a wizard gardener and we were reared on fresh, often raw vegetables, not at that time fashionable but a diet I still enjoy' (Finnegan, 1991, p.48); in later years she herself contributed to her own family's food from her garden and (in the country during the war) from the products of the family's poultry and milk-cow.

Research on housework and on the so-called 'informal' or 'hidden' economy has also drawn attention to the valuable role still played by non-monetary contributions to the domestic economy (see Pahl, 1984; Finnegan, 1985; Wallman, 1984). Some of this consists of unpaid and in a sense 'invisible' tasks like cooking, laundering, gardening, house or car maintenance, child-rearing, DIY and so on – all of which would cost money if someone else had to be paid to perform them! Others are less tangible still, like the provision of information or support, or the sense of identity or network that a particular family can utilize, but these too can contribute significantly to a family's material lifestyle. As Sandra Wallman puts it:

> *The effectiveness of each household system depends on the context in which its resources are being used or assessed, on the particular purposes of its members on particular occasions, and on which options are both available to the household and recognized by its resource-keepers.*
>
> (Wallman, 1984, p.41)

From this perspective, investigating a family's economy entails attention to all that family's resources, not just its money income – far less just the income from one male wage-earner (which is too often the sole focus of researchers). It can be illuminating, therefore, to ask about both paid and unpaid contributions from each family member to the family economy at the particular period under study. What did children do, for example, and when; to whom were their wages paid (to parents?); and how long did they stay at home? Research is opening up on this subject (e.g. Hair, 1982; Davin, 1990) and there is scope for more. What about both the monetary *and* non-monetary contributions of children at various ages, or the income that even small outside tasks bring in to the family's economy? Do your findings coincide with, for example, those of Jamieson (1987) about the ways in which boys' contributions differed from those of girls in families growing up in Scotland early this century? What were the expected roles of teenagers; of those who left for education or marriage; of women as young wives, mothers, earners; of men in their various roles; or of relations outside the household – in terms of remittances to or from family members abroad, for example, or seasonal migration as part of a family's economic strategy? Developing such questions could extend your initial ideas about the domestic economies of particular families and bring your findings into conjunction with recent lines of research.

Following up such points may result in an active picture of family strategies in managing their resources and supporting themselves by a variety of means. As Hareven emphasizes:

> *Strategies involved, at times, calculated trade-offs in order to find employment, achieve solvency, buy a house, facilitate children's education or their occupational advancement, control or facilitate a child's marriage, save for the future, provide for times of illness, old age, and death. Strategies were part of a larger life plan. As people encountered new circumstances, they modified and reshaped their plans and strategies in the context of their own culture and traditions.*
>
> (Hareven, 1991, pp.115–16)

Such questions can only partially be followed up through official sources like the CEBs, which are useful indeed for certain elements but need to be supplemented, as in Holley's study, by more detailed sources. For recent periods, oral evidence can be useful: you might ask questions yourself (see section 4 below) or tap already recorded interviews in a local audio collection.

One example is Elizabeth Roberts' (1993) study of working-class women in Lancashire. Using both official and oral sources she contrasts two sequential forms of working-class family economy. First there was the earlier inter-war situation in which all family members played their part in the 'heroic battles against poverty', with married women centred on the home and taking the crucial role as the household managers, the controllers of the family budget. In the post-war period this gradually changed, with women increasingly turning to paid work – for satisfaction as well as money – and at the same time losing their traditional position of power as budget controllers within the home. Once again this could be elaborated into a series of possible categories (as in Schema B). This checklist could stimulate and perhaps be challenged by your own research, as well as serving as a framework for exploring possible changes and differences by period, class or locality.

Schema B: Some contrasting roles of married women in the domestic economy

o   One home producer among others.

o   One wage-earner among others.

o   Manager of household resources and strategies.

o   Keeper of the home (non-earning).

o   Supervisor of household (including servants).

Notes:

(a)   These roles are not necessarily sequential nor mutually exclusive.

(b)   Comparable economic roles could also be explored for women in other relationships (as daughters, mothers-in-law, grandmothers); for men (as husbands, sons, fathers-in-law); and for children.

Further questions could open up the apparently bounded unit of the household to ask how the family budget is allocated *within* it. This is not an easy area to investigate: it has often been observed that intra-familial finance is more secret than sex! But recent research does at least give some guidance on the kinds of patterns according to which – perhaps differing with situation, period and (probably) wealth – resources can be distributed between husband and wife; or even, perhaps, not distributed, so that the idea of a shared 'household economy' breaks down. The common patterns of money management are summarized below (based on Pahl, 1989, pp.36ff, 63ff; see also Pahl, 1990; Roberts, 1993):

1   *Whole wage system:* one partner is responsible for managing household finances (usually the wife, with the husband's wages handed over to her in total, but some personal spending money kept or returned). This was a common pattern in the nineteenth and twentieth centuries, especially in working-class areas such as parts of Lancashire.

2   *Allowance system:* most commonly this involves the husband giving his wife a set amount every week or month for housekeeping (the husband being responsible for certain other expenditure). This was common in Victorian (and later) families, especially among the middle classes.

3   *Pooling system or shared management:* a common kitty or joint account for both parties.

4   *Independent management system:* each partner has their own income with separate responsibility for specific items.

Have you encountered examples of any of these categories?

We started with questions about domestic economies: about how families supported themselves. This has now drawn us on to more general questions about roles and relationships within families. Even for economic topics, it seems, we need to move beyond the household in the narrow sense to look at changing family relationships. As emerged in the Goodaire example (Chapter 3), 'the household' at any given time only represents one particular stage in the domestic cycle: at different points the same individual(s) may be young; married with no children; parent(s) of young (then of adult and non-resident) children; alone; or with next-generation families in old age. At each point their economic (and other) strategies are likely to be different, and relations with family members outside as well as inside the same household have to be considered as part of the overall equation.

Section 2 follows up these relationships further. But let us first summarize some research suggestions to which you may wish to return in due course.

QUESTIONS FOR RESEARCH

1   From what you have discovered already, how far does the history of a family which you are studying fit with the models summarized in Schemas A or B? How about other families in the same locality; or other branches of your own family; or others you have read about?

2   What roles in the domestic economy were played by the various members of a particular family or household at a given time (or times)? And how does this compare with other cases you know of or have read about?

3   Does examining the sources about your own and comparable families encourage you to take up an approach based on investigating one or more of the kinds of questions raised in this section about family resources and roles? If so, *how* and *why* have your findings led you to this conclusion?

---

2   THE DYNAMICS OF FAMILY RELATIONSHIPS

The analysis of active family processes can also be applied to family experiences and relationships over time. As Tamara Hareven puts it in her overview of recent research, the study of family history, while rooted in historical demography, is now also affected by new interests in 'human experience' and by 'our increasing appreciation of the changing and diverse nature of "the family"' (Hareven, 1991, p.95). These questions too provide a framework for comparison, provoking further research.

One issue to which this developing work has drawn attention is the importance of *internal* roles and relationships within families and households. As will already be clear from the previous section, neither households nor families are undifferentiated black boxes. Once you 'open' the box, you find diverse men and women, each with their own lives and personalities. They are also each influenced by the roles which they are (more, or less) expected to follow.

Section 1 focused mainly on economic roles in the family. But there are other roles too, which again differ according to age, gender or status. There was, for example, the Victorian patriarch – the kind of image conveyed, for example, in Figure 1.4 of Chapter 1; the woman as household manager, or, in other cases, as a feeble lily in need of support; the child as a working contributor to the family resources, or alternatively as full-time scholar; the grandparent as an important source of past wisdom or as a 'burden', marginal to the real business of life. The expected roles vary with culture or region, and can change over time. They can also be resisted or resented by individuals – my mother, for example – rather than blindly followed. But it is essential to take account of these expectations since they directly affect the workings of the family and household.

But even within a family, relationships are not static. People 'grow into' them, going through many different relationships in the course of their lives. This has been a common process for individuals – being born, being a child, growing up, courting, marrying, bearing and rearing children, getting old, being widowed, dying. As we saw in Chapter 3, there is a predictable *cycle* in the life of most families as they change over the years. Hareven (1991, p.106) describes this as 'the progression of the couple from marriage through parenthood, the launching of the children, widowhood, and family dissolution'. It can be illuminating to relate a given family to this basic cycle, and also to note the way the details of its experiences have varied in different periods, as with the more protracted and unpredictable passage between childhood status and household headship in the mid-nineteenth as compared with the mid-twentieth century (Anderson, 1983, p.10) or the increase in non-marital unions and divorce in the late twentieth century.

Additional questions are raised if we widen our focus from *parenthood* (the pivot in traditional views of 'the domestic cycle') to how individuals move into and out of a range of family roles: their life course. These moves regularly involve not just events within the family but also 'outside' activities like work, schooling or travelling. Thus one intensive American study based on census data found that even educational and job transitions were integrated with the family and 'collective family requirements and strategies governed their timing' (reported in Hareven, 1991, p.106). These family ties created dilemmas too:

> *How did individuals and couples cope with conflicting social goals and allegiances to their families of orientation and families of procreation? How did they make their transitions from one family to the other in a regime of economic insecurity, without jeopardizing the independence and self-sufficiency of one or the other?*

(Hareven, 1991, p.106)

The study of life histories can also contribute to our understanding. As Brian Elliott urges in his discussion of 'Biography, family history and the analysis of social change' (1990), the lives of individual people and families throw new light on family experiences, supplementing demographic records about life, marriage and death by such other events as work, success, illness, or perhaps homelessness or unemployment. These too play a part in the experiences of families and their members.

Studying the relationships, life cycle and life course of families and their members means looking at internal family dynamics. But there are further questions too. Families are not isolated units, for individual and family lives also interact with the wider environment.

So what about kinship links outside the current household or beyond the immediate nuclear family? Researchers often focus just on households, the nuclear core or a single genealogical line. But anthropologists and historians are increasingly revealing the significance of family relationships *outside* the household. These can be important in many contexts: for financial support, help in getting a job, accommodation and contacts when away from home (crucial in migration), material assistance in the critical step of setting up a new household (think of wedding presents), support for the elderly or infirm, or, as with my mother's hand-me-down clothes from her cousins, tactful help to less well-off branches of the family. The details vary according to circumstances. Child-care, for instance, could be a grandmother coming in to look after her working daughter's baby, or missionary parents abroad sending their children back to be reared by a maiden aunt 'at home'. Exploring family strategies can be filled out by investigating how these wider ties have been exploited and to what extent they have varied between different families.

This also feeds back into questions about family roles. As Hareven (1991, p.95) reminds us, families have fluid and impermanent boundaries. Relations living together at one point (say, a mother and daughter) may separate on the daughter's marriage, then come together again after the mother is widowed and joins her daughter's household in old age. As will have emerged earlier in Chapter 3 (especially Table 3.6), living together in one household is itself a form of mutual support. So too is parental help to children when they set up a new, separate home, or the potential for support from close relations living nearby (for some information on the latter over time see Table 4.1).

113

Table 4.1 Proximity to elderly parent(s) of nearest child in England, eighteenth to twentieth centuries (percentages)

	Date	Same household	Same parish	Elsewhere	Total	N
Cardington	1782	25	33	42	100	(12)
Stoke Poges	1831	0	75	25	100	(8)
Bethnal Green	1954–5	52	33	15	100	(167)
Swansea	1960	50	18	32	100	(327)
Britain as a whole	1962	42	24	34	100	(1911)
Four towns	1977	14	35[1]	51	100	(1646)
Five towns	1983	—[2]	36[3]	—	100	(432)

Sources of data: Cardington and Stoke Poges calculated from local censuses held at the Cambridge Group; Bethnal Green calculated from Townsend (1957) pp.24, 32; Swansea from Rosser and Harris (1965) p.212; four towns (Hove, Merton, Moss Side, Northampton) calculated from Abrams (1978); five towns (Maidstone, Stockport, Merton, Melton Mowbray, Oakham) from Howes (1984) p.10 and Warnes (1986) p.159f; missing data indicated by dash.

[1] Same street or neighbourhood but presumably extending up to five miles, since a distance from parent(s) of five or six miles is the next category to be specified.

[2] No families with co-resident children were included in the sample.

[3] Within one kilometre (0.62 miles). Fifty-eight per cent of couples lived within five kilometres (three miles) of a child.

Source: Wall (1992) p.75

So have expectations about the mutual obligations and roles of family members changed over time? Or, to take one commonly raised aspect of this, do families support each other more, or less, now than in the nineteenth or earlier twentieth centuries? The question has recently been reconsidered by Janet Finch's (1989) study of the support given by relatives and the patterns of reciprocal help between them. Her conclusion was that people do not necessarily do less now for their relatives or feel less family obligation. But the circumstances have changed over time: for example the demographic structure; the generally smaller size of households; changing housing patterns; the age young people leave home; and the introduction of old-age pensions (from 1908). So the particular forms of support and the nature of family relationships are not the same as earlier.

Not everything has changed, it is true. Take the care of the elderly, for example. In earlier centuries, just as now, many of the aged were in institutional care (see Anderson, 1983, pp.3–4). Complaints about younger generations neglecting their elders also run down the ages: witness the nineteenth-century anxieties – in part from the state – about working-class people lacking an adequate sense of 'filial affection' (Finch, 1989, p.81). Similarly, Table 4.1 provides some support for Wall's suggestion that elderly people in the eighteenth and nineteenth centuries were 'no more likely to have their children close to hand than were their counterparts in the mid-twentieth century' (Wall, 1992, p.75), so there may be little change in potentially supportive children living nearby when you are old. However, the likely size of the household tends to be smaller now than in the nineteenth century, though not dramatically so, and its composition tends to be somewhat different (see Tables 3.8 and 3.10 in Chapter 3 and Finch, 1989, pp.61ff). Overall, Finch concludes:

> *Industrialization and urbanization did not destroy either domestic relations or kin relations but clearly they did ... transform their character ... However, this was not a once-for-all change. The character of family relationships has been changing and continues to change to suit the particular circumstances in which individuals find themselves.*

(Finch, 1989, p.85).

It is not just relatives with whom families and their members interact. Those recognized as kin are probably most consistently turned to for help – a hypothesis that could itself be investigated. But similar support from other people and institutions may supplement or replace them: from neighbours, friends, members of the same church or school, fellow migrants, speakers of a common language, or official governmental and voluntary institutions. These may be directly relevant in extending or constraining family options, as too are the laws of marriage, divorce, or family support. Other questions relate to how family members gain their livelihood in the community – as paid employees, unpaid workers, or perhaps members of a family business whether at board level or in the corner shop. There are many variations at the informal level, too, some almost becoming crystallized into settled conventions, like shared child-care arrangements between neighbouring parents of small children at a certain stage in the family cycle. Others are specific to certain groups. One example is the tradition in some West African families in Britain of sending their children for fostering by white families (Goody and Groothues, 1977). This is a deliberate family strategy that seeks to give their children the advantages of education, good living conditions and perhaps social mobility (not so unlike one role of the nineteenth-century domestic servant system).

Almost all families have a series of links – of kinship (close or distant), neighbourliness, friendship, ethnicity, shared interests – through which they can mobilize resources and design the family strategies. With enough information one can plot such networks on a diagram, as Sandra Wallman did in her study of how people felt about close and distant contacts in eight inner-London households in the 1970s (see Figure 4.3).

The specific links exploited will vary with the family's situation, and over time, but there are always likely to be some. Exploring these internal and external family dynamics adds a further dimension to our understanding of family relationships and resources in both the present and the past.

QUESTIONS FOR RESEARCH

Investigating the kinds of questions raised in this section can add to our knowledge, whether through quantified data at a particular time or through studying individual families over a span of years or generations. Three suggestions for further research are given below, but there are many other possibilities.

1   How far does the evidence from earlier families or households you are studying support Hareven's comments (p.113) on *family* timing or on common dilemmas in family and individual transitions?

Warning: pursuing such questions in a quantified form (as in Hareven's discussion) is time-consuming, with laborious record-linkage for individuals and their families from census to census; it is likely to be beyond the resources of many independent researchers. However, you may already have some such data on a small scale, or perhaps you can get access to it as records increasingly become computerized, in which case you can test out these statements for a small set of families over time. Alternatively, or additionally, you could build on oral sources (particularly effective for exploring people's own perceptions and experiences) for a family or families earlier this century (see section 4 below on oral sources).

2   Support and contact between kin is arguably related to the geographical distance between them. Wall's suggestion above that there has been little change in the proximity of parents and their adult children since the nineteenth century provides a possible hypothesis to test. Does it apply to one or more of the families you are studying? If not, does this suggest that his conclusions are mistaken or are there special factors to consider? This could be tackled through a combination of sources such as CEBs, local maps, family documents, or, for more recent periods, oral memories, perhaps building on information you already possess (see also Exercises 2.5 and 2.6 in Chapter 2).

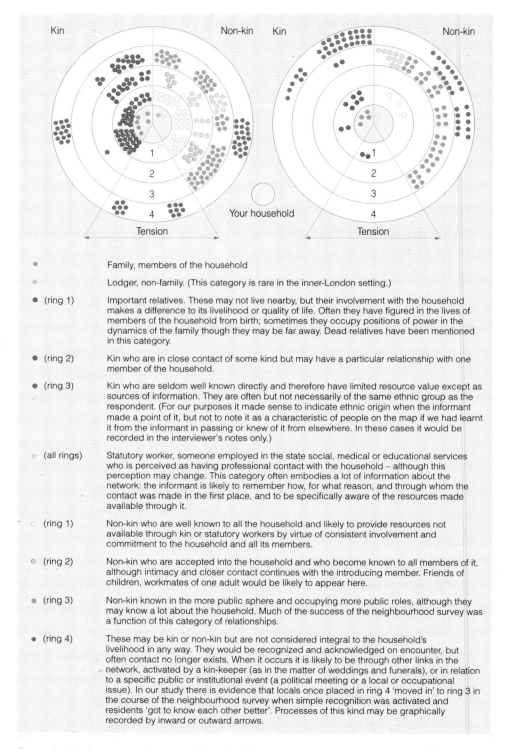

Family, members of the household

Lodger, non-family. (This category is rare in the inner-London setting.)

(ring 1)   Important relatives. These may not live nearby, but their involvement with the household makes a difference to its livelihood or quality of life. Often they have figured in the lives of members of the household from birth; sometimes they occupy positions of power in the dynamics of the family though they may be far away. Dead relatives have been mentioned in this category.

(ring 2)   Kin who are in close contact of some kind but may have a particular relationship with one member of the household.

(ring 3)   Kin who are seldom well known directly and therefore have limited resource value except as sources of information. They are often but not necessarily of the same ethnic group as the respondent. (For our purposes it made sense to indicate ethnic origin when the informant made a point of it, but not to note it as a characteristic of people on the map if we had learnt it from the informant in passing or knew of it from elsewhere. In these cases it would be recorded in the interviewer's notes only.)

(all rings)   Statutory worker, someone employed in the state social, medical or educational services who is perceived as having professional contact with the household – although this perception may change. This category often embodies a lot of information about the network: the informant is likely to remember how, for what reason, and through whom the contact was made in the first place, and to be specifically aware of the resources made available through it.

(ring 1)   Non-kin who are well known to all the household and likely to provide resources not available through kin or statutory workers by virtue of consistent involvement and commitment to the household and all its members.

(ring 2)   Non-kin who are accepted into the household and who become known to all members of it, although intimacy and closer contact continues with the introducing member. Friends of children, workmates of one adult would be likely to appear here.

(ring 3)   Non-kin known in the more public sphere and occupying more public roles, although they may know a lot about the household. Much of the success of the neighbourhood survey was a function of this category of relationships.

(ring 4)   These may be kin or non-kin but are not considered integral to the household's livelihood in any way. They would be recognized and acknowledged on encounter, but often contact no longer exists. When it occurs it is likely to be through other links in the network, activated by a kin-keeper (as in the matter of weddings and funerals), or in relation to a specific public or institutional event (a political meeting or a local or occupational issue). In our study there is evidence that locals once placed in ring 4 'moved in' to ring 3 in the course of the neighbourhood survey when simple recognition was activated and residents 'got to know each other better'. Processes of this kind may be graphically recorded by inward or outward arrows.

Figure 4.3 Affective network maps of households in inner London in the 1970s, recording (a) a large number of 'close' contacts *(left)* and (b) relatively few 'close' contacts *(right)* (Source: Wallman, 1984, pp.66–7)

3   Chart as far as you can the areas of support between members of (a) one or more families you are studying in the past and/or (b) a more recent family (your own perhaps), as far as possible extending this over a generation, i.e. through a full 'domestic cycle'. Do they differ? How far do they fit with Finch's conclusion that the amount of kin support has not changed in the last two centuries, but that its *nature* has? You are unlikely to be able to complete the chart, but even exploring one or two areas could be illuminating. Possible sources are CEBs, family literary sources, observation, oral memories (if using the latter don't overlook the possibility of comparing earlier and more recent family patterns within the twentieth century). Start from one of the following headings:

o   living together

o   financial support and inheritance

o   help in getting a job

o   child care

o   housing or contacts for someone away from home

o   assistance in education

o   support for the elderly or infirm

o   reinforcing family loyalty and identity by attending family rituals

o   political or economic patronage

o   a sense of mutual obligation to help family members

You will find that sources vary in their usefulness according to the question being asked: for instance CEBs are helpful for co-residence, while oral or literary sources are better for questions about experience or values; so which you focus on will partly depend on the sources you have. Your comparisons should be enriched by drawing on the more general conclusions in, say, Finch (1989) (quoted above) or Anderson (1983).

3   FAMILY MYTHS, MEMORIES AND IDEOLOGIES

Family resources are not only material ones. They also include a family's selective memories of the past. As Zeitlin puts it:

> From countless incidents, families choose a few stories to pass on, the funniest or perhaps the most telling. From all of the garbled baby talk, a single utterance may become a family expression. Yet these time-honored images do more than recall scattered people and events; they come to represent the unremembered past, the sum total of a family's heritage.
>
> (Zeitlin et al., 1982, p.2)

Most families have their own stories and traditions, selected from their many memories. Perhaps tellers are not fully conscious that they are crystallizing their family's heritage, telling and re-telling stories that express that family's being. Yet this is a common feature of family experience, and it is another important aspect of a family's resources that can be investigated.

The stories and sayings that have come to represent a family's tradition may not look 'deep' at first sight, nor are they always told consistently. Some may be just about everyday episodes like a funny misunderstanding by an ancestor or a now-grown-up child, or an amusing incident experienced by a grandparent, but they have gradually taken on a symbolic depth. Others may centre on a 'last straw' incident which pushed someone into a momentous course – emigration perhaps. Courtship is another focus, often woven around the motifs of 'love-at-first-sight' or of a test between competing suitors. Quarrels too may get highlighted, or a story built on 'the rogue' theme:

My grandfather mentioned that his ancestors had been, perhaps, for the most part honest – traveling peddlers and merchants – but perhaps with a little bit of piracy. They were in Latvia and Lithuania on the Baltic Sea. I'd like to think they were pirates, but when I think about it seriously, they were probably all hard-working people, to be perfectly honest.

(John Bishop, quoted in Zeitlin *et al.*, 1982, p.vii)

Traditions often emerge or become more formulated in situations of change or crisis. Migration can separate family members drastically, but can also add all the more symbolic depth to selective memories. Think of Wendy's memories of her grandmother's tales of life in Grenada and the 'hows and whys of her moving to England' in Chapter 1; likewise the many nostalgic tales told and sung by Irish emigrants. Stories and images can become especially poignant as a vehicle of family (and ethnic) identity when people make their way against the odds or face discrimination.

The explicit crystallization of a family's shared memories also results from a family history or individual autobiography being written or recorded – something you yourself may have been involved in. Take my own family. I grew up learning many traditions from my parents but did not consciously recognize how these images had moulded my own experience of the world until they were actually verbalized in my mother's autobiography. She repeats there those same stories that I now recall she had told us as children, of the missionaries, scholars and naturalists in her own family, as well as of their close ties to the beauties and battles of the Irish countryside. She symbolizes some of this in her tale of her great-grandfather's father, a nationalist and a Protestant in the United Irishmen's 1798 rebellion, who fled to America from the English soldiers, leaving his unborn son behind in Ulster.

The vision must somehow have entered into the genes of succeeding generations for surely inheritance is not only in bone structure but also in an inclination towards freedom of conscience and the right to revolt against any form of improper power ... The qualities in the succeeding generations might be attributed to the momentum of the past.

(Finnegan, 1991, p.5)

Not everyone in the family may see it exactly the same way, of course: there can be competing images. But still the formulation of such symbols – different for different families or for different people within them – provides the background, the mythic sense of continuance, that can have hidden, deep effects on one's own sense of identity and experience.

Such tales do more than just express a particular sense of history and of one's place in it; they also help shape that experience. Those who enunciate and guard the traditions are thus not just passive transmitters but also in a way active creators of a family's ethos. Often a particular member of a family takes a central role, someone accepted as 'knowing everything about the family'. Stories about the past are also told by their elders to younger family members, sending their influence down the generations. There is often a special bond between grandparents and their grandchildren, an emotive channel through which traditions and identities become formulated between the generations. They result in the 'myths', which, whether or not accurate in factual terms, play a part in moulding a family's views of themselves and their experience.

Have you come across any examples of such family myths?

Such traditions are not necessarily agreed in every detail nor always expressed in textual form. They may even be the focus of dispute, symbolizing feuds among different individuals or different branches of the family. Sometimes there are joint family traditions: relations may have been separated in their youth, or gone in different directions in their adult lives. But memories in such situations may also be the more valued, or even romantically exaggerated; or new families may be created and their shared memories developed. Fragmentation or disputes may not mean an absence of shared traditions. Indeed these may surface long after the individuals thought they had shed their earlier family connections and remain a deep influence on how they experience their lives.

Traditions may not be fully conscious but still have an effect on family memories and actions. This is more controversial perhaps. But it is interesting to consider a psychiatrist's assessment of 'the power of family myths', images that recur through the generations:

> *People have told me of terrible events, tragedies and deaths, which they had not told their spouses or their children: yet nevertheless the theme behind the tragedy is re-enacted by the children ... Somehow the imagery is so powerful for the person who holds it that the rest of the family picks up that imagery and ends by re-enacting it.*
>
> (Byng-Hall, 1990, p.223)

There are further questions to explore. These concern not just what goes on *inside* a family, but also the influence of external ideas and conventions.

Myths and images current in particular epochs or in particular cultures themselves affect family and individual memories, and shape the ways they represent the past, even their own experiences. In nineteenth-century autobiographies, for example, stock themes, like the pursuit of knowledge or progress towards greater freedom, recur again and again (Vincent, 1981). Similarly, life histories among immigrants – Irish, Jews, Italians, Poles, Pakistanis – may each in one way be unique, but also commonly draw on the 'classic' tale of the upward social mobility of an ethnic minority group, so that 'the rise to fortune or success is in fact a favourite tale about immigrants by immigrants' (Werbner, 1980, p.46). Thus personal and family memories are often inspired by the familiar conventions in our culture for expressing and narrating stories about, say, courage or loss or success. Luisa Passerini (1990) illustrates this process from her recordings of Italian women imprisoned for belonging to terrorist organisations in the 1970s and 1980s. Shared images formed part of their collective experience, with only a shadowy distinction between the imaginary and the real. Their memories drew on deeply symbolic themes like

> *the legend of the hero or heroine who leaves home to help the oppressed against the oppressors ... the ideal of a small community united against the world, united beyond separation induced by exile and gaol, even beyond death; fables of the loyalty of mothers who do not abandon their defeated daughters, but are ready to give their lives for them.*
>
> (Passerini, 1990, p.54)

It is too simple to dismiss such images as 'fantasy', for they have their reality in people's lived experience. So in analysing the memories of individuals, whether or not expressed in a family context, we also have to take account of themes and narrative models current in the culture of the time.

Such themes emerge in many stories about family experiences. Ideals like 'motherhood' or the triumph of the youngest child form ready moulds within which experiences can be understood or memories formulated. So too do the motifs running through so many family tales: narratives of adventure, lost fortunes, survival from defeat or humiliation, triumphs, migrations, the odd one out, or the antics of heroes or of rogues and tricksters. The image of 'the stepmother' is another potent symbol, as Natasha Burchardt (1990) illustrates in her analysis of stepchildren's memories: 'myth weaves a thread, helping to shape the memories' (p.249).

Equally influential is the image of 'the Golden Age of the family', the story that in the past 'the family' was stable and united, held together by unstressed love and harmony. This myth, as we have seen, may have little support in literal historical fact, but that does not prevent its being a powerful influence on our self-images and life stories. How many of our spoken or written memories focus on the united family, free from conflicts or everyday annoyances? Does this wished-for ideal – or indeed the 'shocking' reminiscences from reacting against that myth – sometimes unconsciously affect our remembered experience? When we analyse family memories, our own or another's, we need to be aware that they are shaped by such images and counter-images, and not just by simple 'factual recall'.

―――――――――――――――――― **QUESTIONS FOR RESEARCH** ――――――――――――――――――

Further research on family myths, memories and ideology could be conducted at various levels, perhaps as just a passing note, perhaps an in-depth project. Which is appropriate will depend on your interests and opportunities; some families have more developed and explicit stories than others. The most obvious strategy to follow would be to study one family in depth and then put it into a wider context from comparative findings elsewhere and/or from more general discussion such as that above. Below are listed the possible stages in a relatively substantial project, following the kinds of steps discussed in Chapter 2, section 2.

1   Start from your interest in a specific family and its stories (i.e. a particular topic and the related sources).

2   Consider what specific issues you would like to pursue (stimulated perhaps by your own experience and/or from the discussion above): for example, starting from some striking pattern you have already noticed in your own family, or from asking yourself the question of whether there are any memories, stories or images that are particularly significant to some members of your family (in any sense of the term 'family'). If so, what are they, and do they fulfil any comparable roles to those discussed in this section?

3   Further identify and evaluate your sources, i.e. look at your chosen example to see what sources you could tap. These might include written sources like memoirs, letters, diaries, autobiographies from your own family, or people's memories. (If the sources are not accessible or fruitful you may need to modify your aim or turn to some other topic.)

4   Pursue these sources in more detail. A large number of memoirs and autobiographies have been written, many of which are still unpublished; others are published or recorded in collections and bibliographies such as Vincent (1981). (Further comments on autobiographies etc. are given in Volume 4.) There may be material in your own family either hidden away or already published; in fact one common start for the family historian are memoirs by an ageing family member. If such material is available, are there repeated themes or patterns that seem specially significant, and do they fit with ones you have encountered elsewhere? Even written sources need to be consulted with care, of course. Since the use of oral sources is probably less familiar, here are some suggestions:

(a)   Decide what medium you are going to use: face-to-face interview, telephone, recording, or perhaps a mixture. (See also section 4 below, and Volume 4, Chapter 7.)

(b)   Collect and organize your oral sources by asking as many members of your family as you can about:

(i)   any family story or incident they particularly remember or laugh about;

(ii)   their most significant memory as a child;

(iii)   the single thing they most value about their family;

(iv)   the single thing they would like members of the next generation to remember (and perhaps to forget) about their earlier family.

If there is someone in the family widely accepted as knowing all about the family traditions, try to include her (a common assumption is that it will be 'her', but perhaps not in your case).

You also need to reflect on these sources and their significance, for none of this is easy and your results will seldom be final. Such traditions can be emergent rather than fixed, and so become more tightly formulated partly as a result of your own or others' queries.

5   Both during and after considering these sources, reflect back on your earlier questions and see if you want to change or to develop them further. For example, you could try to relate your findings to the roles of family myths discussed earlier (e.g. encapsulating or symbolizing a sense of family identity; formulating and influencing certain values; being a focus of family dispute). Can they be related to comparable themes or genres in, say, memoirs, autobiographies, personal narratives, or to current myths, images or ideologies? How does memory seem to work, i.e. how are the traditions transmitted, formulated and distributed – or perhaps ignored! – among various family members? If there seem not to be accessible family traditions, you might try comparing other families to perhaps elucidate why and how this should be so. If you have uncovered potentially interesting material this might influence which questions you follow and perhaps lead you to further sources.

6   Relate your analysis back to any general questions you started from, to your wider reading (e.g. the earlier discussion in this section), and to any comparable or contrasting evidence you can find, e.g. from one or more families you have read about, researched yourself or drawn (with permission and acknowledgement) from the researches of colleagues. Any comparative evidence you have access to from literary sources would also be worth considering.

Whether or not you pursue research in this area, there is a more general point to notice about both memory and the use of sources, namely the relevance of this discussion not just for the analysis of family stories but for all the products of memory. This includes written documents which themselves ultimately depend on people's memories. It is not so much that memory is fallible, both over short periods and, more especially, over long time spans. This is an obvious enough point, well illustrated in the simple but telling hints in Table 4.2.

What is harder to grapple with, but even more important, is how our memories are built up through myth and images, by the conventions and ideologies around us. In a way our narrative models, drawn from the culture we live in, shape even our own first-hand experience and expression (this is well brought out in such studies as Samuel and Thompson, 1990; Abrahams, 1985; and Bornat, 1989). To understand who we are and what we have done we 'narrate our lives' following out those models.

So when we look at the products of memories, whether autobiographies, life stories, or the records of oral interviews, we should also reflect on how they have been generated and expressed. We can certainly value them as rich sources for our understanding of family and personal history, and for the experiential spheres sometimes neglected in other approaches. But we must also remember that they are not limpid empirical data, transmitted by some mechanical process.

This does not mean that research drawing on oral sources is to be dismissed. On the contrary, it is one of the recognized and growing research methods in family and community history, and consequently it is much emphasized here and in other volumes in the series. It does need to be employed critically, however, and in full awareness of the complexities of remembering: the way people's memories and experiences – not least their experience of family and community – are in part moulded by a series of existing myths, images and ideologies.

Table 4.2 Can we believe these facts from oral evidence?[1]

Place name	Yes – the most accurate item because it is the longest-lasting. Very unlikely to be wrong. Watch spelling; might be spelt as said by illiterate ancestor, or might be confused with another place name familiar to a later ancestor.	*Check:* Ordnance Survey map Census returns
Occupation	Yes – usually at least partly right. Watch: (a) ancestor having different jobs at different times in his life; (b) 'family promotions' – many farmers and master craftsmen turn out to be labourers and journeymen.	*Check:* Trade directories Census returns Parish registers St Catherine's House
Surname	Yes – few lies but many pitfalls. Watch: (a) spelling: might be spelt as said by illiterate clerk/ancestor; (b) ancestor using more than one name interchangeably: maiden and married, mother's and father's, first husband's and second husband's; (c) illegitimate ancestor might use father's, mother's or stepfather's name, or all three; (d) woman using her lover's name (common).	*Check:* Census returns Parish registers St Catherine's House *London Gazette*
First name	No – can be great confusion. Watch: (a) nicknames (very common); (b) use of middle name; (c) use of similar name that ancestor thought was same name; (d) parents giving same name to more than one child (often because earlier child died); (e) ancestor being confused with close relative (parent, sibling).	*Check:* Parish registers St Catherine's House
Date	No – least accurate fact. Never trust a date. Watch: (a) women reducing their age; (b) adding years, especially on marriage certificates; (c) wrong age on census; (d) baptism doesn't mean birth; (e) birth/marriage dates adjusted to mask pre-wedding pregnancies.	*Check:* Parish registers St Catherine's House Family bible

[1]This table was originally compiled to enable family tree researchers to check oral evidence through written sources in record offices etc., but it can also serve as a reminder of points that need checking by consulting whatever sources you have access to (including further oral sources). Such cautions apply to any source: official documentary reports too can rely in part on fallible human memory.

Source: based on Pearl (1990) p.7

4   FOLLOWING UP THROUGH ORAL INVESTIGATION

The kinds of questions raised in this chapter can be investigated through various sources, both written and unwritten. Such sources as CEBs, electoral registers or official surveys are already well exploited, so they are balanced here by some suggestions for using oral sources and interviews. These are particularly appropriate for investigating the topics listed below but could also be adapted to other questions – provided, that is, they are for relatively recent times, within the memories of living people (this can still sometimes take you back to early this century). In many cases they can be linked to information from other sources, both literary and official, and to some of the theories or patterns discussed in this chapter.

Several topics are suggested below. You could follow these up as a limited exercise with one family, or plan a more extended investigation with several families as the basis for a larger project.

_____ *QUESTIONS FOR RESEARCH* _____

Topics: consider the following questions (all related to the subject matter of this chapter):

1   The division of labour within the family: what did boys (and men) do, what did girls (and women) do? To what extent were they different, and to what extent the same? Do your findings fit with your own expectations, or with the patterns discussed in section 1 above or in such accounts as Jamieson (1987), Finch (1989) or Roberts (1993)?

2   What other roles were expected in the family? Did these vary with family life cycle or life course? How do these fit with the discussion in section 2 above?

3   Did wider kinship links play any part in family support or encouragement? If so, in what ways, and how do these relate to the discussion in section 2 above?

4   How far did the children follow in their parents' footsteps?

5   Do particular values and experiences play a role in validating the life of the particular individual (and/or of their family) or in giving it meaning? If so, are they widely shared or specific to (or controlled by?) particular individuals or branches?

6   Do traditions mentioned in (5) affect individuals' (and families') view of the past or experience of the present?

Methods: these questions can be pursued either quickly (by briefly interviewing just two or three people from one family) or much more thoroughly (involving many more people, follow-up interviews, several families). The latter will obviously be more informative if you have time, but either way you can learn something. (The former could be a pilot study for the latter.) One good method would be as follows:

1   Carry out interviews (preferably tape-recorded – see note below) with older members of one or more families. ('Old' can be interpreted according to your own circumstances, but it does not necessarily mean *very* old).

(a)   Conduct these as semi-structured interviews. That is, start by explaining to the person you are interviewing that you want to learn about their earlier life as part of your research into the family's background; allow them mostly to talk informally and more or less in the order they wish; but also ensure that, by the end, the conversation has covered basic personal information plus as much information as you can obtain about whichever topic you have chosen to pursue.

(b)   Make a second set of notes afterwards about general impressions from the conversation: for example, what did the person want to talk about (not necessarily what you wanted)? Did some topics strike an uncomfortable chord (silence can be interesting too)? What comments didn't fit your expectations, and why (this sometimes proves very valuable for further work, so don't ignore it)? Making notes on such points is not easy: doing it effectively means listening, not just 'interviewing'.

(c)   Think carefully and critically about what you are being told, bearing in mind the fallibility of human memory (see Table 4.2), the influence of hindsight, and the possible effects of the interview itself, e.g. of the expectations of both interviewer and interviewee.

2   Consider how far the family you are investigating seems to be typical or otherwise in relation to the discussion in this chapter and any other findings.

3   Consider how far your findings throw light on wider patterns or approaches, or make you change your own questions or assumptions.

4   Finally, in the light of your findings and experience, consider whether you wish to extend or query your investigations (the interviews may have given you further ideas).

Recording or not? Although you will get somewhere by just talking with people (even on the 'phone) and making written notes, one rewarding method is to make your own tape-recordings. First, you get the full flavour of the first-hand words and spoken nuances. Second, you will start building your own archive, creating, not just receiving, the primary historical sources for yourself and future scholars.

Having a structure to organize and stimulate your investigation can be helpful: see Schema C below. Part 1 provides important background information (and will also be useful for other topics later). Completing Part 2 fully may not be possible, so weigh up its importance for your topic against constraints of time, courtesy, etc. Part 3 is to be used selectively: the numbers refer to the topics suggested above. (If you want to engage in extended oral history interviews, there is a longer interview guide in Thompson, 1988, pp.296–306, and further advice in Volume 4, Chapter 7, and Bornat and Kirkup, 1993.)

Schema C: Guide for oral recording

Part 1

Name

Date and place of birth

Parents' names (including mother's maiden name)

Siblings' name(s)

Spouse's name (including maiden name)

Date and place of marriage

Children's names (including date and place of birth)

Part 2 (include dates and places where possible)

Occupation(s) (both paid and unpaid) – own

Occupation(s) (both paid and unpaid) – spouse, children

Place(s) of residence

Education – own, spouse, children

Membership of clubs or organizations

Leisure activities

Religion (if applicable)

Part 3 (numbers relate to the research topics listed above)

(1), (2): Who did what in the family as they grew up? Memories of assumptions or encouragement within the family about education, likely future jobs and aspirations. Occupations of other members of the family. Memories of unpaid work within the family (both growing up and in own later family) and how this did or did not contribute to the family economy.

(2), (3): Did relations outside the immediate family give any help to yourself (or others), for example when travelling, in jobs, in education, when ill, etc? Did relations other than members of the immediate family live in the household? If so, when and why? What happened to infirm, ill or distressed members of the wider family and who took responsibility?

(4): What were the children's occupations, religion, education and/or values compared to those of their parents? Did they leave their home areas for education, jobs, marriage, etc.?

(5), (6): Particular values or traditions emphasized by the individual or their family. Memories of family stories told them as children, and by whom. Family stories or traditions told by themselves or their children.

This chapter has highlighted the many resources that families draw on: economic, social and cultural; and both internal and external. The focus has been on experiences and processes, rather than fixed structures or snapshots at a single time, and on the varied strategies by which families and individuals exploit these resources. But one could not do better than to conclude with Hareven's plea for ultimately integrating the differing approaches to family history:

> It is important to link the new dimensions of the family's private and inner life that emanate from the 'new cultural history' with the demographic patterns of household structure and kinship and economic activity reconstructed over the past two decades and a half. One would then be able to interpret the family's inner life in the past in a rich social-structural context.
>
> (Hareven, 1991, p.123)

REFERENCES AND FURTHER READING

Note: suggestions for further reading are indicated by an asterisk.

Abrahams, R.D. (1985) 'Our native notions of story', *New York Folklore,* 11, pp.37–47.

Abrams, M. (1978) *Beyond three score years and ten: a first report on a survey of the elderly,* London, Age Concern.

Anderson, M. (1980) *Approaches to the history of the western family 1500–1914,* Basingstoke, Macmillan Educational. See especially Chapter 4.*

Anderson, M. (1983) 'What is new about the modern family?', Occasional Paper 31, *The family,* London, OPCS, pp.2–16. Reprinted in Drake (1994).*

Bigger, D. and McDonald, T. (1990) *In sunshine or in shadow: photographs from the Derry Standard 1928–1939,* Belfast, Friar's Bush Press.

Bornat, J. (1989) 'Oral history as a social movement: reminiscence and older people', *Oral History,* 17, pp.16–24.

Bornat, J. and Kirkup, G. (1993) 'Oral history interviews', audio-cassette 1B in Braham, P. (ed.) *Using the past: audio-cassettes on sources and methods for family and community historians,* Milton Keynes, The Open University.

Burchardt, N. (1990) 'Stepchildren's memories: myth, understanding, and forgiveness', in Samuel and Thompson (1990).

Byng-Hall, J. (1990) 'The power of family myths', in Samuel and Thompson (1990).

Collins, B. (1982) 'Proto-industrialization and pre-famine emigration', *Social History*, 7, 2, pp.127–46.

Davidoff, L. (1990) 'The family in Britain', in Thompson, F.M.L. (ed.) *Cambridge social history of Britain,* vol.2, Cambridge, Cambridge University Press.*

Davin, A. (1990) 'When is a child not a child?', in Corr, H. and Jamieson, L. (eds) *Politics of everyday life,* Basingstoke, Macmillan.

Drake, M. (ed.) (1994) *Time, family and community: perspectives on family and community history,* Oxford, Blackwell in association with The Open University (Course Reader).

Elliott, B. (1990) 'Biography, family history and the analysis of social change', in Kendrick, S. *et al.* (eds) *Interpreting the past, understanding the present,* Basingstoke, Macmillan. Reprinted in Drake (1994).

Finch, J. (1989) *Family obligations and social change,* Cambridge, Polity Press. Extract reprinted as 'Do families support each other more or less than in the past?', in Drake (1994).*

Finnegan, A. (1991) *Reaching for the fruit: growing up in Ulster,* Birmingham, Callender Press.

Finnegan, R. (1985) 'Working outside formal employment', in Deem, R. and Salaman, G. (eds) *Work, culture and society,* Milton Keynes, Open University Press.

Goody, E.N. and Groothues, C.M. (1977) 'The West Africans: the quest for education', in Watson, J.L. (ed.) *Between two cultures: migrants and minorities in Britain,* Oxford, Blackwell.

Hair, P.E.H. (1982) 'Children in society 1850-1980', in Barker, T. and Drake, M. (eds) *Population and society in Britain 1850-1980,* London, Batsford.

Hareven, T.K. (1991) 'The history of the family and the complexity of social change', *American Historical Review,* 96, 1, pp.95–124. Reprinted in an abridged form as 'Recent historical research on the family' in Drake (1994).*

Holley, J.C. (1981) 'The two family economies of industrialism: factory workers in Victorian Scotland', *Journal of Family History,* 6, 1, pp.57–69.

Howes, D. (1984) 'Residential mobility and family separation in retirement', Occasional Paper 22, Kings College London, Department of Geography.

Hudson, P. and Lee, W.R. (eds) (1990) *Women's work and the family: economy in historical perspective,* Manchester, Manchester University Press.

Jamieson, L. (1987) 'Theories of family development and the experience of being brought up', *Sociology* 21, pp.591–607. Reprinted in Drake (1994).*

Kiernan, K. (1988) 'The British family: contemporary trends and issues', *Journal of Family Issues,* 9, 3, pp.298–316.

Levine, D. (1987) *Reproducing families: the political economy of English population history,* Cambridge, Cambridge University Press.

Pahl, J. (1989) *Money and marriage,* Basingstoke, Macmillan.

Pahl, J. (1990) 'Household spending, personal spending and the control of money in marriage', *Sociology*, 24, pp.119–38.

Pahl, R. (1984) *Divisions of labour*, Oxford, Blackwell. See especially Chapters 2–4.[*]

Passerini, L. (1990) 'Mythobiography in oral history', in Samuel and Thompson (1990).

Pearl, S. (1990) 'Fact from fiction', *Family Tree Magazine*, August, p.7.

Pennington, S. and Westover, B. (1989) *A hidden workforce: homeworkers in England 1850–1985*, Basingstoke, Macmillan Education.

Roberts, E. (1984) *A woman's place: an oral history of working class women 1890–1940*, Oxford, Blackwell.

Roberts, E. (1993) 'Women and the domestic economy 1940–1970: the oral evidence', in Drake (1994).[*]

Rogers, P. (ed.) (1971) *Daniel Defoe, a tour through the whole island of Great Britain*, abridged, Harmondsworth, Penguin (first published in 1724–6).

Rosser, C. and Harris, C. (1965) *The family and social change: a study of family and kinship in a South Wales town*, London, Routledge & Kegan Paul.

Samuel, R. and Thompson, P. (1990) (eds) *The myths we live by*, London, Routledge.[*]

Thompson, P. (1988) *The voice of the past: oral history*, Oxford, Oxford University Press, 2nd edition.

Tilly, L.A., and Scott, J.W. (1978) *Women, work and family*, New York, Holt, Rinehart & Winston.

Townsend, P. (1957) *The family life of old people: an inquiry in East London*, London, Routledge & Kegan Paul.

Vincent, D. (1981) *Bread, knowledge and freedom: a study of nineteenth-century working-class autobiography*, London, Europa Publications.

Wall, R. (1986) 'Work, welfare and the family: an illustration of the adaptive family economy', in Bonfield, L., Scott, R.M. and Wrightson, K. (eds) *The world we have gained: histories of population and social structure*, Oxford, Blackwell.

Wall, R. (1992) 'Relationships between the generations in British families past and present' in Marsh, C. and Arber, S. (eds) *Families and households: divisions and change*, Basingstoke, Macmillan.

Wallman, S. (1984) *Eight London households*, London, Tavistock.

Warnes, A.M. (1986) 'The residential mobility histories of parents and children, and relationships to present proximity and social integration', *Environment and Planning*, 18, pp.1581–94.

Werbner, P. (1980) 'Rich man poor man – or a community of suffering: heroic motifs in Manchester Pakistani life histories', *Oral History*, 8, 1, pp.43–51.

Young, M. and Willmott, P. (1973) *The symmetrical family*, Harmondsworth, Penguin.

Zeitlin, S.J., Kotkin, A.J. and Baker, H.C. (eds) (1982) *A celebration of American family folklore*, New York, Pantheon Books for Smithsonian Institution.

PART III

AN ILLUSTRATION

✢ ✢ ✢

CHAPTER 5

HOW FAMILIES LIVED THEN: KATHARINE BUILDINGS, EAST SMITHFIELD, 1885–1890

by Rosemary O'Day

Where did your family live? How did your family live? You are perhaps fortunate enough to possess family papers, a diary, an autobiography or correspondence which can help you to answer such questions. More probably, you have few source materials of this kind yet still want to discover the answer to the questions. What can you do? One way is to discover where and how similar families lived in the past. In looking at this we might also move a step nearer towards defining what a 'family' was and what constituted 'family life' for people in a different time and a different milieu from our own.

Ideas about the nature of the family, either as an ideal or as an actuality, vary according to geography, time, income and class. The Victorian middle class had very definite ideas about the ideal family and the desirability of imposing such an ideal upon the whole of society. They also experimented with ways of making the family conform to this ideal. They had views on environmental determinism and its importance. In this study of Katharine Buildings we shall be examining not only the form of the family and family life in a late Victorian block of model dwellings in London, but also the attempted intervention by representatives of the Victorian middle class in that life.

As you read this case study you may be considering its relevance to your own possible investigations, but even if you have no interest in an individual project on this or a related topic, you should still profit from this study since it is designed to be used on several levels.

1   It is a self-sufficient case study of a particular block of flats at a given time. I have identified important historical issues about the history of the family and sought to resolve them. I hope that you will find the chapter illuminating at that level.

2   It is a very special case study, since it is made possible by the survival of rich and diverse sources (some still in manuscript, some published). These include: a large ledger of the inhabitants of Katharine Buildings for the years 1885–1890 (see Figure 5.5); photographs, maps and plans (Figures 5.3 and 5.4); correspondence between two of the visitors/rent collectors (Figure 5.6); a diary of one of the rent collectors; autobiographical material from two of the rent collectors; the evidence of the census of 1891; and information collected by the social reformer and investigator, Charles Booth in the period 1886–1903 (Booth 1902–3; see also O'Day and Englander, 1993). Working through the chapter will give you further experience of the problems and opportunities of making use of such sources. This will be helpful for your own projects,

whatever the detailed topic or sources. (You may reach the conclusion that the sources were inappropriately used in this case study; if so, note down these criticisms as clearly as you can – this too helps to build up your critical skills.)

3   It is rare for such a variety of excellent sources to survive for one block of dwellings. I am not suggesting you could replicate this study, but there are enormous opportunities for similar research in many areas of the country. This study is of flat dwelling, but I hope you will see that you could transfer the skills you have learned in this context to other subjects. Some suggestions will be made following section 3.2 both about issues that could profitably be pursued further and the sources available for such research.

4   While this case study is based on original historical research, both you and I will need to discuss our findings in the light of what other scholars have discovered or asserted about the same subjects and issues (see especially section 3). This interaction between investigating the primary sources and reading the work of professional historians is very important (see step 1 in Schema A of Chapter 2). Through it, your own case study can help to advance the state of knowledge about this important subject.

1   KATHARINE BUILDINGS, CARTWRIGHT STREET, EAST SMITHFIELD

The immediate context of this case study is important. We need to locate Katharine Buildings within the wider community of the East End and then to discuss the circumstances surrounding the construction of the Buildings.

EXERCISE 5.1

Look at the map shown in Figure 5.1 and locate the following: the River Thames; the Tower of London; the Royal Mint; Katharine Buildings; St Katharine's Dock; Toynbee Hall; Whitechapel High Street; Brick Lane; Commercial Street; Flower & Dean Street. (Note: the line of many roads and streets was changed in the nineteenth century and has been changed frequently since; the same street name could be retained for a street following a new route.)

Katharine Buildings, located in Cartwright Street in an area known as the Minories, near the Royal Mint in the East End of London, was erected in 1884–5 to rehouse East End dwellers displaced by slum clearance. Legislation in 1875 (the Artizans' and Labourers' Dwellings Improvement Act) made detailed provision for the clearance of slums and the sale of the vacated land to private companies to build suitable housing for the inhabitants according to a plan approved by the local authorities. High densities were imposed on the building organizations even before they purchased the land: it was a provision of the Act that as many inhabitants had to be rehoused as had lived on the land previously. As these had been areas of severe overcrowding (with between eight and forty people living in one small room), such a ruling inevitably created problems. This stringent requirement was relaxed somewhat in 1879, but densities remained high.

The 1875 legislation was accompanied by a revival of middle-class interest in housing problems; a number of new private organizations were founded and the interest of established organizations was rekindled. Within the Whitechapel and Limehouse area the chief property buyers were the Peabody Trust, the Improved Industrial Dwellings Company, the East End Dwellings Company, and the Rothschild family. The redevelopment of the land was partly

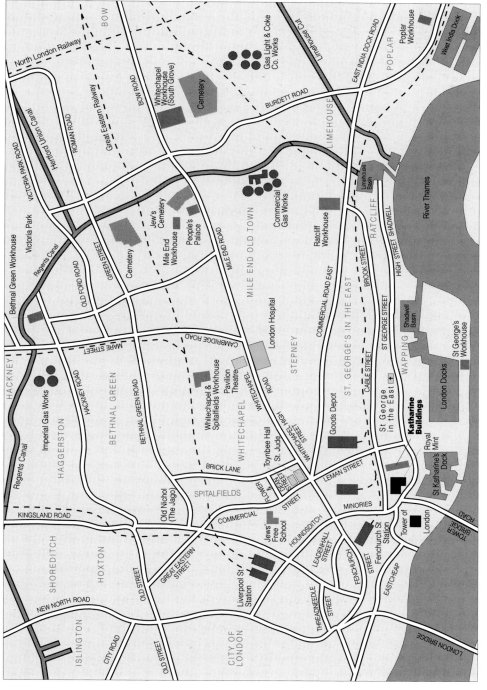

Figure 5.1   Map of the East End of London showing the location of Katharine Buildings (Source: based on Fishman, 1988)

planned by the Metropolitan Board, who did substantial street work before putting the land up for sale. Cartwright Street and Glasshouse Street were reconstructed and extended, while the long narrow site between Cartwright Street and the Mint was purchased for the recently formed East End Dwellings Company by Edward Bond, one of the company's original directors. The shape of the site determined that the building had to be a long narrow one; the terms of the act that it had to have several floors. The architects responsible for the development were Davis & Emmanuel.

There was a good deal of new building designed to rehouse the working poor in Victorian England and Wales, but it did not follow a pattern. Most such housing was private and, in consequence, diverse. Moreover, the term 'working poor' covers an enormous range of occupational and income groups which demanded different types and values of accommodation. I think that housing plans had an impact on how life was conducted within the family and within the neighbourhood, but we should not be trapped into treating Katharine Buildings as 'typical'. There were other types of housing for the poor within London, and other cities possessed their own distinctive forms of housing for the working and lower middle classes. Size of apartments (both in terms of floor space and number of rooms), the physical arrangement, individual amenities, access, and communal facilities did all vary, and this may or may not have had profound effects for the family and community lives of the inhabitants. In part, these idiosyncrasies may have reflected pre-existing local conditions and traditions as much as the ideas of housing reformers and the profit motives of building speculators.

1.1   THE BACKGROUND AND DESIGN OF KATHARINE BUILDINGS

Katharine Buildings belongs to the world of '5 per cent philanthropy' and not to that of speculative building. Five per cent philanthropy was the concept that private companies could redevelop property in the form of affordable and sanitary housing for the working classes, and manage it to yield a reasonable profit and pay a 5 per cent dividend to investors (see Tarn, 1974). Thus individuals could help alleviate the problem of working-class housing and make a personal profit.

We can trace the process with respect to Katharine Buildings. On 1 November 1882 Samuel Barnett, vicar of St Jude's, Whitechapel, chaired a meeting at the vicarage to form a company to provide housing for the poor in that part of London; in February 1884 the East End Dwellings Company materialized. Its prospectus read:

> The main endeavour of the company will be to provide for the poorest class of self-supporting labourers dwelling accommodation at the very cheapest rates compatible with realising a fair rate of interest upon the capital employed. Hitherto little or nothing of this kind has been done on a large scale, the buildings of the existing Companies and Associations being chiefly occupied by a class of industrial tenants more prosperous than those for whom this Company proposes to provide.
>
> (East End Dwellings Co. prospectus, 1884)

This housing, then, was not for the members of the 'residuum', the so-called 'low-lives', but neither was it for the relatively secure working class – the artisans and clerks in permanent employ (Charles Booth's classes E and F; see Booth, 1902–3). The design of Katharine Buildings involved new building rather than renovation, but otherwise closely resembled the influential views of Octavia Hill (1838–1912) as expressed to parliamentary committees:

> [For the moment the organizations should] be satisfied to build clean, light, dry rooms above ground; and instead of building them in suites, build them, as it is very easy to do, opening from a

Figure 5.2   Canon Samuel Augustus Barnett (1844–1913),
vicar of St Jude's, Whitechapel, who took a leading role in the
development of the East End Dwellings Company. He also
founded Toynbee Hall in 1884, the first university settlement,
in memory of Arnold Toynbee, where young men fresh from
university lived and worked in close contact with their East
End neighbours

*little lobby from which four rooms enter, instead of making any of them passage rooms; and they
can let either one, two, three or four rooms, as the people require; and whenever the standard of
working people is raised higher they can take more rooms.*

(Report of the Select Committee on Artizans' and Labourers' Dwellings Improvement,
1882, Q3002)

and

*I think a great deal more simplicity is needed in the construction of the houses. It seems to
me that where you remove the very lowest class of dwelling, and wish to reaccommodate the
same people, you must adopt the very simplest manner of building ... They should build what is
really wanted, and what is essential to health ... Primarily, I should not carry the water and the
drains all over the place; I think that is ridiculous. If you have water on every floor, that is quite
sufficient for working people. It is no hardship to have to carry a pail of water along a flat surface.
You would not dream of altering the water supply in a tiny little house now, and yet people carry
their water up three or four floors there. You would not dream of legislating to prevent that, surely
...?*

(First Report of the Commissioners on the Housing of the Working Classes, 1885,
Q8833, 8852)

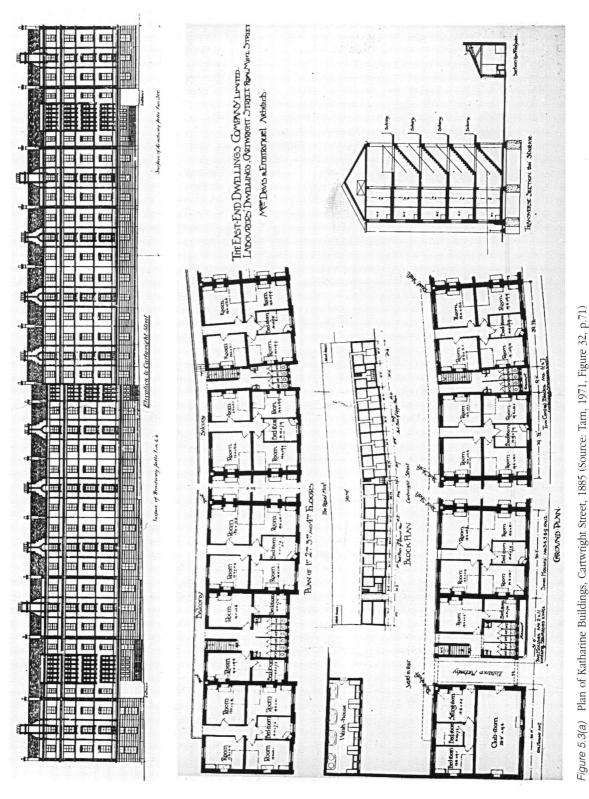

Figure 5.3(a)   Plan of Katharine Buildings, Cartwright Street, 1885 (Source: Tarn, 1971, Figure 32, p.71)

Look at the plan in Figures 5.3(a) and (b). Try to describe the layout of Katharine Buildings in a few sentences.

_____

By examining an architect's plan one can deduce a good deal about the accommodation offered. Of course, modifications may have been made to the design later.

This is what I came up with. The long, narrow building had five floors. There were 18 double rooms. Apparently each double room consisted of a main living room with an adjoining, linked small bedroom. These double suites had the dubious privilege of a location next to the communal WCs and the equally communal staircase. The remaining 245 rooms were in nests of five single rooms (four 'large' and one 'small') which were not interlinked. The dimensions of the rooms are not fully legible, but their comparative proportions are apparent. Each of these rooms opened independently on to a passage leading into the yard in the case of the ground floor, and on to a long balcony on the other four storeys. A suite of three linked rooms for the caretaker and a fairly large, purpose-built club room was set at the south side of the southern entrance to the building. Access to the upper floors was by open staircases from the rear yard where there were dustbins and laundry facilities.

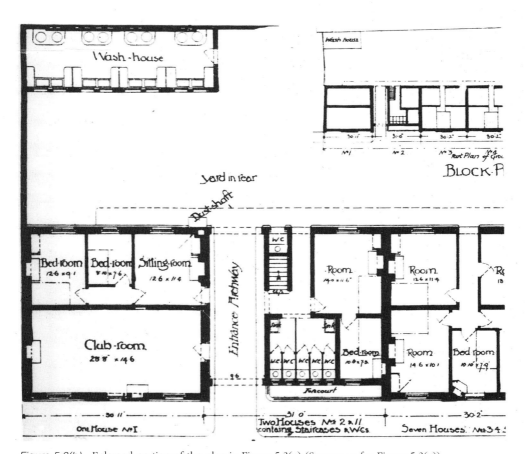

Figure 5.3(b)   Enlarged portion of the plan in Figure 5.3(a) (Source: as for Figure 5.3(a))

This is how Beatrice Webb (née Beatrice Potter) retrospectively described the Buildings in her autobiography in 1926:

> *A long double-faced building in five tiers, on one side overlooking a street; on the other, looking on to a narrow yard hemmed in by a high blank brick wall forming the back of the premises of the Royal Mint. Right along the whole length of the building confronting the blank wall ran four open galleries, out of which led narrow passages, each passage to five rooms, identical in size and shape, except that the one at the end of the passage was much smaller than the others. All the rooms were 'decorated' in the same dull, dead-red distemper, unpleasantly reminiscent of a butcher's shop. Within these uniform, cell-like apartments there were no labour saving appliances, not even a sink and water-tap! Three narrow stone stair cases led from the yard to the topmost gallery; on the landings between the galleries and the stairs were sinks and taps (three sinks and six taps to about sixty rooms); behind a tall wooden screen were placed sets of six closets on the trough system, sluiced every three hours; and these were allotted to the inhabitants of the rooms on either side of them; in the yard below were the dustbins …*

(Webb, 1971, p.269)

We can gain a further impression from the photograph, reproduced as Figure 5.4, which shows the rear of the Buildings.

Why do you think a physical description of the Buildings is important?

First, the design, layout and amenities circumscribed the life of a family in each of these 'apartments'. For instance, if a family had young children, where would they sleep, live, play? Second, the type of accommodation might suggest the clientele for which it was catering.

1.2   REHOUSING THE POOR: RESHAPING THE POOR THROUGH INDIVIDUAL WORK

Octavia Hill wanted to provide a basic standard of housing for the working classes, but from there on her chief concern was detailed individual work with the inhabitants in order to change their habits, reform their behaviour and form their character. (To do her justice, she urged that landlords had responsibilities too: giving tenants security of tenure as long as the rent was paid and keeping their properties in good repair.) Her belief was that 'the improvement of people and dwellings must go hand in hand'.

How would this improvement of the working people take place? On behalf of the landlord, 'lady' managers (they were almost invariably women and middle class) would keep accurate rent books and accounts, keep the building in good repair and sanitary condition, make sure the property paid its way, and provide communal facilities. They would, in so doing, make landlords responsible. But the tenants would also be educated into responsibility. They would pay their rent punctually, which would mean learning to budget and to save. Individual work with the families inhabiting the houses or multi-occupied buildings would take place on the occasion of weekly rent collection – friendships would emerge out of the business relationship. Thrift, sobriety and domestic skills would be inculcated to help the poor be responsible and remain self-supporting. The poor, Hill believed, were destructive by nature but with careful supervision could be trained, provided that such training took place within a context of courtesy, understanding and mutual trust. Monetary doles, however, would play no part.

When the rehousing of the poor in blocks of dwellings was projected in 1883, Canon Barnett wrote that he would 'if possible carry out the plan of having lady rent collectors'. Already within his parish a number of ladies, including the Potter sisters Katherine, Teresa and Beatrice,

Figure 5.4   Rear view of Katharine Buildings (Source: Tarn, 1971, Figure 34, p.72)

collected rents from small houses obtained by one of Octavia Hill's friends. The lady rent collectors for Katharine Buildings were not working for Octavia Hill, but their endeavours were inspired by her vision and the commitment to it by the East End Dwellings Company. The lady manager of the Buildings was directly responsible to that company's board of directors. She was unpaid, and assisted by as many or as few lady helpers as she could recruit. There was a full-time resident caretaker.

Although it has been claimed that Katharine Buildings were named after Kate Potter Courtney and that she was their first lady manager, there is virtually no evidence of her involvement. In practice it was Kate's sister, Beatrice Potter, who shared the early manage-ment of the buildings with Ella Pycroft. This is clear from Beatrice Potter's diary (note: all references to the diary are from the Passfield Papers: Holograph Diary of Beatrice Pot-ter/Webb). In January 1885, after the stoves suggested by the architects proved a failure, she was looking over the fittings for the rooms with Edward Bond. In March 1885 she was trudging through Whitechapel after 'applicants and references'. In January, Ella Pycroft spent three days with the Potter household discussing the task. 'We shall get on', commented Beatrice, 'and we are anxious to have no other workers on the block.' Beatrice, even then, noted Ella's 'decided business capacity, strong will and placid temper'. By March Beatrice, who recognized her own lack of business acumen, had already determined 'in future, when other workers are found, and when once I am fairly started in the practical work', to 'undertake less of the management, and use the work more as an opportunity for obser-vation'.

The principles upon which the Buildings were run and tenants chosen are of immense importance to our study. It was never, and never intended to be, simply a matter of filling the building with tenants and collecting their rents. Beatrice's diary shows that she was fully aware of the responsibilities of the work, exhausted and often depressed:

> *When I look at those long balconies, and think of all the queer characters, tenants and would be tenants, and realize that the character of the community will depend upon our personal influence, and that again, not only on character but on persistent health, I feel rather dizzy.*
>
> (diary, 15 March 1885)

Beatrice's task was to reform the family lives of the working poor within Katharine Buildings; she and Ella were attempting to stamp a new character on the Buildings. In early June 1885 Beatrice pondered the best course of action. The tenants, she perceived, were 'a rough lot – the aborigines of the East End'; disorder in the Buildings and the problems of rent collection made for pressure to take in only the respectable.

Others had dodged the problems of remoulding the family lives of the working poor. An interview with the Superintendent of Peabody's Buildings elicited the following opinion: 'We had a rough lot to begin with, had to weed them of the old inhabitants: now only take men with regular employment'. Following such a policy would mean Beatrice going back entirely on Canon Barnett's principles of directing this housing specifically at the poorest classes of self-supporting labourers. She reflected, 'are the tenants to be picked, and all doubtful or inconvenient persons excluded? or are the former inhabitants to be housed so long as they are not manifestly disreputable?' She did not know the answer and felt mithered by the problems involved. Like Ella Pycroft, she visited lady rent collectors with more experience – for example, Emma Cons at Surrey Buildings, South London – specifically in order to pick their brains.

On 13 August 1885 Beatrice took over the management of Katharine Buildings from Ella Pycroft for a period of six weeks. She approached her task like a new broom:

> *Took over the whole work from Miss Pycroft. Aim during her absence – collecting and accounting, thoroughly and methodically. Arrears diminished; rooms let; first-rate broker engaged; caretaker's work observed; amount of repairs done by him estimated. Morality enforced on buildings. Advantages of clear account of my own tenants written, and general knowledge of Miss Pycroft's. Boys' Club started; notes on reading room taken. To do this must live a great deal on the buildings, but not take rents on all days.*
>
> (diary, 13 August 1885)

These were her aims. On 22 August she assessed how far she had achieved them: 'As to ideal of work: collecting well done; accounts not yet done; arrears diminished and a few rooms let'.

Beatrice was especially critical of the failure of lady visitors (rent collectors) to keep accurate and full records of their work. Emma Cons, for example, 'kept all particulars as to families in her head' (diary, 12 August 1885).

It is very important to describe your sources, to determine their provenance and original purpose, before attempting to 'use' them. In the light of this, why do you think Beatrice considered it important to keep records?

My answer to this question is as follows:

1   It would be difficult for others to continue the work if all the information regarding the past history of tenancies was in one person's head.

2   It would be difficult, even impossible, to measure the success or failure of individual work with particular families without good records.

3 Beatrice, a good friend and disciple of the philosopher Herbert Spencer, believed one should observe people minutely just as the botanist observed flowers and the zoologist animals. Another Victorian philanthropist, C.S. Loch of the Charity Organization Society (COS), wrote in his diary: 'To be a naturalist in social matters is right. Then one should keep a naturalist's notebook'.

Beatrice Potter, Ella Pycroft and Maurice Paul: The United Working Firm of Philanthropic Visitors

Beatrice Potter (1858–1943)
Fabian socialist, famous English diarist and autobiographer. Born into an affluent and large family. Engaged between 1883 and 1885 in Charity Organization Society work and other philanthropic activity. From 1886 to late 1888 Beatrice was an associate of Charles Booth in his inquiry into the life and labour of the people in London (published 1902–3). In 1892 she married Sidney Webb, with whom she was jointly responsible for notable studies of the trades union movement and founding the London School of Economics and Political Science.

Photograph: 1891

Ella Pycroft (known to have lived 1865–1926)
Daughter of a Devonshire physician. Manager and rent collector of Katharine Buildings from 1883 until May 1890, also manager of Lolesworth Buildings, Commercial Street (built by the same company). Left housing management and philanthropy following the break-up of her relationship with Maurice Eden Paul. Trained for a year at the Cambridge Training College for Teachers since she was unable as a 'free thinker' to gain admission to train as a nurse. In 1893 appointed Chief Organizer of Domestic Economy Subjects for the Technical Education Board of the London County Council, where she remained until retirement in 1904

Maurice Eden Paul (known to have lived 1865–1926)
Well-known translator of foreign works and member of the Left of the International Socialist Movement. In 1886 a medical student at one of the London teaching hospitals (probably the London Hospital). Possibly Toynbee Hall student lodger before he moved into a model dwelling. Precise nature of his philanthropic work at Katharine Buildings uncertain, but he is known to have founded the reading room and run the boys' club with Ella Pycroft. Certainly engaged in detailed individual work with tenants. In 1886 also one of Charles Booth's associates.

1.3   NATURALISTS IN SOCIAL MATTERS

During August 1885 Beatrice became increasingly convinced of the importance of 'observation work' and she made plans: 'If I get the facts during the next four weeks, can write up the stories of East End lives later on' (diary, 22 August 1885). When, in September, the books were returned to Ella Pycroft and Beatrice settled back into her role as lady helper on the Buildings, uppermost in her mind was this work: 'Wish to get a complete account of the tenants of Katharine Buildings: must think out facts I want to ascertain about each family and go straight at it. Will be obliged to go more deeply into practical work in order to get opportunities of observation' (diary, 23 October 1885). On 8 November she wrote, 'I have only done my bare duty at Katharine Buildings. I have begun a careful account of tenants. Oh for more energy!'

The result was the ledger of the inhabitants of Katharine Buildings, 1885 to 1889, which has incidentally provided us with data about the tenants themselves for this study. The large ledger contains approximately 320 pages. In most cases, each page represents the history of the tenancies of one room in the Buildings between 1885 and 1890 (see Figure 5.5). There are approximately 750 separate 'household' histories in the book. The handwriting presents few problems in terms of legibility, but rather more in terms of attribution, with many entries being definitely in Beatrice Potter's hand but many more details noted either by Ella Pycroft or less certainly by Beatrice.

_____ **EXERCISE 5.3** _____

Read the extract from the ledger in Figure 5.5 and the extracts transcribed below and note down what questions you think Beatrice Potter was asking about her tenants when she wrote these case histories; in other words, try to deduce, from the categories of information given, what questions she was asking.

Transcription of extracts from the ledger

Tenants December 1885
ground floor
Room 1

double 5/6

Henry **Hofmann**
Came March 23 1885
Left August 24 Bootfinishing at home. Wife ditto
Elder girl works with parents. John b. 1873 August b. 1876
Had lived previously in St George's Buildings under Miss Howell. Returned there. Made great complaints of noise & roughness in the yard & by latrines. Left room in dirty state. Paid rent regularly.
Germans: 20 or 30 years in England

Henry **Auckland**
Removed from no.42
October 5 1885
October 11 1886
In no 2 till Nov. 8th
Commercial traveller at Samuel Tull & co Fenchurch Str very delicate in regular work, violent when in drink.
Jean **Lazarrade** Brother in law, french, cork maker. Henry Aukland pays 3/6 of rent, frenchman 2/-. Find their food separately. Frenchman says he earns some weeks

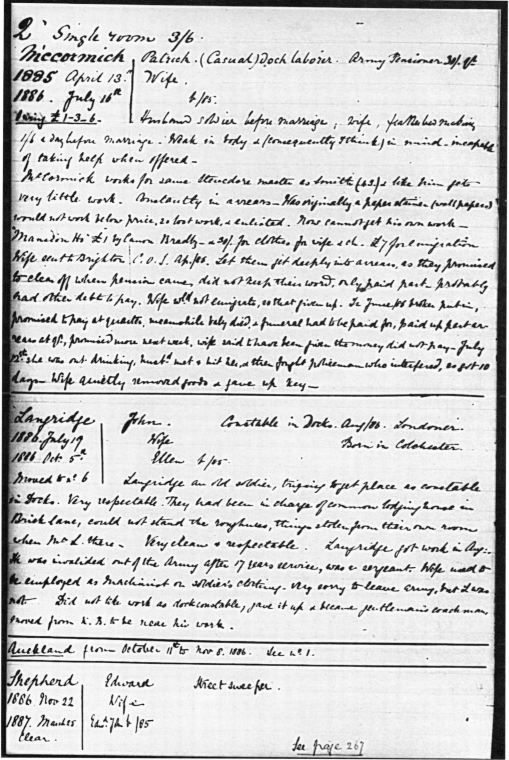

Figure 5.5   An extract from the ledger of the inhabitants of Katharine Buildings (Source: British Library of Political and Economic Science, Coll. Misc. 43)

only 6/- on account of bad legs. Could earn 1.10.0. Began life by marrying widow with money in Champagne: employed 20 workmen in cork making. Lost his money in Revolution '48 migrated to Paris. Preferred being "ouvrier" in London to Paris. Came here 27 years ago: stayed 5 years in New York where he again lost money. His passage back paid by Oddfellows to wch he belonged. Has forfeited membership. In July 1886 sent to French Hosp. by COS [Charity Organization Society]. legs so bad that hardly able to crawl about room. Paralysed — Auckland ill-treated him. Auckland moved to no.2. But having had a bad row with Shearer 146 (who was said to owe him money) the Donovans &c. he was turned out, very abusive at last

Taken as Boys Club Nov 1 1886
to Apr 18 1887

William **Hawley**
April 25 1887
Carman See 54
Wife does office cleaning

| Amelia b.70 away from home | Louisa b.75 | Edward b.79 | John b.84 |
| Margaret b.72 away from home | William b.77 | Harriet b.81 | Dorothy b.88 |

Hawley was ill in autumn/88 – in recovering got little work, & family were almost entirely supported by wife & one daughter who does bead work & looks after the children

[Details for Room 2 shown in Figure 5.5]

[Room] 3
Let with no. 4 & no. 5 at 8/6
> W.D. **Dartford**
> Febry 2nd 1885
> Ap^l 16 1885
> Clear
> Carpenter (permanent) Messr Hoare "Oddfellow"
> Wife mangle on premises
> William (permanent) engraver b.1866
> Emma helps mother — half paralysed b.1869
> Henry   1872   Aldgate School (free with clothing)
> Walter   1874   "   "
> Arthur   1879   "   "
> Henry left Aldgate School July 1889 & is now errand boy with father

Emma sent to the Convalescent Home at St Leonards in September 188[?] She was unhappy there & complained at insufficient food — They left to take three rooms in Royal Mews Square

Taken w^t n° 4
> Ann **Wobey**
> Ap^l 23 1889
> July 9 1889
> Clear
> Mother of Roadnight, the caretaker. Twice married.
> Washerwoman & mangler. Had been living W[est] end.

Found she w^{ld} lose some of W.end work by living here & so returned. For a time was in n° 5 only. Her son bought the mangle for her

Mary **Boylan**

> July 16 1889
>
> See 229 Mangle woman
>
> Has a child to live w^t her (… Blake), & also sees after the boys Blake. 244

[Room] 4

Let with n° 3 & 5 till April /88. Then for a few weeks wt [illegible]

> **Wobey** Ann
>
> 1888 July 9th to 31st
>
> See 3 Stayed on in one room a few weeks. Left clear

Tomlin Ann

> Aug. 6 1888
>
> Nov.19 1888
>
> Owing 4/-
>
> Widow. Had mother living in Royal Albert Bldgs, after a while she said as her mother was ill she must sleep there, & asked if her son & his wife might for a few weeks keep the room — I agreed, but had to turn them out from complaints of their misbehaviour

---

Dee Timothy

> 1888 Nov.19
>
> Young man, blind, earns money by playing concertina — Goes out with the Stapletons, his sister sometimes comes to do his room, oftener Mrs S. Catholic; educated at the L'pool Cath. Sch. for blind. Learnt brush making there, says he can't get enough work to live by it, but thinks 14/- a week too little. Miss Grogan took up the case in Ap^l 89

[Room] 5

Let with no 3 & 4

> Taken on Dartford's leaving by Pack n° 20 See page 20

William **Pearce**

> Sep 3 1888
>
> Feb 25 1889
>
> Clear
>
> Man living alone. Left because a woman with whom he had been, found him out & would not let him alone

---

John **Crawley**

> Ap^l 1 1889
>
> June 24 "
>
> Clear
>
> Foreman at Docks. Widower
>
> Kate b.73
>
> Man brought woman home one night, they turned Kate out & there was a great scene in yard — Next day Kate left. The woman came again in daylight & was turned out by the Roadnights. I gave Crawley notice & he left after a week. Crawley born in Ireland

Source: British Library of Political and Economic Science, Coll. Misc. 43

Here is a list of the 'facts' that Beatrice Potter, writing in November 1885, wanted to record about each family. How many coincide with the suggestions you made? Did you suggest any others?

1 Number of family: alive, dead.

2 Occupation of each member: permanent, casual.

3 Income: from work, charity, savings.

4 Race: English born? foreign?

5 London born? London stock?

6 Reason for immigration.

7 Previous residence in neighbourhood.

8 On site of Katharine Buildings?

9 Religion.

10 Attendance at place of worship.

11 Previous history and present characteristics.

12 Cause of leaving or ejectment.

You may have included surname, first name, room number, floor number, names and dates of birth of children, the date of entry and the date of leaving the room. Sometimes there is detailed information about the sources of income, for instance the paid work of wife and children as well as that of the male household head.

I have included this exercise because it is unusual for the historian or social scientist to be handed on a plate a list of categories of this kind. If you undertake a similar study, in all probability you will have to deduce the questions asked or the categories of information identified. Moreover, as you can see, the information actually recorded may not tally precisely with the categories listed.

2 THE INHABITANTS OF KATHARINE BUILDINGS, 1885–1889

At this point let us turn to the Buildings themselves and their occupants as recorded in the ledger.

2.1 THE COMPOSITION OF THE TENANTRY

Let me remind you of the nature of the accommodation: 18 double rooms for rent, 196 large single rooms and 49 small single rooms, erected to re-house local people affected by slum clearance. It is possible to compare the occupational composition of the male occupants in January 1886 and December 1886. Although a sizeable proportion of male tenants (39 out of 161 and 47 out of 153 respectively) were in dock-related employment, many other occupations were also represented – skilled, semi-skilled and unskilled. We can thus conclude that this was not a community based on occupation. Furthermore, an analysis of the occupancy of each floor suggests that dockworkers did not all cluster together in the Buildings; nor did those in other occupations. It was a varied community in occupational terms.

The rate of turnover was high. At least 72 nuclear families moved *within* the Buildings during the four-year period in which the ledger was kept. There was also a considerable outflow.

The reasons for such turnover were many and various, and not entirely (or even largely) to be accounted for by the alleged preference for mobility among the working poor. As we shall see, turnover was in part a product of the policies followed by Ella Pycroft and her lady helpers, in part a result of poverty itself, and in part a consequence of life in a 'model dwellings' environment.

We know that there was a tendency, deliberately fostered by management, for the tenantry of blocks of dwellings to 'improve' in occupational and social status over time. This does not appear to have happened in Katharine Buildings during the period January–December 1886. If anything the tenantry in late 1886 deteriorated slightly from January in terms of occupational status: policemen, printers and bookbinders disappeared from the list. Before we conclude that this was because Potter and Pycroft had determined to follow the original principles underlying the development – to provide housing for labourers and others from the lowest class of the self-supporting poor – we should turn to Potter's diary again:

> Many of the respectable persons will not come in, owing to prejudice against buildings, & to ours in particular. The coarseness of the arrangements, want of attractiveness, and uniformity of the rooms a great disadvantage.

(diary, 22 August 1886)

There were in fact problems in filling the rooms and in keeping them filled. The position had been reasonably healthy up to January 1886, when all but nine of the rooms were rented. It was less so a year later. One problem, according to Ella Pycroft, was the recent construction of similar buildings directly opposite. Another was the eviction of tenants for a variety of reasons, including non-payment of rent and bad behaviour. Moreover, many of the poor were simply horrified at the prospect of living in such an environment. Also, once a building had been inhabited for a year or more, it was 'dirty' and unattractive to the 'respectable' poor.

A good deal of effort was put into finding suitable tenants. The memoirs of one of the other rent collectors for Katharine Buildings, Mrs Margaret Wynne Nevinson (the first wife of Henry Woodd Nevinson, the war correspondent), give a retrospective glimpse of this tiring and sometimes dangerous work. Her knowledge of Whitechapel came largely from journeys to inquire into the characters of tenants before accepting them. She recalled going to ask about some applicants at Flower & Dean Street, off Commercial Street, 'a well-known haunt of thieves'. She had on her wrist a bag containing £20 in coins, ready for a visit to the bank.

> As I saw the men sitting round a big fire at three o'clock in the afternoon, looking healthy and well, with steak and chips frizzling in the pan, I suddenly guessed that I was in a thieves' kitchen, & £20 would be worth a knock on the head to a woman. I had the presence of mind to go on talking, and politely inquiring the character of Mr. and Mrs.—, but sidled gently towards the door all the time, and was thankful when I stood again outside in the street.

(Nevinson, 1926, p.89)

2.2   INFLUENCES ON THE LIVES OF THE POOR

The work of Pycroft, Potter and Paul depended on the idea that they could influence the working poor so fundamentally that the latter would begin to live their lives according to an entirely alien regime. Poor though the labourers might be and dependent upon irregular earnings, they would learn to save when times were good so as to ride out periods of sickness, unemployment or low earnings. The women would keep their dwellings neat and clean, learn to budget and cook nourishing meals, control their children, send them to school (and to Sunday school), and assist the authorities by reporting infectious disease or infestation. The men would actively look for paid work and not drink their earnings away. They would acknowledge and fulfil their responsibilities to their families, maintaining order and decency and giving the wife the wherewithal to keep the household. Children would attend school and go out to work. They would contribute to the family coffers and, when they left home, maintain their parents in need. These features added up to respectability and responsibility.

In 1889 Octavia Hill outlined what she considered to be some of the major problems involved in rehousing the working poor in flatted accommodation. It was a stern critique. There was 'the enormously increased evil which grows up in a huge community of those who are undisciplined and untrained'. This, she claimed, disappeared with *civilization* and in those blocks where

> *the tenants are the quiet, respectable working class families, who … 'keep themselves to themselves' … Under rules they grow to think natural and reasonable, inspected and disciplined, every inhabitant registered and known, school board laws, sanitary laws and laws of the landlord or company regularly enforced … it is a life of law, regular, a little monotonous, and not developing any great individuality, but consistent with happy home-life, and it promises to be the life of the respectable London workingman.*
>
> (Hill, 1889, p.31)

But civilization, as Hill saw it, was all too easily chased from a 'Dwellings'. Admission of even a small number of the 'undisciplined' to the blocks brought chaos – 'the dirt, the violence, the noise, the quarrels' could not be controlled; the 'tidier ones depart, the rampant remain' and pandemonium prevailed.

> *Sinks and drains are stopped; yards provided for exercise must be closed because of misbehaviour; boys bathe in drinking water cisterns; wash houses on staircases or staircases themselves become the nightly haunt of the vicious, the Sunday gambling places of boys; the yell of the drunkard echoes through the hollow passages; the stairs are blocked by dirty children – and the life of any decent hard-working family becomes intolerable.*
>
> (Hill, 1889, pp.32–3)

'The same evils', wrote Octavia Hill, 'are nothing like as injurious when families are more separate', as in small cottages. The poor, she argued, were not ready for corporate life. People who are gentle when they live in small groups become brutalized in large numbers. Only deliberate isolation of a family within a block would preserve its respectability, she believed. These views appear to echo Beatrice Potter's own opinions:

> *The respectable tenants keep rigidly to themselves. To isolate yourself from your surroundings seems to be here the acme of social morality … Do not meddle with your neighbours is perforce the burden of one's advice to newcomers. The meeting-places, there is something grotesquely coarse in this, are the water closets! Boys and girls crowd on these landings – they are the only lighted places in the buildings – to gamble and flirt.*
>
> (diary, November 1886)

This probably also reflected the reality of the situation. The design of the buildings did to an extent dictate the social behaviour of the inhabitants. The rooms were small and cramped when occupied by two or more generations. They may not have been especially small by contemporary standards, but flat dwelling offered no easy extension to street life such as might be found in a row of terraced houses. There were only two public rooms in the Buildings – a men's club and a boys' club – neither of which was open all the time. Lighting was restricted to the landings where the latrines were placed. The staircases were open to all-comers from the yard which, in its turn, was readily accessed from the street. Small wonder that the social life of the young focused on the landings or that on Sundays the building was troubled by casual visitors. In inclement weather the narrow yard offered little alternative.

However, though we might agree that the physical layout and condition of the Buildings influenced the way of life of families who lived within them, we would be unwise to assume that they 'determined' how the people lived.

2.3   LIFE IN KATHARINE BUILDINGS: DIFFERING LIFE STYLES

We can build up a picture of life styles in Katharine Buildings. On 6 July 1886 Ella Pycroft wrote to Beatrice Potter about an 'elite' member of the tenantry, Margaret Harkness, a novelist living in the Buildings to 'observe' the tenants:

> [She] Must have heard a good deal of noise on Saturday, the hot weather is trying, & then people drink & get more quarrelsome than usual, & being quarrelsome they fought about Home Rule, luckily, the grand fight took place outside the Buildings & the Police could interfere. Roadnight (the caretaker) & his wife were both up till two o'clock, trying to quiet the people.
>
> (Passfield papers, 6 July 1886)

Sometimes such problems reared their heads on weekdays:

> Poor Mrs Shea has twice broken out since she took the pledge & on Monday I had to give them notice. She was so drunk that though she would come into the room for me, I could not make her stay there long – she promised me she would if I'd give her half a pint more beer!
>
> (Passfield, 23 September 1886)

Miss Pycroft had heard that her husband 'did manage her by promising more when she was in bed'. In her report to Edward Bond in January 1887, Ella Pycroft lamented:

> It has been much to my disappointment that the tenants of the lowest class can not be kept in the Bgs if order is to be preserved, & I have been obliged to turn out the rough set ... [However] the fights which used to take place every Saturday are now events of rare occurrence – at Christmas there were none.
>
> (Passfield, 22 January 1887)

Employing a second assistant caretaker had eased another problem, since he occupied a room next to the north entrance and impeded entry to the yard by strangers intent on loitering.

Beatrice Potter and Ella Pycroft lived in Katharine Buildings only to a limited extent. Between November 1885 and January 1886 Beatrice paid rent on two rooms, leaving Ella in their sole occupancy until May 1886, when Ella and Maurice Paul moved to Wentworth Dwellings on Goulston Street, a more desirable Buildings. It seems, however, that little time was spent in the Katharine Buildings room. Beatrice moved in and out between York House, the Potters' townhouse, and her country home, while Ella apparently spent Saturday nights in the Buildings to maintain order and quiet. The rooms provided a base for their day-time involvement in managing the Buildings. 'Slumming it' hardly describes their way of life.

It would be easy to exaggerate both the problem of disorder and the resort to eviction. Most tenants were orderly – most of the time – and it was a question of removing a disorderly, and therefore infectious, element. The rent collectors, moreover, put a good deal of effort into working with individual 'problem' cases and into providing an orderly corporate life within the Buildings.

The rent collectors were aware that the physical layout of the Buildings had an effect on sociability and was the cause of many of the troubles of the early days. Beatrice told her father in September 1885 that

> The Buildings are undoubtedly healthy, but the facts of structure are against decent and orderly behaviour and must be counteracted by an amount of moral force no company should count on getting in management and superintendence. It remains to be seen whether Miss Pycroft and I with the help we are able to attract are equal to giving it.
>
> (Mackenzie, 1978, p.42)

Countering the physical environment was clearly a problem. In February 1886 Ella Pycroft wrote to Beatrice: 'I find that the impossibility of having a division between the compartments [WCs] with the trough system have led to indecencies of which I should never have dreamt.' Changes were put in hand only after Beatrice had drawn public attention in the *Pall Mall Gazette*. Then the water closets were provided with doors, and keys were supplied to the tenants. One tenant suggested that the men's and women's latrines should be on separate balconies, and Ella asked the caretaker to discover tenant opinion on this (Passfield, 26 February 1886, Ella to Beatrice). In her report to Edward Bond, Beatrice argued that all the rooms in a new block to be constructed by the East End Dwellings Company should be self-contained, so that the latrines could not become the focus of social life. Octavia Hill's penny-pinching recommendations of the early 1880s had come back to haunt the housing reformers. Interestingly, several of the 'respectable' tenants vacated Katharine Buildings precisely because of the 'arrangements'.

Thought and effort were also put into alternative forms of sociability and entertainment. A men's club was held in the club-room every night except Sunday. Papers, games, cards and chess were supplied. So was a bagatelle board, donated by Miss Potter and shared with the boys' club. Concerts were given once a month during the winter (in practice men-only affairs); tickets were also given away for concerts at nearby Toynbee Hall. A subscription lending library at a halfpenny a week proved popular, appealing to a different sort of tenant from the club. Maurice Paul ran a reading room. On Sundays the club-room was let out for a Bible class (by a teacher from Derby St School) and a prayer meeting (run by Canon Bradby) in the afternoons, and for an evening service led by one of the city missionaries. Once a week there was a mothers' meeting. In November 1886 Ella Pycroft rented number 51 as a club-room for the boys, following an earlier (but failed) attempt in 1885/6. Careful consideration of this earlier failure and a handsome subscription from Beatrice Potter led to its re-opening. Pycroft and Paul attended wood-carving classes so as to teach it to the boys. Twenty boys were offered opportunities to play games and box and, on two evenings a week, to learn carving and drawing although they reported that 'no great advance has yet been made in these arts'. The bagatelle board attracted the boys back from the larger local boys' clubs, including Toynbee Hall's Whittingham Club, because at Katharine Buildings they were not forced to queue so long for a turn. Beatrice held a party for the tenants of the Buildings in 1885, attended by Joseph Chamberlain. The following spring, Ella took about 32 tenants down to visit some of her relatives in Reigate. On one occasion a tea party was given for some of the young girls. And it was common to take parties of tenants to the 'houses of the rich and great'.

> *Sometimes we were received in stables and coachhouses, and tea was served in workhouse fashion … More often our hosts spread tables on green lawns, or in stately halls with full glory of ancestral plate, so that we trembled for the temptations of needy men; but … our people were poor but honest.*

(Nevinson, 1926, p.97)

There were, in other words, corporate activities on offer, and in the 1885 report Ella attributed the friendly feelings among the tenants in part to the clubs and meetings of various kinds.

What do you think was the purpose of these activities?

The civilizing purpose of such activities was uppermost in the minds of the rent collectors. There was also, probably, a desire to divert those working men who wanted a social life outside the home from recourse to the pub and music hall, and from subsequent rowdyism.

Entertainment was what some working men craved, and it was not always of a kind congenial to civilizing middle-class ladies. What was provided by the lady manager was a 'lady-like' concert or play. One lady visitor, Margaret Wynne Nevinson, was to recollect:

We got up entertainments for our tenants and I could always rely on my former pupils in Hampstead to give us a good show. The people were good critics and quite capable of recognising the best in music and acting, though we were distressed to find they liked a comic song, however bad, better than our well-meant attempts to elevate their taste.

(Nevinson, 1926, p.97)

Early in February 1886 this preference was forcefully stated when a group of working men at the Buildings staged a 'regular mutiny' at a Tuesday night concert. Ella described the scene to Beatrice:

They (the men) sang songs I very much disapproved of, & Mr Aarons brought forward a friend to sing & dance though Mr Paul & I had distinctly said we would not have it. My black looks stopped the men, & Aarons went off to the back of the room in a huff … then Elliott came forward to sing (to help me out of my difficulty I thought) but he made a speech most insolently finding fault with my conduct & I had to answer him & assert my authority; and then Aarons appealed to the people to know if he hadn't succeeded in amusing them, & all the low set applauded him. It was horrid. I talked to the two men after the concert was over & said we were not going to quarrel but such a thing must never happen again & that I should talk to them about it another time – & then went away with my friend Miss [Clementina?] Black, the only lady who was there, & got hissed by the rough set as we went out.

(Passfield, 9 February 1886)

Two days later Ella discussed the occurrence with Aarons and Elliott for some hour and ten minutes.

I made them … acknowledge that it was possible to laugh without having vulgar jokes or worse, & that we ought to try and raise the tone of the people & so on; & made them clearly understand that the Club room was let to me & I'd have no disputing my authority in it & we parted with smiles all round … They must never have a loose rein again, it has all been my fault for trusting them too much.

(Passfield, 11 February 1886)

Such experiences may have put paid to Beatrice Potter's hopes of setting up a tenants' committee to assist in managing the Buildings. After this, the concerts were often poorly attended and tickets had to be given away. Mrs Nevinson saw people bored to tears by 'being compulsorily uplifted'. If the culture of many tenants offended the visitors, no less did their ways of living. Mrs Nevinson commented in her memoirs on the inadequate home-making skills of the tenants, which were not just due to poverty. She compared the lack of culinary know-how with that of working people in France and Germany, which she had visited. In Whitechapel tenants despised cereal foods as 'work'us stuff' and the staple diet was stewed tea, bread and butter, and fried steak, liver or 'lights'.

Most of the mothers had worked in pickle or jam factories and knew nothing of housekeeping. Their ill-nourished husbands pardonably took to drink, and the unfortunate babies, brought up on strong tea, sips of beer and gin, stuffed with adulterated sweets, tempted with whelks and winkles, died quickly.

(Nevinson, 1926, p.94)

Alternatively, babies lived to be sickly and mentally defective. Interestingly, Mrs Nevinson observed that 'a few men, who had the foresight to marry domestic servants, had their food properly cooked and their homes kept clean' (Nevinson, 1926, p.94).

Beatrice Potter also describes taking several young girls from the Buildings to see life above and below stairs at York House and their enthusiasm to go into service. She thoroughly approved of their ambition and did her best to find placements. She must have found dispiriting, however, the number who left service soon after they had entered it.

Dirt and infestation were a feature of life that could not be countered by hygienic house-keeping by the few. 'Even our speckless, Leicestershire maid could not keep us free from vermin', exclaimed Mrs Nevinson.

> However much we whitewashed and fumigated Katharine Buildings, the fauna of the district were too strong for us … Within a year of the opening of a new building it was rendered uninhabitable by the cleanly and respectable. The sheer impossibility of maintaining cleanliness caused most to give up the struggle.
>
> (Nevinson, 1926, p.83)

'A good deal of the dirt and vermin came from abroad', either with the Irish or with Russian and Polish Jews whom the prejudiced Mrs Nevinson denounced as having 'brought their dirty habits with them'. Against such enemies as dirt, vermin and disease, the proposed remedy of 'window-boxes and pot-plants' was to no avail. Ella Pycroft was determined to impress upon tenants the need to report immediately cases of infectious disease. In spring 1886 'there was an alarm of scarlatina amongst some children' and a danger of it spreading because the parents had not reported the cases and precautions had not been taken. As a result printed notices were posted in the Buildings requiring residents to tell the authorities of such illnesses (*Inhabitants of Katharine Bulidings*, Ella Pycroft's report to Bond, 22 January 1887).

Potter and Pycroft were aware that the impoverished condition and overcrowding of the tenants were to a large extent outside their own control, and they groped towards an appreciation that dirt and disease may have been products of the situation rather than its causes.

'Babies and beer', reported Mrs Nevinson (1926, p.95) 'were the only things that never seemed to run short in the Buildings'. According to her, marriage came early for most girls: 'Many young wives told me they were only fourteen or fifteen "though I said seventeen to the clergyman" but as twelve was the legal age for marriage in England no one seemed shocked' (Nevinson, p.100). In consequence, it was not uncommon for a young couple to start their married life on an errand boy's pittance combined with what the girl could earn at the pickle or jam factory. Babies abounded, for birth control was never mentioned and apparently never practised (or at any rate with no success), and received with 'scanty welcome'. ''E was awful angry because I had another baby … 'e swore at me shocking, and now 'e's taken 'isself to the public-'ouse because there's no dinner for 'im' (Nevinson, p.95).

How significant do you think drinking was in family life?

Drink is often highlighted by scholars as a problem of nineteenth-century working-class life. The lady visitors remembered it as such. The ledger, however, indicates that it was far from omnipresent (it was identified as a problem in some 84 households out of 483). But the trouble caused was out of all proportion to the numbers. Drink was cheap and opening hours long. Saturday night brought a fair share of domestic violence directed against the womenfolk. One old soldier wounded in the Crimean War used to unstrap his wooden leg to beat his wife (Nevinson, p.91). It was to try to protect the women that Ella Pycroft began to stay at the Buildings each Saturday night, but she had little success. The rows between men and women became public spectacles, attracting large crowds of neighbours and passers-by. In general, the women bore 'their sufferings with a patience that seems to me a sin against the race … "He didn't lay a finger on me", said one young woman proudly, as I stood in her wreck of a home where everything breakable lay smashed in a thousand pieces' (Nevinson, p.92). But drink was by no means a male prerogative. In 33 cases, the wife alone was said to be 'in drink' as against 36 cases where the man was the only partner in drink; in eight further cases both drank. While the visitors tried to impress upon tenants the need for sobriety, in only 12 out of 107 cases of eviction was drink given as one of the reasons for ejection.

2.4   VISITING

Detailed individual work with families, designed to improve them into middle-class norms and values, was the main occupation of the lady visitors in Katharine Buildings. Through regular rent collection, the visitors aimed to form friendships with tenants, and within these friendships to work to help families by inculcating certain behaviours and standards. Paying the rent on time was regarded as a regular and invaluable discipline. In a world where unemployment, underemployment and sickness were prevalent, tenants would be urged to save towards a 'rainy day'. Drink would be out of the question. Work would be a priority. There would be domestic harmony and the provision of a fitting nest for the children.

The visitors probably found it difficult to meet the adult male tenants. Charles Booth and his associates were told by their clerical informants that while they could often visit the women, the men would sidle out of the back of the house as soon as the clergy were admitted (British Library of Political and Economic Science, Booth Collection, B305 fo.243). The information therefore came from the women – a point worth remembering as this may have affected both the nature and the quality of the evidence.

Not all tenants found this 'friendship' congenial. On one occasion an Irishman declared to Mrs Nevinson, 'I wish to give notice'. 'And Why?', she asked. 'Well, Ma'am, it's like this; me and the missis can't have a row in any peace. All the ladies come a-knocking and a-fussing at the door and a-carrying their tales to you ladies, so I'm going now to a little house where we shan't be interfered with' (Nevinson, p.91). The disastrously 'misbehaved' were evicted; those who kicked against the levels of 'supervision' left of their own accord; those who could not or would not pay the rent were ejected; left behind were the self-supporting 'respectable' families who could not afford more salubrious accommodation elsewhere.

How much influence the lady visitors really had over the people of Katharine Buildings is uncertain, but there can be no doubt that they were diligent in their attempts to know the inhabitants. Close acquaintance with individual circumstances generally came from regular visitation of families. The ledger permits us to look at each individual family in some depth – in a detail which reflects the careful work done by Potter and Pycroft. Here are a few examples of family histories and the approach to them taken by the visitors.

The Nagles   Mrs Nagle, her husband and disabled son lived in room 188 from 23 March 1885 until 30 August 1886. John Nagle was a plasterer with 'seldom any work'; his wife was an old (second-hand) clothes dealer and the sister of Mrs Lyons, who lived in no.183; their son John had been injured in an accident and helped either parent as occasion demanded. Amongst the first intake of tenants, they were regarded favourably: 'Regular in payment. Clean, respectable, hardworking.' In May 1886, to the visitor's dismay, the mother and son quarrelled with the father, and moved to room 129. Eventually the quarrel was resolved and the Nagles decided to take a large and a small room together. But then Ella Pycroft found that 'Mrs N. had quarrelled with her son because of his courting Mr Debond's daughter' and said she must leave altogether. John Nagle had told the Debond girl that he could earn £2 a week. Miss Pycroft stepped in and 'tried to make Mrs Debond see the madness of letting her girl marry such a cripple but she couldn't.' The summer came, the Debonds went off 'hopping' (picking hops in Kent) and by the time they returned the romance was over. The Nagles then moved to no.133 on 30 August 1886 and rented in addition room 131 in September 1887. In winter 1887 John Nagle junior was taken extremely ill with rheumatism; John Nagle senior 'was seized with one of his maniacal fits of jealousy of his wife. He was almost, if not quite, dangerous.' The rooms were rented in John junior's name so Ella Pycroft made him give notice for room 133 'as he & his mother were in 131' (remember that the rooms were not linked in any way.) 'Then I told the old man he was either a trespasser or a tenant, as the latter I gave him notice – He went to the workhouse – returning his wife threw water over him; so he left again.' The advice of Edward Bond was sought. 'In the end Nagle came back to his wife. I said if he stayed they must leave – However, finally I agreed to let them stay. Nagle got work in the summer & behaved well'. In May 1888 they moved to room 274, then to room 134. Unfortunately in summer 1888 Mrs Nagle had a bad leg which prevented her working. 'I paid her rent for 2 weeks on condition she stayed in bed', recorded Pycroft, and 'later on helped her in same way with Lord Airlie's money [a philanthropic bequest]'.

_____ *EXERCISE 5.4* _____

Clearly one should attempt to relate such individual examples to the rest of the inhabitants of Katharine Buildings. Three features of the Nagle case history are readily identifiable: their frequent moves within the building and the large number of rooms they occupied at different times; the presence of disabled occupants in the family; and the fact that the visitors extended 'a helping hand'. How 'typical' of the families were disability and illness or the intervention of the visitors to assist? Look at Tables 5.1 and 5.2 (which, like all the tables in this chapter, have been drawn up from the households on the ground, first and second floors of the Buildings).

Table 5.1 Incidence of disability and illness among households and household heads in Katharine Buildings

| | Total | With: | | With illness or disability | |
		Illness	Disability	Total	%
Households	483	81	57	138	29
Heads	483	45	30	75	16

Table 5.2 Features of households in Katharine Buildings according to household type

Type	Total	Lodger	COS assisted	Visitor	MABYS	MHS	Violence	Criminal	Neighbours	Bad feeling
All	483	22	35	57	18	26	29	17	115	13
Nuclear	217	3	19	32	12	16	11	14	51	8
Conjugal	81	1	3	4	0	2	6	1	21	3
Cohabiting	2	0	0	1	0	0	1	0	1	0
Separated woman	20	1	2	4	2	3	2	0	4	0
Separated man	5	0	0	0	1	1	0	0	2	0
Deserted woman	2	0	0	0	0	0	0	0	0	0
Widow	69[1]	5	8	11	2	2	8	0	14	0
Widower	11[2]	1	0	1	0	0	0	1	2	1
Single woman	12	2	0	2	0	0	0	0	4	0
Single man	45[3]	7	2	1	N/A	1	1	0	11	1
Other	19	2	1	1	1	1	0	1	5	0

[1] Total includes one widow with an adult child excluded in Table 5.3.
[2] Total includes two widowers with children or mother who are excluded in Table 5.3.
[3] Total excludes two single men who lived with a relative and who appear under 'other' in Table 5.3.

Key:
Lodger = presence of lodger(s)
Visitor = mention of direct intervention by visitors
COS = assisted households with Charity Organisation Society help
MABYS = households with service placements by the Metropolitan Association for Befriending Young Servants. Many of these girls came from workhouse schools and were the responsibility of MABYS until they reached the age of 20. MABYS visited them every quarter, tried to sort out their problems in employment and provided lodgings when they were out of employment. MABYS was also available to all young servants who wished to use its services.
MHS = Mansion House Relief Scheme mentioned
Violence = incidence of
Criminal = identified as criminal
Neighbours = mention of relationship with neighbours
Bad feeling = definite evidence of bad feelings towards management

The tables indicate that while a majority of tenant families did not share these features, they were far from uncommon in the Buildings.

The Bullocks   Not all 'families' contained husband, wife and own children (i.e. were a nuclear family). 'Family' life could involve several distinct 'households'. Mrs Clara Bullock was a widow who inhabited a single room, no.133, from 11 January 1886 until 8 March 1886. She had two married daughters living elsewhere in the Buildings (Mrs Lewis at no.148, Mrs Larmar at no.113), another married daughter, Mrs Green, at 114 Wentworth Street, two unmarried daughters in service (Clara, born 1870 and Alice, born 1872), and she shared her room with two children, John and Mary Ann. She was also reputed to have had six dead children. She took in washing and sometimes did other work such as 'making umbrella cases' at $1s\,2d$ a gross. Mary Ann, born in 1866, 'helps', but during the day worked for Mrs Bullock's married daughter in Wentworth Street. John, born in 1867, was out of work and the mother declared that she 'wants smaller room to get rid of him & force him to support himself'. As a result she moved to no.121 and John left home. However, Mrs Bullock 'could get no work' during the winter 1886/7 and 'there seemed no prospect of her paying rent, so I had to eject them'. When they were gone two neighbours, Mrs Kelly and Mr Hagerty, reported that they had been a noisy lot and they were glad they were gone. Miss Pycroft was not too keen to hear that the son had continued living with them after all – there were limits to her oversight of the tenants.

One of Mrs Bullock's daughters, 'a good tempered little woman', was married to Albert Lewis, a packing-case maker, and her rooms, first no.148 and then no.100, were 'the meeting place for all of her family living on the block'. Between September 1886 and November 1888 hard times hit the Lewises. Albert could not obtain work and Ella Pycroft helped them with Lord Airlie's money in the winter of 1887/8. Mrs Lewis had two babies within two years. 'She behaved badly then for the first time', commented Ella, 'taking away & pawning things I had lent her. But they were almost starving.' They were evicted for non-payment of rent.

Such examples indicate that it was perhaps important for families to live near one another and maintain frequent contact. What help does the data in the ledger give in deciding whether kin could or did maintain close links? A rough count suggests that 14 per cent of married women and 21 per cent of female household heads had kin elsewhere in the Buildings, whereas only 6 per cent of male household heads claimed kin in the Buildings – indicating that women maintained such habitation links more frequently than men.

The Roberts   Another colourful family history was that of Michael Roberts and his wife, who moved into the Buildings in October 1888. They took two rooms (first nos.115 and 118, later 115 and 114), for Michael was a clerk in the Tower of London – regular, well-paid work. His son Harry and his eldest daughter were also employed. At the time they moved in Mrs Roberts had gone to Ireland on a visit 'and came back bringing fowls – bantams, which she allowed to run about the room till I remonstrated'. She assured Ella Pycroft that she would remove them to the Tower, 'but she sent them to the back room, & made a cage for them of the shelf of a wash-hand stand, till I found them out again!' Ella judged her to be a 'Rough, coarse woman, very well to do – Didn't like to be honest.' The Roberts were evicted for non-payment of rent and summoned to the county court. Mrs Roberts was much put out that she was not allowed to leave with a clear rent book, when she proffered the rent after eviction.

2.5   PHYSICAL CONDITIONS

In describing the family life of the inhabitants we need to establish the physical conditions in which the people lived. For this we have to rely on clues from case histories like those above and general inferences from the architecture and the 'arrangements'.

What features might we look at?

I would suggest the following:

1   The facilities in the rooms – was there a cooking range, water, or light? (Tenants complained there were no shelves for storing pots and pans, which made it difficult to keep the property clean and tidy. It was a long way to bring water to the wash-hand stands in the rooms from the taps on the landings. No artificial light was provided.)

2   The communal facilities – WCs, latrines, laundry, yard.

3   The ease of living – a baby could be put out in the fresh air on the balcony so there was no need to trek down and up three or four flights of stairs, but those who rented two rooms which were unlinked had to make considerable efforts to 'socialize' with other members of their so-called 'household' (although doors were occasionally cut through partition walls to provide access).

4   Inconveniences caused to the sick and disabled (of whom there were very many in the Buildings).

And finally, a crucial feature:

5   The density of the population – how many people lived in each of these small rooms?

Details of household occupancy by household type are given in Table 5.3. You should note that some scholars apply the term 'nuclear' (or 'conjugal') to a household containing (a) a husband and wife with children *or* (b) a husband and wife alone, *or* (c) a widow/er and offspring. I think the historian should explore the varieties of experience within the family, so I have used separate terms to distinguish 'nuclear' (a household of husband, wife and children) from 'conjugal' (husband and wife alone, or with lodgers); widow, widower, etc. are self-explanatory.

Table 5.3   Occupancy of households by household type in Katharine Buildings

Type	Total	Average occupancy	Number of members										
			1	2	3	4	5	6	7	8	9	10	UNK
All	483	3	82	125	70	60	67	30	25	11	0	2	11
Nuclear	217	5	0	0	41	47	61	26	25	10	0	2	5
Conjugal	81	2	0	79	2	0	0	0	0	0	0	0	0
Widow	68	2	27	15	16	6	2	1	0	1	0	0	0
Widower	9	2	3	4	1	0	1	0	0	0	0	0	0
Separated woman	20	3	4	8	1	3	2	2	0	0	0	0	0
Separated man	5	1	4	1	0	0	0	0	0	0	0	0	0
Deserted woman	2	4	0	1	0	0	0	1	0	0	0	0	0
Single man	47	1	34	9	4	0	0	0	0	0	0	0	0
Single woman	12	1	10	2	0	0	0	0	0	0	0	0	0
Other multikin households	22	3	0	6	5	4	1	0	0	0	0	0	6

UNK = unknown

2.6   ASSESSING THE FAMILY AND THE INDIVIDUAL

For the lady managers and visitors, deciding whether it was 'worth' continuing to work with a family who had failed to pay the rent consistently or who were disorderly or dirty was tricky. If a family or an individual could never be self-supporting in a million years – whether through sickness, 'want of character', or vice – the decision had to be made to evict them. Assessing the family was, therefore, an important part of the rent collector/visitor's work. We know from Ella Pycroft's letters that she did not always feel that she was particularly adept at this. In July 1886 she told Beatrice Potter:

> I am trying to bolster up a woman in Kath. Buildings now who has been half starved, & she will come back from a Convalescent home to which she is going pretty strong – & then it will begin all over again – & I know, (or I think I do) that if I had left her to die, it would have been one less to struggle for food here.
>
> (Passfield, 15 July 1886)

One tenant, Mrs Panrucher, once told Ella that her husband had found work for several other inhabitants. 'Oh that Gibbs is a lazy man', she exclaimed, without prompting, of one of the Buildings' unemployed, and she went on to explain that Mr Panrucher had got Gibbs a work ticket but he had failed to get up and go to work. Moreover, Gibbs beat his wife. Ella reflected comfortingly to Beatrice, 'It is just one more instance of how long it takes to find the truth about people – & of the fact that if a man is constantly out of work it is generally his own fault' (Passfield, 9 February 1886).

Another case was that of John Shermann. Already a cripple, his health had been shattered and his chances of future employment destroyed when a cart ran over him and badly damaged his hand. A married sister who lived elsewhere looked after him (her sense of obligation arising from her responsibility for his original disability by dropping him in infancy), but was unable to help financially. Ella Pycroft obtained 5 shillings a week from the Charity Organization Society when he first came out of hospital, but this was temporary relief. A convalescent home was out of the question because it would not improve his chances of employment. He had tried taking in a lodger but the tenant had been so objectionable that Ella turned him out.

> I have had to tell Shermann that he must face the fact that there is nothing for him but the Infirmary till his hand is strong. But the tears run down his cheeks at the thought, the one thing he has is his liberty to sit in his room or hobble to the balcony. He said he might as well drown himself & for the first time in my life I thought suicide might be justifiable.
>
> (Passfield, Ella Pycroft to Beatrice Potter, 21 August 1886)

Between them Ella and Maurice Eden Paul persuaded Beatrice to pay Shermann a pension of 7*s* 6*d* a week while they tried to find him some kind of gainful employment (see the extract from a letter written by Ella to Beatrice shown in Figure 5.6). Paul held out little hope. 'He will never be able to use the thumb of his right hand again, as the lead tendons have been cut right through & have contracted & I doubt if he will be able to clean boots properly using his fingers alone even if they recover their strength.' In his better days Shermann had scarcely been able to walk to his spot on Leman Street (for location see Figure 5.1) to clean boots, but now he was further disadvantaged. He was illiterate and also insufficiently vigorous to act even as a gate man. 'He really wants some sinecure post & though there are plenty such for men in the higher walks of life, they are difficult to find for people of his class', wrote Maurice Paul to Beatrice. Pycroft and Paul searched hard and long for work for Shermann, quizzing tenants on the availability of work as a toll-taker in the local cloth market, for example, but they were unsuccessful. Eventually Ella advised that the pension be discontinued because Shermann was in such straits that he would be better off in the workhouse. However, when Shermann entered the workhouse he was found to have a little money in his pockets and was turned out. Back he came to another cheaper room in Katharine Buildings where he and his lodger caused further problems for the managers.

Why do you think this case caused problems for Potter, Pycroft and Paul?

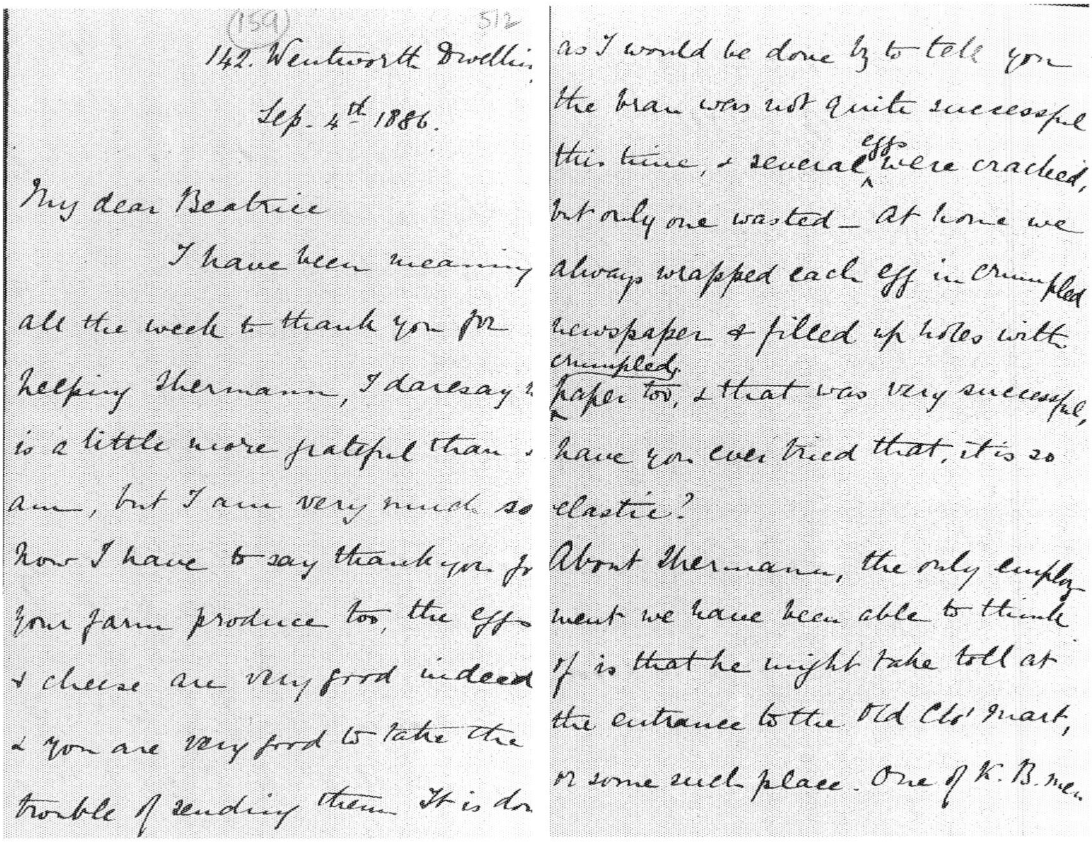

142. Wentworth Dwellin[gs]
Sep. 4th 1886.

My dear Beatrice

I have been meaning all the week to thank you for helping Shermann, I daresay he is a little more grateful than I am, but I am very much so now I have to say thank you for your farm produce too, the eggs & cheese are very good indeed & you are very good to take the trouble of sending them. It is do[ne] as I would be done by to tell you the bran was not quite successful this time, & several eggs were cracked, but only one wasted – at home we always wrapped each egg in crumpled newspaper & filled up holes with crumpled paper too, & that was very successful, have you ever tried that, it is so elastic?

About Shermann, the only employment we have been able to think of is that he might take toll at the entrance to the Old Clo' Mart, or some such place. One of K.B. men

Figure 5.6 Extract from a letter written by Ella Pycroft to Beatrice Webb, 4 September 1886 (Source: British Library of Political and Economic Science, Passfield Collection)

Shermann wanted to work, he was 'respectable', and his difficulties were no fault of his own. Even so, the philosophy of the COS philanthropist went that those who could not be self-supporting should not be artificially supported by money doles but sent to the wall – in this case the workhouse. However, personal knowledge of the case, human compassion and emotion got in the way for a while and made all three question the wisdom of such a philosophy.

3 KATHARINE BUILDINGS IN PERSPECTIVE: IMPLICATIONS FOR THE STUDY OF THE FAMILY

This case study relates to the housing of a particular group of working-class families in a specific location and a specific context. We need to decide how usual the circumstances were. There are several ways of doing this.

One is to see Katharine Buildings as part of the provision of model dwellings in London during the last two decades of the nineteenth century. There were several such buildings, although few were designed for the portion of the working class that Katharine Buildings served. But the entire 'movement' could have housed only a tiny fraction of the self-supporting working-class population of London, so relatively few London working-class families would in fact have been affected by the particular features of life in Katharine Buildings, such as the difficulties in maintaining contact with one's family in an inaccessible second room, or the problems of noise and disorder associated with living in the Buildings. Presumably, though, there were features of family composition and life in Katharine Buildings that were unrelated to the design of the Buildings themselves, namely size of household, structure of household, nature of employment, and sources of income.

If, however, we see Katharine Buildings as part of the housing of the metropolitan working class which came under the sway of the 'Octavia Hill system', we can make some attempt to assess how successful this was in 'reforming the values and way of life of the working class population'. Hill's methods, we should remember, were thought to be transferable from ordinary housing to flatted accommodation. The individual case-work method pioneered by the Christian Socialists and Hill fed into the case work characteristic of later public sector housing management and social work in general.

The example of Katharine Buildings illustrates the 'class' dimension of such 'caring' relationships and the narrowing of vision that led Beatrice Potter and Ella Pycroft to abandon this kind of work. The work strove to impose middle-class norms and ways of life on families without middle-class incomes. Those who could not match up to this conception were thrown to the wall. The idea that the structural causes of poverty had to be tackled before progress could be made was anathema. That the working class might have norms which were different from but as valid as those of the middle class was rarely entertained. Charles Booth (1902–3) was one of the very few who seems to have valued the working class of London for what they were. Beatrice Potter certainly despaired that individual case work could 'reform' the working poor – for her the underlying poverty had to be tackled. But she had little empathy with the poor as people and her brand of socialism preserved the regulatory relationship – the state would regulate the economy, banish poverty and bring the lives of all into conformity with broadly middle-class values.

Another way of setting life in Katharine Buildings in context would be to compare our knowledge of family composition and sources of income with information derived from else-where about the working population as a whole. The census is the obvious source here.

One might also compare life in Katharine Buildings with that in other model dwellings, always bearing in mind the differences in accommodation and in the class or income group of the inhabitants.

So where does this leave us?

Our case study is just that – a case study of a particular block of dwellings in a specific context. Moreover, although we can extract 'objective' data from the ledger, the ledger itself is the fruit of the effort of the Victorian middle class to shape the family life of the labouring poor. We see the 'real' working-class family through a middle-class prism.

Oddly enough there is no general history of the working-class family in Britain from which to take our bearings. Nevertheless, there have been many interesting contributions to such a history. A further step, therefore, is to compare what we have learned about family life in Katharine Buildings with what other historians and social scientists have said about family life in late Victorian Britain. This will put Katharine Buildings in perspective but may also lead us to contest, modify or add a new dimension to existing descriptions of family composition, life and structure.

3.1   THREE COMPARABLE STUDIES – OR ARE THEY?

Let us take some of the important work on the family and set against it the Katharine Buildings experience.

1   Anderson on the structure of the nineteenth- and twentieth-century family
Michael Anderson's article 'What is new about the modern family?' (1983), may be regarded as

representative of the sophisticated and historically aware historical demography of the later twentieth century. Anderson, of course, used very different data from the sources we have employed here. His figures are largely derived from census samples of the entire population of Britain, with no separate calculations of a class- or employment-specific nature. He does, however, speak of 'diversity of experience' in the family, suggesting that this was yet more prevalent before the twentieth century, and contrasts the family life of the working class with those 'above them' in the social hierarchy. We cannot simply place our information about Katharine Buildings against Anderson's and draw direct comparisons. Nevertheless, our data certainly seem to echo some of Anderson's general conclusions, as set out in Schema A.

Schema A: Some possible characteristics of nineteenth-century family life

- o   There was a lack of privacy for marital and familial life.
- o   The family was an economic unit: women worked at home or outside the home; children worked.
- o   Family experience was varied.
- o   There was a high incidence of disrupted families.

Are there areas where our data might amplify or modify Anderson's statements?

Anderson, like most modern scholars, tends to ignore the fact that, as Charles Booth demonstrated, there were different sections to the working class. Significantly, contemporaries called them 'the working classes', not the 'working class'. The data for Katharine Buildings suggest how people in the lowest self-supporting section of the working classes lived. These were families who could hope to earn enough to pay a rent of between 3s 6d and 8s 6d (out of the whole family's income) and bring up a family with no or minimal resort to relief. Their existence as self-supporting families was precarious in the extreme – an element understandably ignored by Anderson, for it has little to do with life tables and all to do with life experience. For the historian it is important not only to establish that there was diversity of experience but also to define that experience. For example, it must have mattered little to the families of Katharine Buildings that most households of the time (statistically) contained only 2.0 offspring when your own contained five. Note the wide range in household size in Table 5.3.

Social class and income must also be taken into account when analysing the data. After all, Beatrice Potter's own family contained ten daughters yet her parents were well off and well connected and therefore able to provide good prospects for all and excellent living conditions. A family with this number of children in class C or D would have been overcrowded, cramped and near destitution. Also, a census provides a snapshot of conditions at one time. The ledger makes us aware of the fluidity of the household as well as the precarious livelihood of the individual families of the labouring poor.

2 Ross on working-class marriage in late nineteenth-century London   The American historian Ellen Ross has argued (1982) that gender relations between working-class men and women in London followed a set pattern, with a clear demarcation between the spheres of husband and wife, man and woman. 'Despite the ties of marriage, and their intense economic interdependence, women and men lived in quite separate material worlds organized around their responsibilities' (1982, p.578). The wife was responsible for childcare and domestic labour, while a husband's primary obligation was to work and to hand over a customary amount of pay to the wife. If he failed, there was dreadful domestic tension and violence. Within the household money and goods were not held in common by the married couple. Ross argues that stealing between spouses was common, as was stealing from fathers and siblings by children. Properly speaking, 'family socialism' – a true family economy – existed only between mothers and children. The wife budgeted for herself and the dependent children. The husband lived on a budget quite separate from theirs. The man's diet had a superior nutritional content and the woman used her skills as a shopper and pawner and member of the neighbourhood of women to scrape together sufficient for herself and the children. Strike pay provided for the man's dietary needs but made no provision for the wife and children.

The division between husband on the one hand and wife and children on the other was reinforced by endemic wife- and child-beating. Ross holds that the 'fissures present in the family thus encouraged husbands in their failure to consider sex, or its products – children – as a joint responsibility' (1982, p.595).

Many criticisms can reasonably be levelled at Ross's work. For example, she incorrectly uses 'Cockney' to refer to the whole of working-class London! More damning from our point of view is her failure to acknowledge that her work describes just one small sector of the working class – those brought before the Old Bailey for trial, scarcely a typical sample. These were not the respectable poor but the low-lives among the poor. Evidence provided in court cases must also be suspect if only because participants are highly likely to exaggerate the opposition's faults and misbehaviour.

Because Ross claims to describe the pattern of working-class marriage in the very area in which Katharine Buildings is situated, we should take care to compare our findings with hers. There are, of course, many examples of married life which resemble those Ross cites – but are these 'colourful' examples in the majority?

Do our data (or indeed your own) support or modify Ross's conclusions?

3 Scott and Tilly on women's work and the family economy   The Katharine Build-ings ledger contains evidence regarding the tenants' sources of income and the types of economic activity occurring both without and within their households. In an influential article, 'Women's work and the family in nineteenth-century Europe', Joan Scott and Louise Tilly (1975) constructed a general interpretation of the impact of changing economic circumstances on lower-class women's working lives and, incidentally, the family economy. They describe the female labour force as composed overwhelmingly of members of the working and peasant classes who were normally young and single. Most held jobs in domestic service, in garment making and in the textile industry proper – all preserves of female labour.

Why was this the case?

Scott and Tilly argue that such women worked to maintain the economic viability of the household economy and that young, unmarried daughters could more readily be spared from the household than could married women with husbands and young children to care for.

Their thesis is an important one. The nineteenth-century female workforce owed its salient characteristics to the persistence of traditional family forms and values, even during the period of rapid industrialization and beyond. It was an extension of women's household work and commitment. Admittedly the movement of young and unmarried women into the paid work-force was not a new development: even in pre-industrial times women, married and unmarried, had been expected to contribute to the family economy. According to Scott and Tilly, the family economy disappeared once unmarried girls were removed from the family home to undertake paid work: living a distance away from home, factory girls escaped parental control and came to regard their incomes as their own.

There are, however, problems with this thesis. First, it assumes that the traditional family economy they describe was a universal one, i.e. that before industrialization the norm was of husband, wife and children contributing to the shared household economy by their labour, paid or unpaid, and living together. But paid labour was taken out of the household for many male and female members long before industrialization. Factories and increased population densities may have accentuated tendencies towards the breakdown of parental control, but can scarcely be said to have caused it. Also, there were many regional variations in female labour patterns. In a spa town, for example, domestic service was often the main form of paid female labour, whereas in industrial towns and cities factory work was more important.

Moreover, it is agreed by economic and labour historians that London presented a special case. There was no large industry capable of absorbing the plentiful supply of female labour. Rates of pay for skilled and semi-skilled males were relatively good. The wives of skilled artisans, if they worked at all, did not compete for low-paid factory work or enter the sweated trades, but instead became small shop-keepers. But most did not work. As a result, in London, women's work was identified with poverty and low status. When the man could not obtain work, when 'his' wages were low, when 'he' was sick or disabled – then the women, married and unmarried, worked. Dockers' wives, for example, were more likely to work than the wives of skilled workers (see also the findings from the 1890s reported in Booth, 1902–3). The adequacy of the man's wage or the constancy of the work determined whether or not a married woman entered paid employment.

Scott and Tilly, then, seem to have overstated their case. The results of our study of Katharine Buildings enable us to test it out in one part of London in some detail.

Table 5.4 Number of female spouses in Katharine Buildings who worked relative to total number of married males and to the number of married heads of household in dock-related employment

Male heads	Married	No. with working wife	% of married heads with working wives	Dock-related	Dock-related married	Dock-related and working wives	% of married heads in dock-related employ with working wives
375	302	90	30	83	70	26	37

EXERCISE 5.5

Tables 5.4 and 5.5 and the text as a whole present data relating to the involvement of the various family members in the economic activity of the household and the sources of income of each household (the data are derived from my own database of the inhabitants of Katharine Buildings). On the basis of these try to answer the following questions:

1   Did many married women work outside the home?

2   Did more dockers' wives work than those of skilled workers?

3   Did most dockers' wives work?

4   To what extent was there a shared household economy?

5   What other information would we require to add more sophistication to the picture?

Answers/comments p.185.

Where does this leave us as regards the assertion of Ross that there was no shared family economy in working-class households, or that of Scott and Tilly that there was? I leave the conclusions to your judgement.

Table 5.5 Source of household incomes within Katharine Buildings

	Category of household														
	All	N	C	WF	WM	SW	SM	DW	CO	MK	SIM	SIW	SIB	SIBGP	UNK
Source of income	483	218	81	69	9	20	5	2	2	5	45	12	7	2	6
1 Head only	269	119	45	34	4	10	4	1	2	4	32	8	3	0	3
2 Head and spouse	49	24	24	0	0	1	0	0	0	0	0	0	0	0	0
3 Head, spouse and child	35	34	0	0	0	1	0	0	0	0	0	0	0	0	0
4 Head, spouse, child and charity	1	1	0	0	0	0	0	0	0	0	0	0	0	0	0
5 Spouse only	2	0	1	0	0	1	0	0	0	0	0	0	0	0	0
6 Children only	5	1	0	3	0	0	0	0	0	1	0	0	0	0	0
7 Charity only	0	0	0	0	0	0	0	0	0	0	0	0	0	0	0
8 Head and lodger(s)	12	2	0	3	1	1	0	0	0	0	5	0	0	0	0
9 Head and charity	9	5	1	1	0	0	0	0	0	0	2	0	0	0	0
10 Head and pension	2	1	1	0	0	0	0	0	0	0	0	0	0	0	0
11 Head and child(ren)	43	16	0	20	2	3	1	1	0	0	0	0	0	0	0
12 Parents	1	0	0	0	0	0	0	0	0	0	1	0	0	0	0
13 Children and charity	1	0	0	1	0	0	0	0	0	0	0	0	0	0	0
14 Head, spouse and charity	6	4	1	0	1	0	0	0	0	0	0	0	0	0	0
15 Spouse and pension	0	0	0	0	0	0	0	0	0	0	0	0	0	0	0
16 Pension	2	0	0	1	1	0	0	0	0	0	0	0	0	0	0
17 Spouse and children	3	2	0	0	0	1	0	0	0	0	0	0	0	0	0
18 Head, spouse and pension	1	0	1	0	0	0	0	0	0	0	0	0	0	0	0
19 Head, children and charity	4	1	0	2	0	1	0	0	0	0	0	0	0	0	0
20 Parental home	1	0	1	0	0	0	0	0	0	0	0	0	0	0	0
21 Head and parent	3	0	0	0	0	1	0	0	0	0	1	1	0	0	0
23 Head and brother	2	0	0	0	0	0	0	0	0	0	0	0	0	2	0
25 Head, children(ren) and lodger(s)	1	0	0	1	0	0	0	0	0	0	0	0	0	0	0
26 Head and sister	3	0	0	0	0	0	0	0	0	0	0	0	3	0	0
30 Sister	1	0	0	1	0	0	0	0	0	0	0	0	0	0	0
31 Brother	0	0	0	0	0	0	0	0	0	0	0	0	0	0	0
32 Head and cohabitee	1	0	0	1	0	0	0	0	0	0	0	0	0	0	0
33 Head, child(ren) and pension	1	1	0	0	0	0	0	0	0	0	0	0	0	0	0
66 Pension and charity	0	0	0	0	0	0	0	0	0	0	0	0	0	0	0
67 Pension, charity and child	1	1	0	0	0	0	0	0	0	0	0	0	0	0	0
68 Head, lodger(s) and charity	1	0	0	0	0	0	0	0	0	0	1	0	0	0	0
69 Head and savings	1	0	0	0	0	0	0	0	0	0	0	1	0	0	0
70 No source identified	22	6	6	1	0	0	0	0	0	0	3	2	1	0	3

Key:
N = nuclear (husband, wife and children)
C = conjugal (husband and wife)
WF = widow
WM = widower
SW = separated woman
SM = separated man
DW = deserted woman

CO = cohabitees
MK = multikin
SIM = single man
SIW = single woman
SIB = sibling
SIBGP = sibling + grandparent
UNK = unknown

The Katharine Buildings study brings out the incomplete nature of our knowledge of the working-class family. The contributions of Anderson, Ross, and Scott and Tilly are, in their own ways, as partial as our own. With many more case studies our knowledge of the working-class family of the past will be enriched.

3.2   HOUSING AND FAMILY LIFE

The study of Katharine Buildings also raises larger issues about the British housing experience. There was enormous variety both in London and elsewhere. This particular study should not tempt us to exaggerate the importance of flatted accommodation in the later nineteenth century. As Anthony Sutcliffe reminds us:

> *Even as late as 1911 when, significantly enough, the rise of the purpose-built flat prodded the census authorities into enumerating flats for the first time as distinct from separate houses, it was still very much in a minority. Over England and Wales as a whole structurally distinct flats accounted for 3.4 per cent of the total stock of dwellings, but this bald average conceals the fact that the great majority of flats were to be found in two parts of the country, the London area and Tyneside. The predominance of flats in the latter area was the result of the proliferation during the later nineteenth century of that fascinating phenomenon, the terrace of two-storey 'Tyneside' (or 'Newcastle') flats. In the city of Newcastle itself, 55.67 per cent of dwellings were flats and South Shields scored even higher, with 72.00 per cent.*

(Sutcliffe, 1974, p.14)

In London, within the London County Council area, 17.83 per cent of all dwellings were flats, but the percentage within the boroughs varied from a mere 2.31 per cent in Woolwich to 60.8 per cent in Holborn. Flats were not always for the working class. In prosperous Kensington 17.41 per cent of dwellings were flats. Not all multi-occupancy was represented by flat-dwelling, however. In early twentieth-century London it is estimated that as many as 40 per cent of households did not enjoy exclusive occupancy of a separate house. This did not imply structural separation but a more informal adaptation of housing for shared occupancy. When structurally separate flats were built in the suburban areas they were often of the two-storey terrace or 'Newcastle' type, which appeared to formalize the already common occurrence of shared occupancy.

While flats were common in the North of England, in Scottish cities and in Dublin, outside these areas separate flatted accommodation was the exception. In Liverpool, for example, only 1.76 per cent of dwellings were flats.

Katharine Buildings pointed to the future. By 1966 one dwelling in ten in England and Wales was a flat. Flats were common in all large cities and most bigger towns. Half were local authority flats but a third were privately rented and nearly a tenth owner-occupied. Now that the British experiment in council or public housing has run its course, it is timely to reflect on that experiment. In its time millions of people were brought up in council flats and on council estates with housing policies derived from 5 per cent philanthropy. Many are still occupied. Some idea of the type of study that is possible can be gained from Alison Ravitz's (1974) study of Quarry Hill, Leeds, but we still know next to nothing about the council house phenomenon and its impact on working-class families. Now is the time to interview those who shared this experience and to engage in local studies using the readily accessible architects' plans and designs, photographs, minutes of council and housing committees, records of house-exchange bureaux, records of tenants' associations, contemporary survey research, newspapers and so forth. Equally important will be studies of families living in the 'luxury' flats built to attract middle-class residents from the 1920s onwards. You should not expect to discover identical sources to those used in this Katharine Buildings study or the Leeds study, nor should you seek to replicate exactly such studies. They provide flexible models for your own research.

The opportunity should not be missed. The moment for such research is now, while the record lives and breathes. This moment will all too soon be past.

_____ **QUESTIONS FOR RESEARCH** _____

The wider relevance of the case study of Katharine Buildings is, I hope, self-evident. If you think that you would like to devise a similar project you might consider these questions first:

1   What issues/questions particularly intrigue you? Here you might include such items as: the physical, economic and social circumstances in which some family – perhaps your own – or its ancestors lived (if so, which part of the family or which ancestors and at what time?); the nature of the family (as a general concept) in the past (if so, which period?); the extent to which the physical environment determined family forms and experience; the existence of a household economy; the role of external agencies in moulding the family; the methodological problems involved in studying the family and the household in the past.

2   What sources are readily available to you? It is all very well to decide what interests you. Perhaps you want to study the circumstances of your own relatives, but if you have no easily manipulable data then such a study might have to be approached indirectly. For example, you might decide to study a family or a group of families of a similar socio-economic background in the same area, or even a different one. If so, what archives or printed works are available to help you?

3   How manageable is the task you are setting yourself? It is easy to underestimate the amount of time required to complete even a tiny historical project. It is better to set your sights quite low at first. There is rarely any difficulty in 'expanding' a project which turns out to be too limited, but it is both frustrating and disheartening to be unable to complete an over-ambitious project. The following are the types of project which you might find both interesting and manageable and which would contribute to the state of knowledge about the family in the past:

(a) A project that seeks to describe and then analyse the various family 'experiences' of a wider family. You could make a short list of the categories of data you wish to collect about the individuals in the family (many of these details might be at your fingertips already if you have already done research on a family tree). You could assemble other information in the form of diaries, papers, photographs and interviews. Your study would indicate the size and structure of the nuclear families involved but could also seek to describe the meaning and 'strength' of the concept of 'family' and try to identify patterns and dissimilarities among the families. For example, you might examine the evidence for the existence of a shared 'household economy' in one or more of the various families being studied and relate _your_ findings to those of other scholars and this case study. Any such study would clearly describe and reflect on the methodology and the sources employed therein.

(b) Should you feel that you have to concentrate on contemporary or near contemporary cases, you might explore the attitudes and opinions expressed by individuals within the family about 'family' and 'household'. If you are taking Katharine Buildings as your inspiration you might discuss the impact of environment on family life by asking questions of your family (or that of your neighbours), both directly and indirectly. For example, you might seek information about the physical environment and their views about how it determined the way they lived. Verification of the data would provide a challenge. You might wish to slant the project towards other issues: did members of the family seek to emulate other life-styles; did they feel that they were encouraged or pushed into so doing, and if so, how; why did the women work or not work; who controlled the purse strings; who did the tax returns; who booked the holidays; who made the decisions? The Katharine Buildings case study might also tempt you to seek information and opinion about the intervention of external agencies in family life – the church, social services, landlords, even the media. A variant would be to use the papers of a tenants' association or a house exchange bureau to analyse attitudes to housing and family life. For example, what were the main criticisms of the housing provided?

(c)   All the reading you have done in this volume about the census may spur you on to further research in this area. For instance, you might compare a detailed study of households in a short street or a landing of a block of flats with the published census statistics or to the more detailed census findings (the CEBs) for the area in 1881 or 1891.

(d)   A project studying architects' plans for philanthropic or, later, council housing for a given area: what types of housing were considered appropriate, what features were deemed necessary/desirable, what space and facilities were allowed? It would be important to set the study in context by discovering to which development the plans related; the proposed clientele; any contemporary discussions that took place; any relevant legislation to be obeyed; evidence of the realization of the development; other visual evidence such as photographs; how this evidence fits with general evidence for the period. There would be considerable scope here for individual interests. As always, source criticism would be extremely important. It would also be possible to study housing provision for the middle or professional classes using similar techniques and perhaps contrast the findings with those for council housing.

(e)   A study of council housing policy. The minutes of the relevant committees can be used not only to describe the politics involved but also to deconstruct middle-class attitudes to the working-class family and household. You would need to choose a short time-period during which major decisions about housing were discussed and taken. Newspapers can provide an interesting perspective on council policy-making.

(f)   Rent/tenant records of the type used in this study of Katharine Buildings do exist in some numbers both for blocks of flats and ordinary housing. Late nineteenth-century and early twentieth-century records have often been deposited in the local record repositories. Consult their card indexes and their archivists. While you may set out hoping to study your 'buildings' in the way I have studied Katharine Buildings, remember that the nature of the record must to a great extent shape your study, so be both flexible and critical in your approach.

(g)   You could take a hypothesis and test it for a particular locality and period; for example, 'That the shared household economy had ceased to exist by the late nineteenth century', or 'That women and men in the nineteenth century lived in quite separate material worlds organized around their family responsibilities in a rigid sexual division of labour, and that in the family, women and children dwelt on one side of the divide, and men on the other'.

NOTE ON MANUSCRIPT AND ORIGINAL SOURCES

This case study is based for the most part on the following manuscript sources:

Inhabitants of Katharine Buildings, 1885–90, Miscellaneous Collections 43, British Library of Political and Economic Science, London School of Economics.

Correspondence of Beatrice Potter, Ella Pycroft and Maurice Eden Paul, Passfield Collection, II(i) II.7–8, British Library of Political and Economic Science, London School of Economics.

Diary of Beatrice Webb, Passfield Collection, Holograph Diary, British Library of Political and Economic Science, London School of Economics.

Diary of C.S. Loch, University of London Library, Senate House.

East End Dwellings Co. Prospectus, 1884, held by Charlwood Alliance Group.

Report of the Select Committee on Artizans and Labourers' Dwellings Improvement with Minutes of Evidence, HC 235 of 1882, London, HMSO, 1882.

First Report of the Commissioners on the Housing of the Working Classes (England and Wales) with Minutes of Evidence and Appendix, 1884–85, reprinted in *British Parliamentary Papers*, Shannon, Irish University Press, 1970, pp.386–406.

REFERENCES AND FURTHER READING

Note: suggestions for further reading are indicated by an asterisk.

Anderson, M. (1983) 'What is new about the modern family?', Occasional Paper 31, *The family*, London, OPCS, pp.2–16. Reprinted in Drake (1994).

Barnett, H. (1921) *Canon Barnett*, London, John Murray.

Black, C. (ed.) (1983) *Married women's work*, London, Virago.

Booth, C. (1902–3) *Life and labour of the people in London*, 17 vols, London, Macmillan.

Daunton, M.J. (ed.) (1984) *Councillors and tenants*, Leicester, Leicester University Press.

Drake, M. (ed.) (1994) *Time, family and community: perspectives on family and community history*, Oxford, Blackwell in association with The Open University (Course Reader).*

Englander, D. (1983) *Landlord and tenant in urban Britain*, Oxford, Clarendon Press.

Hill, O. (1989) 'Blocks of Model Buildings; (2) Influence on Character', reprinted in Booth, C. (1902–3), *Life and labour of the people in London*, Poverty series, vol. 3, London, Macmillan.

Lewis, J. (1991) *Women and social action in Victorian and Edwardian England*, Aldershot, Edward Elgar.*

Mackenzie, N. (ed.) (1978) *The letters of Sidney and Beatrice Webb*, 3 vols, London, Virago.

Mackenzie, N. and J. (eds) (1982–86) *The diary of Beatrice Webb*, 4 vols, London, Virago.*

Muthesius, S. (1982) *The English terraced house*, New Haven and London, Yale University Press.

Nevinson, M.W. (1926) *Life's fitful fever: a volume of memories*, London, A. & C. Black.

O'Day, R. (1993) 'Before the Webbs: Beatrice Potter's investigations for Charles Booth', *History*, 78, June.

O'Day, R. and Englander, D. (1993) *Mr Charles Booth's inquiry: life and labour of the people in London reconsidered*, London, Hambledon Press.*

Ravitz, A. (1974) *Model estate: planned housing at Quarry Hill, Leeds*, London, Croom Helm.*

Ross, E. (1982) 'Fierce questions and taunts: married life in working-class London', *Feminist Studies*, 8, pp.575–601.*

Scott, J.W. and Tilly, L.A. (1975) 'Women's work and the family in nineteenth-century Europe', *Comparative Studies in Society and History,* 17, pp.36–64.[*]

Sutcliffe, A. (ed.) (1974) *Multi storey living, the British working class experience,* London, Croom Helm.[*]

Tarn J.N. (1971) *Working-class housing in 19th-century Britain,* London, Lund Humphries Publishers Ltd.

Tarn, J.N. (1974) *Five per cent philanthropy,* Cambridge, Cambridge University Press.[*]

Webb, B. (1971) *My apprenticeship,* Harmondsworth, Penguin (first published Longmans, Green & Co., 1926).

PART IV

REFLECTING ON THE ISSUES

CHAPTER 6

CONCLUSION

Section 1 by Ruth Finnegan; section 2 by Ruth Finnegan and Michael Drake

1   SO WHAT DO WE MEAN BY 'FAMILY'?

This volume has focused on ideas for research, giving both practical suggestions on projects you could undertake, and information about the relevant findings and approaches of other scholars. In this final chapter we want to alert you to a problem that needs to be confronted head on. If you are to make comparisons or link your work with that of others, you need to be sure that you are comparing like with like – or at any rate be aware of the range of possible contrasts or meanings of words or concepts.

So what *is* 'the family'? Here we further unwrap some of its many meanings.

1.1   DIFFERENT TYPES AND MEANINGS OF 'FAMILY'

You will have already encountered some of the issues in earlier chapters or in your own work. Let us review them briefly.

EXERCISE 6.1
---

1 What are the main terms used to distinguish or define types of (a) families, and (b) households, and what do they mean?

2 What other technical or semi-technical terms have been used to describe or classify families or domestic groupings and their activities?

Answers/comments p.185.

The first step, then, is to recognize these different *types* of family and of household. We are often so bound up with our own personal experience that it is easy to forget that the domestic groups in which people live can differ according to culture, historical period and individual circumstances. Thus there is no one form of *the* 'family'. Even the co-resident nuclear family, which Laslett and his colleagues discovered had existed much earlier in English history than had once been supposed (see Chapter 3, section 2.2), comes in several shades and forms. Furthermore, most people have experience of more than just nuclear relationships at some point in their lives. Indeed, as the Katharine Buildings case study shows, there is not even just one fixed 'English' type at a particular period, but variations existed according to class, area, or perhaps religion. Domestic groupings and family relations change over time, too, following changes in, say, birth, death or marriage patterns, or historical events like the massive number of male deaths in the First World War (of those aged 20–24 in the 1911 British census, 16.2 per cent or one in six died – see Winter, 1985, Table 3.7, p.82) or the huge numbers of people migrating from these islands in the nineteenth century when so many families had at least one member overseas. Household composition also varies at different stages in the family life cycle, or following local economic or housing opportunities. Knowing about these different forms of domestic and family organization and the appropriate terms to describe them, enables researchers to set their own case in a wider perspective and see how it resembles or differs from those of others.

But there is also the further problem of different *meanings*. Whether in everyday conversation or in formal research, people are liable to use the central terms in several senses. This is partly because words can change their meaning over the centuries. ('Family', for example, was earlier used to cover all members of the household, including servants and apprentices.) More confusing still is the way that, even in the same culture or historical period, 'family' is used in different senses. Which one is intended varies according to the context and to the speaker's (and perhaps listener's) situation.

What do *you* think is meant by 'the family'?

If you attempt to answer this question from your reading or by asking people (try it), you will probably find 'family' used for all or any of the meanings listed in Schema A.

Schema A: Some meanings of 'family'

o   Parents and their offspring, living together – the co-resident 'nuclear family'.

o   Other co-resident groups based on *some* sexual or blood relationship (actual, or by analogy as with adopted children), irrespective of the strict legal situation; many different variants on these themes, e.g. composite families, step-families, lone-parent families, 'extended' families of several generations.

o   A recognized relationship between previous members of such groups, whether or not now living permanently together, e.g. children of separated parents.

o   A relatively restricted group which includes yourself and your siblings, parents and grandparents, whether or not living together.

o   A wider group of relatives including aunts, uncles, cousins (usually never having lived together in the same household).

o   An open-ended network of kin, not constantly in touch but contacted as and when the opportunity arises.

o   Everyone that could with enough effort be put onto a family tree going back through the generations, and right out to fourth or fifth cousins.

'The family' is commonly used in *all* these senses, and more too. None is incorrect, but the consequence is that there is much room for confusion.

As far as your own research goes, such a multiplicity of meanings presents a challenge, rather than a cause for despair. There are two main lessons. The first is obvious (if often neglected): you need to be clear about *which* of these you or others are studying at any given time (the co-resident household? a wider group of non-resident relatives? your close relatives? – or what?).

The second point is more interesting. It is not a matter of chance that there are these different usages, for our concept of 'family' is itself a relative one. Thus, like kinship, it is commonly conceived of 'in terms of widening circles and degrees' (Phillips, 1986, p.145), with the current close domestic household often being seen as at the centre, surrounded by enlarging circles of weaker but still recognized relations like aunts or uncles or cousins, who are family in a way, then further out the living or ancestral relatives, who are also family but less immediately so. The key elements in our concept of 'family' seem relative too, drawing on overtones to do with: (a) recognized relationships and obligations; (b) living together; and (c) blood ties. Which of these should count for most depends on your viewpoint, and in particular what questions you are pursuing in your research. Furthermore, these elements can be split apart: someone can be a member of one 'family' by co-residence, of another by blood ties, yet another by shared obligations. So 'the family' is not some self-evident entity that can be described by one unambiguous 'correct' definition. People are members of *several* 'families' both over time and simultaneously, depending on how you (and they) look at it.

Precisely because there *are* several acceptable meanings, researchers have some choice about which they wish to concentrate on in any study of the 'family' or 'family history'. This, of course, is one reason for the varying approaches to studying family history that you will have noticed in this volume. So part of the obligation of critical and informed researchers in family history is to unpack and scrutinize these different (implicit) definitions.

EXERCISE 6.2

1 What varying meanings have been attached to the term 'family' in discussions earlier in this volume? Try to note down two contrasting examples and how they differ.

2 Consider the definition of 'family' given in FitzHugh's *Dictionary of genealogy*: 'all people of the same name and blood descended from a common male-line ancestor' (FitzHugh, 1991, p.107). What do you think of this usage?

3 What meaning(s) have *you* assumed in any research you have conducted or contemplated in family history?

Comments p.186.

This exercise will probably also have confronted you with another feature of the term 'family': its *evaluative* connotations. It is impossible to select any *one* usage that would always be equally acceptable to everyone or appropriate to every piece of research, for any such selection immediately runs into non-neutral assumptions about what is most 'important' or most 'real', and even into what kind of questions we *ought* to be pursuing to give a balanced account of human affairs.

This emerges clearly in current debates about the nature of 'the family' and about how we should define and study it. There are disagreements about whether we should focus on demography, individual experience, administrative role, economic make-up, personal values, place in the class structure, internal power relations, or perhaps a mixture of all of these. Some writers prefer to select from the various Marxist analyses, perhaps emphasizing the economic and socializing role of the domestic group in maintaining the current power structure in society.

Others focus on gender issues, arguing for example that ideologies associated with certain concepts of 'the family' have been used to perpetuate women's oppression within the domestic group or the wider society; or pointing out that the family is essentially a contested concept (Strathern, 1992, p.24). Others, like Bernardes (1985), say the term 'family' is so confused and debatable that we should give it up completely as a research word.

That last, extreme position has some appeal! But for present purposes it surely goes too far. The term is an emotive one, certainly, used in different senses and with differing implications. But an alternative conclusion is that for this very reason it is all the more interesting to study, the one proviso being that we do this in full awareness of its different usages, and on our guard against hidden evaluations.

1.2   MYTH, SYMBOL AND IDEOLOGY

A final complication is that 'the family' is often used to refer more to an *ideal* than to any empirical description of how it actually is or was in reality. The focus is implicitly on what the family *ought* to be.

What do *you* think 'the family' ought to be like? Would everyone agree?

We saw an interesting example in Chapter 5, when, without fully realizing it, the lady rent collectors were imposing their middle-class views about family life on the inhabitants of Katharine Buildings. We too can impose our own modern images when we look back from the present. Precisely because the term 'family' is an elusive but stirring one, *idealized* senses are easily invoked to make what are really debating points about modern issues rather than dispassionate historical descriptions. The trouble is that it is often not clear that this is happening – also that there is a series of *different* ideals. For example, there is the nostalgic myth of the happy, stable families of a golden past; the ideology of the norm as 'naturally' a family consisting of man, wife and two children; the image of female support and solidarity within war-time working-class families; or the appeal to 'Victorian family values'. What looks like objective, historically supported 'fact' may equally be wishful thinking or a rhetorical claim, or even an attempt to manipulate present realities towards some particular political ideology.

At the level of an individual family or community, the accepted images can shape, and not just reflect, our experience (see Chapter 4, section 3, or, for a community example, Strathern, 1981). So too do wider myths and ideals about the family. These can change from time to time, influenced perhaps by current political, religious or cultural developments; they may even exist alongside a series of other, potentially conflicting, ideologies. Either way they can directly affect both everyday perceptions and scholarly research.

We cannot just wish this situation away. 'The family' will continue to be a potent concept, used for a variety of symbolic evaluative purposes, not just cool description. What you *can* do, however, is look at such images with caution, be clear about your own usage, and not be afraid to explore how far our myths and symbols are *in fact* supported by the evidence.

The final point, then, is that there is no one single prescriptive meaning of the term 'family'. You will not want to expatiate at length on the different theories and meanings, nor to engage in unending theoretical debates. But it *is* useful to have some awareness of the issues discussed here, if only to avoid using ambiguous and evocative terms naively. This should alert you to the occurrence of differing meanings of 'the family', give you some sensitivity to its often loaded connotations, and help you reflect in an informed and critical way on research in family history, including your own.

2   LOOKING BACK: WHERE ARE YOU NOW?

This volume has moved a long way: from the series of possible starting points and research strategies in Chapters 1 and 2, to population studies, family myths and resources in Chapters 3 and 4, and finally to the extended case study in Chapter 5. Have you perhaps been so busy negotiating each and every thicket that you have lost sight of the wood? This last section looks back over the path you have taken.

2.1   YOUR OWN INTERESTS?

You may have been inspired initially by a particular case – perhaps the history of a specific family (in some sense of that elusive word). Or you may have started from a more general interest in the family, now or in the past, or be 'adopting' a set of families as you go along. Or perhaps you are extending your original interests through new topics or perspectives. Whatever your background, why not return to your own experiences and interest within the framework provided in this volume?

EXERCISE 6.3

Set out briefly (a sentence or two will do) four ways in which this book has helped you to extend your understanding of a particular family history, or your general interest in the family, past or present.

Comments p.186.

Your answers will no doubt differ from those of others, because of your background or interests. But our recurrent theme has been the value of putting particular cases into a wider framework, together with the sources, methods and approaches that can be exploited in order to do so. You, we hope, will have ended up with fresh insights into an example you already know well; the motivation to explore new ones; a greater awareness of ambiguities to be clarified or controversies to explore; and an increased understanding both of current scholarly work on family history and openings for your own contribution.

2.2   WHAT NEXT?

Our hope is that you will now want to make your own contribution to this developing field of study. Equipped with these new insights, aware of the problems and the possibilities, recognizing there are sources to be explored and tools to help you to do so, we imagine you can hardly wait to begin! But let us first make a couple of final checks of your academic luggage, to make absolutely sure that you haven't forgotten anything.

EXERCISE 6.4

We have highlighted two research strategies: 'testing hypotheses', and 'questioning sources'.

1   How do they differ?

2   What do they have in common?

3   Give a couple of examples of each.

4   Set out the steps or stages in each.

Comments p.186.

Some topics can be researched in more than one way, so your interests could be formulated either as *questions* to which you want to discover answers (which might then mean reformulating the questions or posing new ones) or as *hypotheses* to be tested. One piece of advice is crucial: unless you have long experience and, more to the point, lots of time and resources, start with a *limited* enquiry. Do not (initially anyway) aim at the scale of some of those illustrated in this volume. Michael Anderson's study of Preston or Rosemary O'Day's of Katharine Buildings took many years' work. But research on a smaller scale is also valuable. It can interact with these larger academic works, and indeed lead to amplifying, qualifying or perhaps challenging their conclusions.

Another limitation you will meet lies in the *sources* you can get at. For however brilliant a strategy you have, it won't help you unless you can find the data. Exercise 6.5 refreshes your memory on that too.

_____ *EXERCISE 6.5* _____

Primary sources are essential to all historical research. List half a dozen that are of key importance for the family historian working on the nineteenth and/or twentieth centuries.

Answers p.187
_____

Your suitcase is now getting pretty full. But it is right and proper that the most important item of intellectual luggage should be near the top – a knowledge of the insights of fellow researchers, without which your own imaginative leaps and research endeavours will be sorely curtailed. Some of these we have discussed in detail (e.g. Michael Anderson's work on family and household; Lynn Jamieson on the experience of being brought up), others in passing (Kussmaul on marriage seasonality; Hair on pre-marital conception; Holley on the link between work and status, domestic cycle and residence; Hareven or Finch on family strategies and kin support; Scott and Tilly on women's work and the domestic economy). Yet others can be found in our lists of references, in other volumes in this series, and in the collection of articles and extracts from other works (Drake, 1994) that accompanies them.

_____ *EXERCISE 6.6* _____

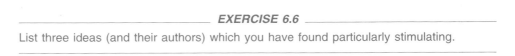

List three ideas (and their authors) which you have found particularly stimulating.
_____

We have covered a good deal in this volume, though there is more to come (see Volumes 2–4). You may already have seen a niche here or there, where you feel you can contribute to our understanding of the history of the family. If so, fine. Alternatively you may be feeling a trifle overwhelmed by the new knowledge brought to your attention. For that reason we have decided to conclude this volume by drawing attention, briefly, to some of the findings discussed earlier, with an eye open to the contributions you can make.

2.3   YOUR FAMILY: TYPICAL OR NOT?

Underlying this volume is the idea that in order to understand your own life or family you need to know about the lives and families of others. How many others and over what time span are, of course, difficult questions to answer. There are, as the late Professor Postan said (cited in Schürer, 1991, p.100) 'microscopic' and 'microcosmic' studies. We might say that the creation of a family tree is an example of the former since its 'outlook, aims and interest are restricted' (Postan again, p.100) to one specific family. Here we have tried to show how family studies, based on local enquiries, can take a 'microcosmic' form, through setting the 'situation or issues in question' into a wider context.

One place to start, we suggest, is with some of the rituals associated with demographic processes, e.g. baptism, marriage, burial. What can the timing (day of the week) or seasonality of these events tell us about the families who took part in them? Looking at the demographic events themselves, what can local studies tell us about the variation in experience that lies behind the national or regional aggregates? How far can the Malthusian theory of demographic change explain local experiences?

And in that long fight against premature death – a fight that has occupied much of the past two centuries – what further insights are to be gained from microcosmic studies focused on a few families or a local community?

Demographic structures – the families and households that provided the locale of most demographic experience – lend themselves to microcosmic study. Indeed, much of the progress that has been made has come about in this way. The source material, principally the CEBs, is readily available on microfilm or paper, and this is a great help for more adventurous studies crossing local, regional or indeed national boundaries. For instance, should your family be of Irish or Scottish origin but now settled in England, you could compare demographic structures in the place of origin and the place of settlement. Who lived with whom, and in groups of what size? What changes in family and household structure occurred over the family or life cycle? In a particular community, were the contrasts great or small in these matters, or less or more pronounced at different times?

As you will no doubt have spotted, these suggestions were mostly based on Chapter 3. They are *examples* of the kinds of questions that you can draw out for your own research from the earlier chapters in the volume.

EXERCISE 6.7

List three possible research projects suggested by the discussion in Chapters 4 and 5 (Chapter 2 also, if you like), with a brief indication of the strategy and sources that could be used.

Comments p.187.

2.4   THE HISTORY OF THE FAMILY?

Finally, what point have we reached in investigating the history of the family? Can we identify wider findings and issues that are broader than individual family histories or family trees? If so, this would make it easier for you to develop 'microcosmic' studies by relating specific cases to more general contexts (such as the 'higher' levels in Figure 1.7, which depicts ways of generalizing).

As you now know, the conclusions are not fully agreed if only because 'the family' is not just one single thing. The subject is still developing (it will continue to do so as a result of your and others' collective efforts). However, it is worth noting the following findings and questions, since they can give you effective channels for relating particular cases to larger social processes.

THE DEMOGRAPHIC PATTERNS

In spite of the crudity of the measures and the tangle of lines, Figure 3.2 does encapsulate central elements affecting family life over the past two centuries. For many families comparatively high birth and death rates meant a fresh face every other year or so, followed fairly quickly by a visit to the cemetery – see, for example, the experience of Benjamin and Rachel Goodaire in Figure 3.1. Nevertheless, the gap between births and deaths was a sizeable one too, the result being that families were faced with finding *new* means of livelihood for their offspring (see Volume 3 for studies on the work they found).

Not until the twentieth century did birth and death rates begin to fall substantially, at first in parallel, but then with the former gathering pace until it finally overtook the latter. Today there is virtually no difference in the two rates in Scotland, England and Wales, a state of affairs likely to come about shortly in both the Republic of Ireland and Northern Ireland. This fall in the rates has had an impact on family size and composition, since it has produced a dramatic change in the age composition of the population, with a sharp fall in the proportion under 20 years of age and an increase in that over 60. Many of the latter are widows or widowers, which has contributed to a dramatic rise in the number of one-person households (Table 3.8). The fall in the birth rate has meant that even if such people wished to live with relatives, many could not do so: in England and Wales, one-third have no relatives to live with. Here are trends into which you can nest your own research.

From the point of view of family history, however, Figure 3.2 is misleading, principally because it is based on information for political entities. This is how such information is presented to us and conventional thinking leads us to pass it on unchanged. However, if or when you come to study Volume 2 of this series you will recognize that such has been the extent of migration between the islands that constitute these political entities, that hundreds of thousands of family histories will bear the mark of the demographic experience of two or more. When we add to this the differences in the demographic experience of regions, cities, towns and villages within these islands, family history will be seen to be a truly hybrid phenomenon – demographically speaking.

In examining your own family history, or one that interests you, consider which of the following have impacted upon it:

o   Movement(s) from:

rural area to town

town to town

town to city

Scotland to England, Wales, Ireland

England to Wales, Scotland, Ireland

Ireland to England, Scotland, Wales

Wales to England, Scotland, Ireland

Scotland, England, Wales, Ireland to overseas

overseas to England, Wales, Scotland, Ireland.

o   The Irish famine of 1846–8.

o   The Bengal famine of 1943.

o   The cholera epidemics.

o   The influenza epidemic of 1919.

o   Deaths in the First World War.

o   Deaths in the Second World War.

o   A civil marriage in the nineteenth century.

o   Marriage between partners of different national origins.

WHAT IS THE RELATION BETWEEN THE FAMILY AND INDUSTRIALIZATION?

What are your general conclusions on this question?

You will doubtless have noticed that the current trend is to reject the idea that industrialization had one single 'impact' on 'the family'. Leading scholars as different in their general approaches as Michael Anderson and Tamara Hareven are united in rejecting earlier assumptions about industrialization. 'Research over the past 20 years', writes Anderson,

> *has significantly modified at least the academic if not the popular view of the past. It is clear that industrialisation as such cannot have been primarily responsible for many of the most salient features of the modern family if only because many of the most significant 'new' features are a product of the twentieth century.*
>
> (Anderson, 1983, p.3)

Similarly, Hareven, in her review of recent work on the history of the family, rejects earlier 'myths and grand theories', such as the assumption that

> *in pre-industrial societies, the dominant household form had contained an extended family ... and that the 'modern' family, characterized by a nuclear household structure, family limitation, the spacing of children, and population mobility, was the product of industrialization ... [There was] also the popular myth that industrialization destroyed familial harmony and community life. But historical research on the family ... has led to the rejection of these assumptions and to the resulting questioning of the role of industrialization as a major watershed in American and European history.*
>
> (Hareven, 1991, p.96)

That is not to say that there is *no* link. The processes of industrialization over time clearly interacted – perhaps differently in different places and periods – with many of the features of family life discussed in this volume. They were related, for example, to such factors as work, income and the domestic economy, together with the relationships linked to those (Chapter 4); residential patterns and the composition of households (Chapter 3); demographic changes (Chapter 3); family support for elderly people (not necessarily diminishing, but changing – see Chapter 4); the emerging class structure and, perhaps, the consequent contrasts between different ideologies of the family, and the specific ways in which people and their families lived in particular places and times (as in the example in Chapter 5). But questions remain. There is the usual chicken-and-egg problem of what causes what. There is also the question – perhaps especially relevant for your own research – of how such changes were experienced and affected by individuals and families, and worked out at the local level.

The subject is still being investigated (we hope by you, among others); one of our pressing needs is for local and small-scale studies to inform – as well as be informed by – the wider picture.

THE DEVELOPMENT OF THE FAMILY: ONE THEORY TO CONSIDER

One 'classic account' of the development of the family in the nineteenth and twentieth centuries was presented in Chapter 2 (see Schema B in section 2 of that chapter; for a fuller account see Jamieson, 1987; Hareven, 1991).

As you saw there, not all researchers' findings support this theory. However, it is well worth returning to, for whether or not you accept the theory and its various constituent sub-theories, it is a good jumping off point for more detailed studies. *Did* the family become a 'haven in a heartless world'? *Was* there a change from loyalty to the family to more respect for individual rights and fulfilment, and if so, when (Anderson, 1983, p.14 suggests post-1945)? Was Jamieson (1987) right in her rejection of at least part of the theory?

Your own findings could support, challenge or qualify this classic account. As with other general theories, it gives small-scale researchers an opportunity to relate their detailed findings to more general theories, or, using the terminology in Figure 1.7, to both 'split' and 'lump'.

GREATER DIVERSITY OF FAMILY LIFE – OR NOT?

Some writers (such as Anderson, 1983, 1985) have suggested that one feature of 'modern' family life in at least the thirty years following the Second World War was its greater security and predictability over the life cycle compared to the nineteenth century – there was the opportunity to plan one's life in advance. Others disagree (e.g. Elliott, 1990, p.73). Where does your own research lead on this, or on Anderson's further surmise that we may now be seeing increasing diversity again in family experiences (a theme also taken up by writers such as Kiernan and Wicks, 1990)?

FAMILY ECONOMY AND RESOURCES?

Have there been interrelated changes in domestic economies, work patterns, or family resources over the last two centuries? One possible set of generalizable changes was summarized in Chapter 4, Schema A (p.107). As suggested there, such a theory is probably too simple to encompass the many social, chronological and geographical differences. But again, this Schema (as well as Schema B on p.111) may be worth returning to as a testing ground for more detailed findings, whether your own or others'.

COMPLEXITY AND DIFFERENTIATION

Another possible view might be that *all* these theories are too simple to encompass the *variegated* family and personal experiences resulting not only from regional, local, class or religious differences but also from individual personalities. This could be one possible conclusion from the Katharine Buildings case study in Chapter 5, for example. Perhaps we need to look more to individual or family strategies in changing circumstances rather than some overall direction of development in 'the family'; or to gradual 'inch-by-inch' changes (Laslett, 1987, p.274) rather than any dramatic revolution. This would imply further research through specific case studies, with a special emphasis on the particular (the 'splitting' end of the continuum), but preferably without totally neglecting more general theories (the 'lumping') which can give it perspective. Indeed, further research through case studies could well contribute to the discovery of different or additional patterns, both in family life or in people moving and settling over time (the subject of Volume 2).

So where do you go now?

General overviews like those above can take you back to questions we raised near the start – those controversial statements considered in Chapter 1, p.22, for example – as well as on to the wider literature in this volume and elsewhere, and to the related topics explored in Volumes 2 and 3. They can also form the basis and the testing ground for your own investigations. There is still much to discover.

REFERENCES AND FURTHER READING

Note: suggestions for further reading are indicated by an asterisk.

Abbott, M. (1993) *Family ties: English families 1540–1920*, London, Routledge.

Anderson, M. (1980) *Approaches to the history of the western family 1500-1914*, Basingstoke, Macmillan.*

Anderson, M. (1983) 'What is new about the modern family?', Occasional Paper 31, *The family*, London, OPCS. Reprinted in Drake (1994).*

Anderson, M. (1985) 'The emergence of the modern life cycle in Britain', *Social History* 10, 1, pp.69-87.

Bernardes, J. (1985) 'Do we really know what "the family" is?', in Close, P. and Collins, R. (eds) *Family and economy in modern society*, Basingstoke, Macmillan.

Cheal, D. (1991) *Family and the state of theory*, Hemel Hempstead, Harvester.

Cochrane, A. and Muncie, J. (eds) (1993) *Politics, policy and the law*, Milton Keynes, The Open University. See especially Chapters 1 and 4.*

Cohen, A.P. (ed.) (1986) *Symbolizing boundaries, identity and diversity in British cultures*, Manchester, Manchester University Press.

Davidoff, L. (1990) 'The family in Britain' in Thompson, F.M.L. (ed.) (1990) *People and their environment*, volume 2 of *The Cambridge social history of Britain 1750-1950*, Cambridge, Cambridge University Press.*

Drake, M. (ed.) (1994) *Time, family and community: perspectives on family and community history*, Oxford, Blackwell in association with The Open University (Course Reader).

Elliott, B. (1990) 'Biography, family history and the analysis of social change', in Kendrick, S. *et al.* (eds) *Interpreting the past, understanding the present*, Basingstoke, Macmillan. Reprinted in Drake (1994).*

Finch, J. (1989) *Family obligations and social change*, Cambridge, Polity Press. Extract reprinted as 'Do families support each other more or less than in the past?' in Drake (1994).

FitzHugh, T.V.H. (1991) *The dictionary of genealogy*, third edition, London, A & C Black.

Hareven, T. (1991) 'The history of the family and the complexity of social change', *American Historical Review*, 96, 1, pp.95-124. Reprinted in an abridged form as 'Recent historical research on the family' in Drake (1994).*

Jamieson, L. (1987) 'Theories of family development and the experience of being brought up', *Sociology*, 21, pp. 591-607, reprinted in Drake (1994).

Kiernan, K. (1988) 'The British family', *Journal of Family Issues*, 9, 3, pp.298-316.

Kiernan, K. and Wicks, M. (1990) *Family change and future policy*, London, Family Policy Studies Centre.

Laslett, P. (1987) 'The character of familial history, its limitations and the conditions for its proper pursuit', in Hareven, T. and Plakans, A. (eds) *Family history at the crossroads: a Journal of Family History reader*, Princeton NJ, Princeton University Press.

Marsh, C. and Arber, S. (eds) (1992) *Families and households: divisions and change*, Basingstoke, Macmillan for British Sociological Association. See especially the Introduction.*

Phillips, K. (1986) 'Natives and incomers: the symbolism of belonging in Muker parish, North Yorkshire', in Cohen (1986). Reprinted in Drake (1994).

Schürer, K. (1991) 'The future for local history: boom or recession?', *Local Historian*, 21, 3, pp.99–108.

Strathern, M. (1981) *Kinship at the core: an anthropology of Elmdon, Essex*, Cambridge, Cambridge University Press.

Strathern, M. (1992) *After nature: English kinship in the late twentieth century*, Cambridge, Cambridge University Press.

Wall, R. (1983) 'The household: demographic and economic change in England 1650-1970', in Wall, R., Robin, J. and Laslett, P. (eds) *Family forms in historic Europe*, Cambridge, Cambridge University Press.

Wallman, S. (1986) 'The boundaries of household', in Cohen (1986).

Winter, J. M. (1985) *The Great War and the British people*, Basingstoke, Macmillan.

EXERCISES: ANSWERS AND COMMENTS

Exercise 1.4

Question (a):

1 False.

2 False.

3 True.

4 Doesn't say (but you can find some answers in Chapter 2, section 2, and Chapter 4, section 2).

5 False.

Question (b): Read on in the main text.

Exercise 2.1

1 They are supposed to mark the end of the entries for each house (i.e., according to the instruction to the enumerator, 'a separate and distinct building and not a mere storey or flat'). Here, therefore, we appear to be dealing with four houses in one street, each with its own number. Often this was not the case. You may also come across 'a similar line under the last name of each Occupier in the same house, in this case [commencing] a little on the left hand side of the third column' (again quoted from the instruction to enumerators). One might have expected such a line after the name of Ann Eastham, so making Thomas Roscaw a second occupier. But perhaps he and his wife shared Edward Eastham's table? In that case they should have been described as 'boarders'.

2 See the last two sentences above. But the matter goes deeper than the distinction between 'lodgers' and 'boarders', for in what way can Thomas Roscaw and his wife have a 'family relation' with Edward Eastham? Perhaps Ann Roscaw was his sister or some other relative, in which case an 'extended' family relationship could be detected. Clearly we are dealing here with matters of definition, with those who drew up the forms seemingly believing that houses were occupied by husbands and wives, their relations, servants and apprentices. What we get in fact, between each of the long horizontal lines in Figure 2.1, are more properly, if less simply, described as 'co-residing groups' (for the best recent discussion of the issue see Higgs, 1989, pp.57–66).

3 Whether one was unmarried, married or widowed. Note the abbreviations ('U' for unmarried, 'Mar' for married). Various changes were made at subsequent censuses, but it is obvious what they stood for. Abbreviations occur throughout the books, some officially encouraged, others at the whim of the individual enumerator. However, they are used sparingly and rarely create a problem.

4 All were wives. In the cases here it could well be that the women concerned were housewives and had no other employment. Then as now, however, many wives had part-time employment, a fact rarely entered on the census form. Similarly many men had more than one source of income. This too was rarely noted. One assumes the most important source was the one put down.

5 These marks were made by the census clerks in London while they were checking the CEBs and preparing the printed tables. Sometimes they are a nuisance because they obliterate letters or figures vital for making sense of the original entries. Prior to the 1841 census the analysis was done locally. This proved unsatisfactory, since many Poor Law officials were not up to the task. From 1841 onwards the copying of the household schedules into the CEBs was done locally. These were then sent to London for processing.

6 These give the number of houses on the page that were inhabited (I), uninhabited (U) or being built (B).

Exercise 2.2

Nine out of twenty – almost exactly what Anderson found for Great Britain as a whole. No doubt a fluke!

Exercise 2.3

I am assuming William Marley came from Caton (near Lancaster), with 'Keton' being a misspelling. Caton is 22 miles from Preston. I adjudged the distance from Ribchester to Preston to be 8 miles; from 'Claton le dale' (Clayton-le-dale) 9 miles; from Adlington 11 miles; from Chorley 8 miles; from Penwortham 2 miles. Thus the mean distance travelled was 22 + 8 + 9 + 8 + 8 + 11 + 11 + 8 + 2 = 87 ÷ 9 = just under 10 miles. This is a rough-and-ready calculation suited to a map that makes a more precise measurement impossible.

Why not try this exercise on some entries in a CEB for a community that interests you. (Refer to Volume 4, Chapter 8, for different methods of calculating averages, their strengths and drawbacks.)

Exercise 2.4

1 Five (i.e. 20 ÷ 4).

2 One (i.e. William Marley, his wife and two children). John Jones heads what is called a stem family household. Such a household consists of two conjugal families: in this case that of John Jones and that of his daughter and her husband. The household headed by William Kirkham consists of siblings (i.e. brothers and sisters) only. And that headed by Edward Eastham consists of two conjugal families, one of which is a lodger and his wife.

3 Three or five: three if just the conjugal families living alone are counted (William Marley's, Edward Eastham's and Thomas Roscaw's); five if all conjugal families are included, i.e. John, Elizabeth and Luke Jones (one family), and Thomas and Alice Taylor (another).

4 3.7 (i.e. 11 ÷ 3) or 3.2 (i.e. 16 ÷ 5).

5 Three (see the answer to question 2 for details).

6 Read literally, John Marley is the son of William Marley and his wife Nancy. However, as the child is three, Nancy would have been about forty-five when he was born, which is, of course, possible. Another possibility is that John is the son of William and Nancy's daughter Ann. If so, he should have been described as 'grandson', but son was sometimes used instead. For this and other nineteenth-century usages see Higgs (1989) p.65. But where is the husband? Was there one? If he were away on census night he would, quite properly, not appear in the CEB. I also think it not unlikely, though impossible to prove on this evidence, that Ann Roscaw might have been the daughter or another relative of the head of the household, Edward Eastham. If you have already investigated your own family you may be in a position to know more about this than social historians do more generally, through other details of family links that can throw additional light on such a document as appears in Figure 2.1. The extent to which kin lived with other members of the extended family or nearby is an important question during industrialization. Michael Anderson was one of the first to discuss this, as we shall see later.

7 The occupants of Savoy Street seem a pretty homogeneous bunch. All in employment have manual jobs, mostly in the textile industry. Note that they are all relatively young, the mean age of the adults (twenty-one years or over) being thirty-two years.

8 There seem to be an awful lot of them!

Exercise 2.5

You may have found this exercise easy or difficult, but whatever the details you will almost certainly have come up with some relevant findings and/or with a greater appreciation of the problems and potential of the method. For some further comment read on in the main text.

Exercise 2.6

Once again the answer is up to you. What you were doing was replicating Jamieson's work by using similar methods and questions on a smaller scale, and testing out her conclusions on your own case. It would be interesting to see how your own findings from (presumably) later this century and perhaps a different area fit with hers (something we will be returning to later in this chapter).

Exercise 2.7

The main phases could be summarized as follows (with phases 2 and 3 simultaneous and iterative):

1   Starting with interest in a topic and/or very general question.

2   Checking the availability and relevance of appropriate sources and methods.

3   Reading further about related work on the topic or question resulting in modifying or refining the theory.

4   Modifying the questions in the light of (2) and (3).

5   Consulting and interpreting the sources and relevant comparative evidence (perhaps further recasting the initial assumptions and questions to handle insights from the sources).

6   Gathering together and reporting on the conclusions, taking account of comparative evidence as well as specific findings and perhaps opening up new questions and further research possibilities.

Exercise 2.8

1   Principally, I believe, by examining other sources to cast light on the single issue discussed above; and by mining the letters more thoroughly, i.e. not confining one's attention to the health/wealth, social, and psychological issues. To take the first of these, one could examine rate books, wills and CEBs to see how Joseph's relations and friends, who remained in England, fared; local newspapers might indicate something about the success or otherwise of the quarrying industry; official sources (e.g. government reports) should give an indication of wages and business conditions; there may be other business records; local health reports could provide information on morbidity and mortality. Of course, there must be sources in the USA too: membership lists from the Wesleyan chapel that Joseph and Rebecca attended; records on the state of the local economy; an obituary notice in a local newspaper.

2   In one sense it is crucial, since it shifts the emphasis of the strategy from the exploration of theory to that of empirical data. On the other hand it is negligible, reflects the realities of the research world and, providing the various stages are treated with equal seriousness, is not likely to lead to a very different outcome.

Exercise 3.1

Question 1

1701–6
Labourers: 8.5 days
Non-labourers: 13.5 days

1831–6
Labourers: 26.5 days
Non-labourers: 31 days

It would appear that both labourers and non-labourers waited quite a bit longer in the early 1830s than in the early 1700s before baptizing their children. This is in line with most findings and suggests that the birth–baptism interval did lengthen during the period 1700–1830. As for the difference between labourers and non-labourers, both moved in the same direction, suggesting a common cultural shift so far as this ceremony is concerned. In both cases labourers baptized their children earlier than non-labourers. (See Volume 4, Chapter 8 for more measures of central tendency and for sampling techniques.)

Question 2

(a) 1701–6

Monday	Tuesday	Wednesday	Thursday	Friday	Saturday	Sunday	Total
8	1	4	2	14	10	18	57

Of the 57 baptisms, 42 took place on Friday, Saturday or Sunday. Although Sunday had more baptisms than any other day, it does not stand out very prominently. Monday to Thursday were not days for baptisms, it would seem – at least not under normal circumstances. For the 15 cases that did take place on these days, nine would appear to fit into an emergency category, i.e. baptized within two or three days of birth, suggesting their lives were at risk.

(b) 1831–6

Monday	Tuesday	Wednesday	Thursday	Friday	Saturday	Sunday	Total
3	1	1	3	3	2	45	58

Sunday was obviously *the* day for baptism in this period, though whether this was the popular choice or dictated by the incumbent clergyman we do not know. If this shift to Sunday was widespread, it explains some of the increase in the gap between birth and baptism. What determined the choice of the other days? Various reasons suggest themselves. In three cases it would appear that the upper-class parishioners were setting themselves apart from the rest: an Esquire and a Gentleman had their children baptized on a Saturday, whilst a Lieutenant Governor of the island of St Vincent chose a Monday. In four other cases the child was baptized within a day of being born. This suggests an emergency, the child being sickly and likely to die. The other cases do not provide any obvious explanation.

Question 3

Topic of interest: Popular attitudes and the family.

Articulate problem: Do shared attitudes and values within a particular socio-economic group affect the organization of family life?

Formulate hypothesis: That the timing of baptism within a particular socio-economic group at a given period follows a common pattern, indicating shared values.

Devise test: Plot the days on which baptisms took place and the birth–baptism interval: (a) over time; (b) between socio-economic groups.

Collect data: From a Church of England or nonconformist register (or registers) abstract 200 baptisms for each of two five-year periods, noting: (a) the day of the baptism; (b) the birth–baptism interval; (c) the occupation of the father.

Test: Work out the number of baptisms per day; the birth–baptism interval both by socio-economic class and for each period. For this you will need to use a system of classification (e.g. Armstrong, 1972, or see Volume 4, Chapter 8). If you have drawn a sample you will need to test for the significance of any differences that emerge (see Schofield, 1972, or Volume 4, Chapter 8).

Result: The extent to which the hypothesis is upheld and any inferences you draw from the particular data used.

Exercise 3.2

Put simply, the family tree shows a dramatic fall between the number of children born to Rachel and Benjamin Goodaire from the 1830s to the 1850s and those born to the last three generations of the family. Those born to Joseph and Caroline Goodaire in the 1860s and 1870s occupy an intermediate position.

Exercise 3.3

1   There might be a number of people 'at risk' of being entered in the baptism or marriage register who have the same name, so the wrong people may be matched.

2   Aids to identification, such as occupation or address, might not be given.

3   People might leave the parish after marriage and have their children baptized elsewhere. One way of overcoming this is to discard all marriages which do not result in a baptism within three years of the marriage. Thus pre-marital conceptions would be expressed as all couples who produced a baptism within nine months of marriage as a percentage of all couples producing a baptism within three years of marriage.

4   Some people may die shortly after marriage, and as a result have no children. One way of checking this is to look through the appropriate burial register.

To overcome these problems, Hair (1966 and 1970) advised:

(a)   Use, where possible, printed registers that are indexed.

(b)   Use only registers which include the names of both parents in a baptism entry, e.g. 'Nancy, daughter of John and Betty Whittaker'.

(c)   Use only registers for rural parishes. This is because many couples, for a variety of reasons, went to a town to get married and 'subsequently produced and registered offspring in their home, rural parish' (Hair, 1966, p.234, footnote 7).

Exercise 3.4

They married on 4 April 1831 and their first child, Catharine, was born on 8 September 1831. For a discussion of pre-marital conception see pp.70-1.

Exercise 3.5

In Figure 3.A you see John Heaton Goodaire (with the circle round him). He is living with his father and mother, brother and sister, in a household headed by his maternal grandfather. The only other member of the household is his maternal grandmother. Here is an example of a multiple family household.

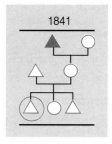

Figure 3.A

Exercise 3.6

In 1851 John Heaton Goodaire (again, circled in Figure 3.B) was living in an extended family household in category 4(d). Here we see a household extended both upwards (Elizabeth Myers, the head's mother-in-law) and downwards (John Heaton Goodaire, the head's nephew). One would depict it as shown in Figure 3.B. Here we see the conjugal family (inside the red shaded area) with its head, Joseph Goodaire, in solid red. The extension upwards is shown above Joseph and his wife; the extension downwards is below them.

In 1861 we find John Heaton Goodaire with his wife at his side and three sons beneath him. His father-in-law (a widower), as head of the household, is above him. Here we have an extended family, this time linked through a married daughter. This is category 4(a) and is shown in Figure 3.C.

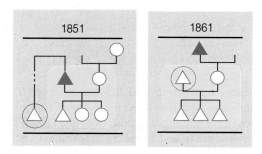

Figure 3.B   Figure 3.C

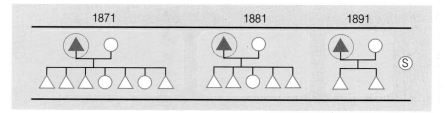

Figure 3.D

In 1871, 1881 and 1891, John Heaton is living in his own household: a nuclear (conjugal) family unit of type 3(b). Note, however, that in 1891 the household also contains a non-family member, namely a female servant (Figure 3.D).

Exercise 5.5

1 Yes – 30 per cent.

2 Yes.

3 No.

4 In only 56 per cent of households was the income supplied solely by the head.

5 I can think of four:

o the types of work working women engaged in

o whether their work was as 'casual' as that of their husbands or fathers

o the occupations of household members and when the work was carried out

o the extent of income supplement.

Exercise 6.1

Question 1
(a) Family: One set of terms distinguishes: nuclear (or simple) and extended families, i.e. vertically or horizontally extended (for further discussion see Chapter 3, section 2.2). There are also lone-parent families; composite or multiple families (e.g. step and reconstituted families; or two co-resident kin-linked simple families), conjugal families (sometimes used synonymously with nuclear, sometimes of just spouses without children – see, for example, Chapter 5, Table 5.3). These are all essentially definitions based on co-residence, thus often overlapping with households (see below). Another approach is to look at family in terms of relationships (outside as well as inside the residential unit at any given time); in this sense family and, more broadly, extended family are relative terms which refer to all those whose links are recognized more or less directly – through their obligation, for example, to partake in family rituals or family support systems (see Chapter 4, section 2). Kinship or extended kinship relations overlap with this sense, but are also often used to include even more distant relations.

(b) Household: people living together in a particular house, flat or, as in Katharine Buildings, a room, and sharing some communal activity. In censuses (the basis for much research) communal activity was defined as eating together; in 1981 this was extended to sharing a living room. Housing opportunities and constraints thus affect the nature of households (for example one-, two- and three-roomed tenement housing in Scottish cities and Dublin). Households often have a family core (one reason why 'family' and 'household' are sometimes used interchangeably; in the nineteenth-century CEBs, the head of household was usually followed by wife of, son of, etc.). But households can also be made up of more than one family (see examples in Chapter 3, section 2) or of unrelated people (e.g. young single people sharing a flat). So households can also be classified by how many and what kind of people live in them (see, for example, Chapter 3, Table 3.7, and the detailed distinctions in Chapter 5, Tables 5.2 and 5.3).

Question 2
Other terms include *natal family* or *family of orientation* (the one you're born into); *family of procreation* (the one in which *you* are the parent); *domestic* or *family cycle* (pp.91ff, 112–13); *life course* (p.113); *affines* (in-laws or relatives by marriage). These and other terms are often used to distinguish different stages of the family cycle, or different aspects of family or household activity.

Exercise 6.2

1   For some contrasting meanings see the examples given in answer to question 1 of the previous exercise. Work based on research by Anderson, Laslett and some other members of the 'Cambridge Group' tends to focus mainly (though not totally) on the co-residence, household aspect (see Chapter 3). The idea of family as defined through recognized obligations or symbols both within *and* outside the co-residential unit draws on the approaches of writers like Finch or Elliott (see Chapter 4). Hareven is similar, but particularly emphasizes the relative and fluid nature of family relationships, and the family not as a static unit at one particular time, but as 'a process over the entire lives of its members' (1991, p.96) including their personal experiences. This approach is generally consistent with that of Rosemary O'Day's case study in Chapter 5, but did you also notice how careful she was to sort out a number of different forms – see Tables 5.2 and 5.3?

2   Note the *male* focus in this 'genealogical usage' as stated by FitzHugh. Many of the scholars represented in this volume would regard this as too narrow and selective a definition to be appropriate for the kinds of questions they themselves are interested in investigating.

3   Over to you!

Exercise 6.3

Here are four possible answers (you might have thought of others), that you can explore in a local or specific context:

1   It has provided you with ideas, based on current academic literature, that you can explore in a local or specific context.

2   It has described wider frameworks and approaches into which you can fit your own specific findings and interests.

3   It has suggested the kinds of sources you can use in research projects and pointed to the need to treat them critically.

4   It has suggested research strategies you can follow. .

Can you think of examples from earlier chapters to illustrate all these answers?

Exercise 6.4

1   The hypothesis testing strategy tends to have a more circumscribed goal, a series of distinct stages followed in a linear progression, and a more explicit use of theory (from which the hypothesis being tested is derived). By contrast, the questioning sources strategy can be likened to a research spiral, along which one circles in order to move upwards. There is then more interaction between the various research stages, more to-ing and fro-ing. This strategy also tends to emphasize interpretation and understanding rather than measurement. (For further discussion look back at Chapter 2, sections 2.1 and 2.2; see also Volume 4, Chapter 1).

2   They draw on a common battery of sources, techniques and academic literature. Both involve skills in assessing sources, identifying issues, drawing comparisons, and utilizing the literature. Both require clear thinking as to topics under investigation and the articulation of questions. Both demand communication skills. (For further points, see Chapter 2, section 2, especially Schema A (p.38) and Schema C (p.47); also Volume 4, Chapter 1).

3 Here are some examples from earlier chapters:

(a) *Hypothesis testing:* the hypothesis that 'the residences of sons (living outside the parental home) and those of their parents are closer to each other than would be found if such persons were not making a positive effort to ensure this' (see Chapter 2, section 2.1); the hypothesis relating to the Hartley letters in Chapter 2, section 3; and various hypothesis-based suggestions for research, for example in Chapter 3, section 1.2 on Malthus, Chapter 4, section 2 on Wall, and Chapter 5, section 3.2, Question for Research 3(g).

(b) *Questioning sources:* Jamieson's use of oral sources in Chapter 3, section 2; the Katharine Buildings case study; the research suggestions in Chapter 3, section 1.1 on pre-marital conception, Chapter 4, sections 1 and 4, and Chapter 5, section 3.2, Questions for Research 3(a)–3(c).

4 See the steps listed in Chapter 2, sections 2.1 and 2.2 (also the summary figures in Volume 4, Chapter 1).

Exercise 6.5

Here are eight important sources (others have been mentioned too):

o CEBs

o Religious registers

o Oral sources (recorded by yourself or others)

o Private letters

o Diaries and autobiographies

o Local and national government reports

o Social surveys (e.g. Booth)

o Maps and plans.

For further sources and their uses see later volumes in the series, especially Part II of Volume 4; look back also at Chapter 1 in this volume.

Exercise 6.7

You may already have your own plans, but you could glance back through these chapters for further ideas. Look particularly at the Questions for Research; the examples of other people's research (which you might wish to replicate or challenge, but on a smaller scale); and the Schemas, which lay out questions, issues or models to which you can relate your own findings.

ACKNOWLEDGEMENTS

Grateful acknowledgement is made to the following sources for permission to reproduce material in this book:

Chapter 1

Text   Alo-wa: Black Women's Oral History Group (1990) *Our story*, Willowbrook Urban Studies Centre and Southwark Women's Centre; Anderson M. (1982) 'For better, for worse – property, know how, fertility. What's love got to do with it?', *The Guardian*, 10 February, 1982.

Figures   Figure 1.3: Office of Population, Censuses and Surveys (1891) *Census enumerator's book for Rastrick*, Yorkshire, reproduced with the permission of the Controller of Her Majesty's Stationery Office; Figure 1.4: courtesy of Ruth Finnegan; Figure 1.6: Wicks B. (1988) *No time to wave goodbye*, Bloomsbury Publishing Ltd.

Chapter 2

Text   Jamieson L. (1987) 'Theories of family development and the experience of being brought up', *Sociology*, 21, British Sociological Association; 'First surviving letter from Joseph Hartley', 9 June 1858, courtesy of Michael Drake.

Figures   Figure 2.1: extract from the 1851 *Census enumerator's book for Preston*, © Crown Copyright, reproduced with the permission of the Controller of Her Majesty's Stationery Office; Figures 2.3, 2.5, 2.6: courtesy of Michael Drake; Figure 2.4: National Archives and Records Administration/Temple University – Balch Institute for Ethnic Studies, Center for Immigration Research; Photos: Professional Color, Philadelphia.

Chapter 3

Figures   Figure 3.1: courtesy of Michael Drake; Figure 3.3: Diamond I. and Clark S. (1989) 'Demographic patterns among Britain's ethnic groups', in Joshi H. (ed.) *The changing population of Britain*, Basil Blackwell Ltd, © Centre for Economic Policy Research; Figure 3.7: Mary Evans Picture Library; Figure 3.8: adapted from Laslett P. and Wall R. (1972) *Household and family in past time*, Cambridge University Press; Figure 3.9: Ruggles S. (1987) *Prolonged connections – the rise of the extended family in 19th century England and America*, The University of Wisconsin Press.

Tables   Table 3.2: Encyclopaedia Britannica, 15th edition, 1974, *Micropedia*, Vol ii, p.455; Table 3.7: Knodel J. (1979) *Local Population Studies*, 23, Local Population Studies; Table 3.9: Ruggles S. (1987) *Prolonged connections – the rise of the extended family in 19th century England and America*, The University of Wisconsin Press; Table 3.10: Wall R. (1989) 'Leaving home and living alone: an historical perspective', *Population Studies*, 43, pp.369–89, Population Studies; Tables 3.11, 3.12, 3.13, 3.14: courtesy of Carol Pearce.

Chapter 4

Figures   Figure 4.1: courtesy of Agnes Finnegan; Figure 4.2: Bigger D. and McDonald T. (1990) *In sunshine or in shadow: photographs from the Derry Standard 1928-1939*, Friar's Bush Press; Figure 4.3: Wallman S. (1984) *Eight London households*, Tavistock Publications.

Tables   Table 4.1: Wall R. (1992) 'Relationships between the generations in British families past and present', in Marsh C. and Arber S. (eds) *Families and households: divisions and change*, Macmillan; Table 4.2: adapted from Pearl S. (1990) 'Fact from fiction', *Family Tree Magazine*, August 1990.

Chapter 5

Figures   Figure 5.1: adapted from Fishman W.J. (1988) *East End 1888: a year in a London borough among the labouring poor*, Duckworth, © 1988 by W.J. Freeman; Figure 5.2: reproduced from: Henrietta Barnett, *Canon Barnett, his life, work and friends*, London, John Murray, 1918 (frontispiece); Figures 5.3 a,b, 5.4: Tarn J.N. (1971) *Working class housing in 19th century Britain*, Lund Humphries Publishers Ltd, photos courtesy of Professor John Tarn, University of Liverpool School of Architecture; Figure 5.5: courtesy of the British Library of Political and Economic Science; Figure 5.6: Passfield Papers II 1 (11) 7 Item 159 (extract) courtesy of the British Library of Political and Economic Science.

Covers

Front (clockwise from top left)   Family with child in pram: Northamptonshire Libraries and Information Service, Local Studies Department, copyright Mrs J. Chennells; Evacuee children: *Derby Evening Telegraph*; Family group: Mrs Iris Moon/Photo: Rural History Centre, University of Reading; Part of envelope containing letter from Joseph Hartley, 1861: courtesy Michael Drake; Soldier on leave: Rural History Centre, University of Reading; Family of John Maxwell Finnegan, c.1903: courtesy Ruth Finnegan; Villager with boys: Garland Collection, West Sussex Record Office/Photo: Beaver Photography.

Back (clockwise from top left)   The Abrahams family: Bedfordshire County Record Office; Three generations of a labouring family: Northamptonshire Libraries and Information Service, Local Studies Department, copyright Canon P.J.M. Bryan; The Doms family, Belgian refugees, 1914: Bedfordshire County Record Office; Mother and daughters during Second World War: Northamptonshire Libraries and Information Service, Local Studies Department, copyright Mr P.E. Lewis; Emigrating family on ship: from Bigger D. and McDonald T., *In sunshine or in shadow*, Belfast, Friars Bush Press; Aerial view of West London; Man with child in arms: Northamptonshire Libraries and Information Service, Local Studies Department, copyright Mr S. Tapp; Aerial view of West London.

INDEX